THE LANGUAGE OF YOUTH SUBCULTURES

Social Identity in Action

Sue Widdicombe
University of Edinburgh

Robin Wooffitt
University of Surrey

HARVESTER
WHEATSHEAF

New York   London   Toronto   Sydney   Tokyo   Singapore

First published 1995 by
Harvester Wheatsheaf
Campus 400, Maylands Avenue
Hemel Hempstead
Hertfordshire, HP2 7EZ

A division of
Simon & Schuster International Group

Typeset in 10/12pt Times
by Dorwyn Ltd, Rowlands Castle, Hants

Printed and bound in Great Britain by
T J Press (Padstow) Ltd

British Library Cataloguing in Publication Data

A catalogue record for this book is available from
the British Library

ISBN 0 7450 1419 4

1 2 3 4 5   99 98 97 96 95

THE LANGUAGE OF
YOUTH SUBCULTURES

CONTENTS

ACKNOWLEDGEMENTS

For all their support, help, and advice, we would like to thank the following individuals and institutions: Rad Babic, Farrell Burnett, Kate Burningham, Jimmy Cuthbert, Departments of Experimental Psychology and Psychology, Universities of Oxford and Edinburgh respectively, Department of Sociology, University of Surrey, Economic and Social Research Council, Derek Edwards, Ann Greenwood, Nick Hopkins, Nicola Horton, Kay Lattimore, Marina Maclean, Jonathan Potter, Pauline Stewart, and Dave Wilkinson.

INTRODUCTION

This book is about how personal and social identity and group affiliations are constructed, maintained and negotiated in ordinary, everyday language. In particular, we focus on the accounts, stories and anecdotes produced by members of youth subcultures: punks, skinheads, gothics, rockers and so on. Through the analyses of these accounts we try to address three crucial issues and debates in the social sciences: arguments about the extent to which language is constitutive of personal and social identity; theoretical attempts to chart the relationship between the individual and social groups or society; and the degree to which identity is tied to social action.

Our empirical focus is on the way the people use words to do specific kinds of work; in this case, to characterise their own identities, and to portray the relationship between their selves and the subcultural group. However, in keeping with recent developments in sociology and social psychology, we do not treat these accounts as passive verbal representations of pre-existing identities or attitudes. Rather, we are interested in the constitutive nature of language use. We are keen to explore how accounts are constructed, and to describe the interpersonal functions served by these constructions.

The data presented in this book were originally collected as part of conventional social psychological research. The goal of the research was to establish whether a particular theoretical framework, the Social Identity approach (Tajfel, 1978; Turner *et al.*, 1987), could be used to explain why some young people joined subcultural groups. Much previous research in Social Identity Theory had relied heavily upon experimental or laboratory-based studies. To try to extend the methodological scope of the approach it was decided to collect data in more naturalistic settings. Consequently, instead of administering questionnaires to individuals in social psychology laboratories, we conducted informal interviews with members of subcultures in places where they gathered: rock festivals, street corners, alternative markets and so on. These interviews were tape recorded.

However, it was at this point that our appreciation of these data changed. First, the accounts were far too variable to permit a straightforward interpretation in terms of Social Identity Theory. But more important, we were influenced by arguments that language is not a neutral medium for the transmission of values, attitudes, opinions about a world of events 'out there', but rather a medium through which social acts are accomplished. It became apparent that we could not simply treat these accounts as passive *resources* in our research. Consequently, we began to treat these data as the *topic* of our research, and to re-evaluate the research questions we wished to address.

We can illustrate this methodological shift with a brief example. One of the issues we initially wanted to explore was the extent to which an individual's social identity as a member of a specific subculture was tied to ways in which that individual compared him or herself to other members of their own group and with members of other groups. Therefore, our questions were designed to elicit information which would enable us to provide evidence that respondents' identities were derived through comparisons, and to chart the cognitive dimensions on which comparisons were made. Consequently, we treated people's accounts as being somewhat 'transparent' insofar as we assumed that they would reveal the workings of psychological processes which underpinned the individual's perceptions of him or herself in relation to others. However, once we realised that language use is itself a form of social activity, it became untenable to treat accounts as transparent representations of inner mental events, like cognitive processes or attitudes and so on. Instead, we began to examine accounts which dealt with comparisons between the individuals and other members of the group, or other groups, to see how these comparisons were constructed, and to try to discover the kinds of interpersonal or inferential work which was being addressed through these accounts.

This important methodological shift in our approach to language permeated our interest in all the data we had collected, not just accounts in which comparative issues became relevant. Broadly, we started to treat these data not as accounts produced by 'punks', or 'gothics' or whatever. Instead, we became interested in exploring how it was that specific subcultural identities become salient in specific moments in the accounts. We began to look to see how our respondents constructed their identities as members of subcultures; and how they constructed accounts of their relationship as members of subcultural groups to wider society. It is the result of these empirical analyses that we present in this book.

A focus on language and identity differs markedly from more traditional sociological approaches to youth subcultures. However, we feel that our approach intersects with themes in conventional sociological research in a number of ways. Consequently, in the first chapter, we provide an account of previous sociological research on subcultures. By doing this we can illustrate the kinds of questions which sociologists have tended to ask, and set these against issues which emerge from our own research agenda. One of the aims of this book is to see what kinds of contributions we can make to existing research programmes (both in sociology and social psychology) and so it is crucial to set out clearly the kinds of questions that are asked in existing approaches, and to sketch the kinds of answers they provide. Of course, it may be that our emphasis upon the way that identity is produced in language may lead us to ask entirely novel research questions, and may ensure that we cannot contribute to research issues generated in conventional approaches. However, we believe that it is important to attempt to mesh new work with existing perspectives, even if only to clarify the kinds of differences which exist.

Positioning our own perspective in relation to existing work also allows us to identify what we feel are weaknesses in that literature which our own approach avoids. For example, we focus on the complaint that sociological research has tended to be overtly theoretical in its treatment of youth subcultures and that, consequently, there has been no significant attempt to incorporate into the research process accounts produced by members of subcultures themselves. We also raise the general issue of the relationship between the individual and society, and the self and identity, which we feel has been poorly conceived in previous sociological studies of youth subcultures.

These are crucial theoretical issues which have permeated social scientific debates. These key issues of identity, the social group and the relationship between the self and society therefore allow us to situate our project within wider debates in the social sciences; in particular, ways of conceptualising the interrelationship between self and society, identity and agency, and how these have stimulated a turn to language amongst some social scientists. Thus, in Chapter 2 we show how the approach we adopt fits into these wider issues.

We begin the chapter by reviewing a variety of sociological and social psychological attempts to conceptualise the relationship between individuals and society. These include macrosociological theories and role theory, as well as social cognition and the Social Identity approach in social psychology. In the course of our review we argue that these conceptualisations are based upon, and reinforce, dualistic assumptions which prevent the proper realisation of their aims. In brief, the aim is to show that individuals and society are inseparable, the one utterly implicating the other. But the different approaches start by assuming that individuals and society are separate orders of things, so that the problem becomes one of understanding their relationship. We argue that a more fruitful approach is to overcome the dualistic assumptions intrinsic to more conventional approaches. We discuss ways to help us think beyond dualism. In particular, we will consider a range of arguments which claim that the notion of 'the individual' is itself a social and cultural product. Indeed, some have gone so far as to say that the concept of the individual is a *product* of academic disciplines like psychology. This in turn raises the possibility that concepts like the self and personal identity are not properties intrinsic to human beings, but a legacy of attempts by the human sciences to establish their legitimacy by defining a distinctive subject matter.

In the final part of this chapter we outline a variety of attempts to introduce new starting points. These include the focus on interaction and situations, the development of theories of social selves and the postmodern death and reconstruction of the subject. Despite the diversity of these approaches, they share a common premise: the centrality of language to selves, society and social life. These theoretical issues strike right to the heart of the human sciences, for they raise questions about the status of concepts which have become central to many streams of social scientific research.

The consequences of these debates have very real methodological implications. For example, arguments about the death of the subject have led to an attempt to try to refashion the proper subject matter for psychological research. Some have argued that it makes no sense to build research around the concept of the individual, but that we should focus on the matrix of relationships in which notions of 'individuality' and 'identity' become salient. Others have argued that the proper focus for empirical research should be those discourses – systems of meanings and concepts which provide a coherent way of representing the world – through which persons are ascribed identities. It is important to review these arguments because they focus attention on language, and the ways in which identities are produced in language. Although the perspective we have adopted shares many broad assumptions with this 'linguistic turn' in the social sciences, there are points of divergence, and these need to be marked carefully. Indeed, throughout the book we discuss these divergences, and common assumptions, not only with perspectives which are part of the linguistic turn, but also with the more traditional approaches.

In Chapter 3, we describe the empirical stance we pursue in the analytic chapters. We draw primarily from conversation analysis in sociology and discourse analysis in social psychology. There are, however, many different kinds of research which are known as discourse analysis. The kind of discourse analysis we refer to here is an empirical perspective that developed from sociological studies of scientific knowledge (Gilbert and Mulkay, 1984) and which has subsequently been developed in social psychology (Potter and Wetherell, 1987). It seeks to examine how language is used variably, constructively, and attempts to chart the social functions of language use. However, for many radical social psychologists, discourse analysis, as developed by these researchers, does not challenge traditional social psychological assumptions as much as it should. Consequently, there are claims that discourse analysis could do more to address topics such as power, gender relations and class, and could profit by drawing from the work of social philosophers such as Foucault, Derrida and Lacan. In the early part of Chapter 3 we shall examine the divisions within discourse analysis in social psychology, before turning our attention to conversation analysis.

Conversation analysis sets out to describe the orderly properties of verbal interaction. It examines how utterances in talk are designed to address specific interactional tasks, and how these actions are produced with respect to the sequence of conversational actions in which they occur. Thus there is an emphasis upon examining the turn by turn development of verbal interaction.

Some features of conversation analytic research are sketched by reference to ethnographic studies which have broadly addressed the relationship between social identity and talk.

A conversation analytic approach is used in Chapters 4 and 5, which are the first two empirical chapters. In these, we examine some features of the interviews we conducted with our respondents. We show how issues of the respondents' identity became particularly relevant during a specific section of the interviews: the opening two or three recorded exchanges. We try to show how respondents use their communicative competencies to address specific fine-grained interactional tasks. In particular we argue that respondents may address these interactional tasks by exhibiting a specific type of social identity: that of an 'ordinary person'. Chapter 6 continues our concern with ordinary identities; in this chapter we examine ways in which this identity is used as a resource in the pursuit of a specific social action, making a complaint. We conclude by situating our empirical analysis within broader debates concerning the relationship between social identity and action.

In the first three empirical chapters (4, 5 and 6) we examine ways in which the respondents' identity becomes relevant in verbal social interaction. That is, we focus on identity as an interactional resource in the production of discursive action. In the last three empirical studies (Chapters 7, 8 and 9), however, our analytic emphasis shifts. Instead of focusing at the level of verbal interaction we take more account of the substantive content of our respondents' talk. While not relinquishing our interest in the functional consequences of our respondents' discourse, we examine sections of their accounts in which they address topics which resonate with issues addressed in social psychological and sociological studies, for example, how and why people join subcultures, and the nature of the relationship between youth subcultures and wider society. This allows us to establish the extent to which our approach, and its emphasis upon the constructive properties of language use, enable us to say anything about more conventional sociological perspectives on youth subcultures. More than this: a key concept in the literature on youth subcultures and the Social Identity approach has been the way that individuals constitute society through their membership of groups. Moreover, the social identity which is derived from group membership or social category ascription is often regarded as the link between individuals and society. This, then, makes issues of group affiliation and social identity a significant issue in the relationship between individuals and society. Nonetheless, our analyses in these chapters reveal some unexpected themes. For it is not issues of social identity and celebrations of the group which permeate these accounts, but themes of individuality, autonomy and authenticity. The ways that these issues emerge as recurrent participants' concerns allow us to say more about the group, the subculture and individual members.

In our concluding chapter we assess the kinds of empirical gains our approach has yielded for the study of youth subcultures, and our understanding of broader issues concerning the relationship between the individual and the social group. We then consider a number of benefits yielded by taking a pragmatic approach to the understanding of the relationship between self and identity, and pursue the implications of our analyses for issues concerning authenticity, personal motivation and the concept of the social group.

Chapter 1

YOUTH SUBCULTURES AND SOCIOLOGY

Youth subcultures[1] attract a lot of attention, both from the mass media and from academics. This is not surprising. Members of youth subcultures tend to be highly visible, and occasionally engage in activities that most 'ordinary' people would find incomprehensible or worthy of censure. Youth subcultures have tended to generate 'moral panics'; successive subcultures have been identified as new 'folk devils', and media reaction has further ensured their prominence. Moreover, the activities of members of subcultural groups, and developments in youth subcultures more generally, have always tended to make good 'copy' for journalists.

Academics have been interested in subcultures because they have assumed a centrality in what Davis (1990) calls the 'youth question' debate: they are taken to represent, albeit in extreme form, what 'youth of today are up to'. Moreover, the 'youth question' in general, and youth culture in particular, have come to be seen as indexes of the condition and direction of wider society. So, youth cultures are seen as the product or epitome of social change, or a barometer of future changes. Consequently, youth subcultures have been given a significance and prominence within much wider sociological debates, and beyond the lives of the minority of adolescents who are involved.

One of the objectives of this chapter is to sketch a brief history of subcultural developments up to the present day. Our historical account draws upon sociological and conventional wisdom concerning the nature and succession of various subcultural groups, and the time period within which they are primarily located. Later in this book we show how the constitution and meaning of the subcultural group are flexibly constructed, and we shall argue that the concept of the group is as nebulous as its constitution. Our intention in this chapter, however, is simply to portray the starting points for traditional sociological explanations: the common and accepted assumptions about the attributes of the phenomena to be explained.

Furthermore, in the course of this review, we draw upon Davis's (1990) analysis of the ways youth subcultures have been interpreted within the context of social, economic and political changes. This will also permit us to chart media interest in youth subcultures and its often ambivalent reactions of condemnation and admiration. These reactions are due, in part, to the association forged between youth subcultures and images of delinquency, progressiveness and social commentary. In the following section of this chapter, we will show how these themes are picked up and developed within the kinds of sociological explanations which have been produced to account for youth subcultures.

A brief history of subcultural forms

The first post-war, high-visibility, working-class subculture was the teddy boys. They appeared in the working-class districts of south and east London in about 1953, and died out in the late 1950s. They came mainly from unskilled backgrounds (Fyvel, 1963). Their elegant appearance, which consisted of an Edwardian style suit, thick crepe-soled suede shoes and hair greased and combed into a quiff, was offset by their butch, territorial, masculine image and their possession of flick knives and other weapons. Their music was rock'n'roll imported from North America (for example, Elvis Presley, Bill Haley, and Eddie Cochran).

'Teds' are significant because the way society in general reacted to them set the scene for public, media and academic concern with subsequent youth subcultures. From the outset, they were associated in the media with public disturbances (including race riots and disturbances in dance halls and other public places); sudden violence directed at other people; and with the increase in juvenile delinquency after the Second World War. The teddy boy image thus served as a symbol and focus for adult anxiety over juvenile delinquency and violence, and more generally as an indication of something seriously wrong with at least a significant sector of the younger generation and therefore, by implication, with contemporary society at large.

According to Davis (1990), the negative stereotyping of the ted was also closely related to a common and growing perception from the early 1950s onwards that Britain was 'not what it used to be'. He suggests that the roots of this anxiety lay in the decline of the British empire and the nation's loss of its status as a primary economic and political power. In the new climate of apparent widespread changes, it seemed that Britain's established value system was under threat; what was regarded as the certainty and stability of the old order was perceived to be disintegrating fast, and the teddy boy provided the ideal screen onto which many of the most deep-rooted anxieties about and hostile evaluations of the new order could be projected.

Academic explanations for the teddy boy spectacle included the psychological impact of the experience of a childhood spent in wartime (absent fathers, evacuation, and the context of violence) as well as contemporary social ills such as boredom inherent in an affluent society, the breakdown of the family and traditional authority patterns, materialism, too much sex and so on (Fyvel, 1963).

Alongside such fears, however, there coexisted a more optimistic perception of the state of the nation and its youth who had 'never had it so good'. This perception was related to the idea that society was more affluent, and that traditional class divisions were becoming eroded in politics and lifestyle. In turn, these myths (Clarke *et al.*, 1976) were reflected in a growing preoccupation with the teenager. For example, the *Daily Mirror* initiated a trend in the mid-1950s for the press to report on and interpret the dress, customs and habits of teenagers and this quickly spread throughout the popular press. In addition, the activities of pop and rock stars became newsworthy material and, by the 1960s, they were singled out as spokespeople for the teenagers. It was thought that knowledge of the habits and behaviour of teenagers could indicate the way in which British society might develop in the post-war era. By the end of the 1950s, images of youthful violence and delinquency, and of newness and progressiveness were well established, permeating discussion of youth in general. Existing alongside these images was a belief that a unified, classless, consumption-based youth culture had emerged. The more cynical commentators, however, argued that the emergence of the new youth culture was aided if not created by an expansion in the music and media industries which was aimed specifically at the youth market (see Frith, 1983).

The 1960s witnessed the emergence of a variety of new 'folk devils': mods and rockers, and skinheads, as well as the more middle-class hippies and student activists.[2]

The mods (or modernists) originated in the early 1960s in east London and the new towns of the south-east of England, and came from the lower white-collar, upwardly mobile sections of the working class. In contrast to the teddy boys, the mods were more subtle and subdued in appearance. They wore conservative suits with neat, narrow trousers and their hair was generally short. Mods were associated with speed, both in their lifestyle (nightclubbing and scooters) and in their use of amphetamines. Their music was ska or West Indian popular music, together with some commercial spinoffs like The Who and Rod (then 'the Mod') Stewart and the Faces. Mods were characterised as consumers, and specialist mod boutiques and mod clubs opened up, demonstrating that there was an industry waiting to capitalise on the new enthusiasm for all things mod. However, mods were not merely passive consumers of a commercial subcultural product: Hebdige (1976) argues that they modified what they consumed. Scooters, for example, which had formerly been a respectable means of transport, were transformed and customised with a flamboyant use of scooter accessories.

The term 'rockers' encompassed both bikers and greasers; they were distinguished in terms of the extent to which they were involved in the 'cult of the motorcycle' (Brake, 1985). They were low paid, unskilled manual labourers (Barker and Little, 1964). Their style consisted of black leather jackets, studs, boots and faded jeans and, for some, the motorcycle. Their music taste, rock'n'roll, was shared with the earlier teddy boys. Their image was violent, studiedly working-class, butch, wild, anti-domestic, anti-authority and sexist; in keeping with this the motorcycle was regarded as a symbol of freedom, mastery and intimidation.

The media tended to focus on the supposed rivalry between mods and rockers. Mods were said to ridicule the crude, traditionally masculine self-image of the rockers, counterposing their own coolness and sophistication to the rockers' oafish crudity; and the rockers focused on the effeminacy of the mod style in contrast to their ostentatious masculinity. Murdock (1974) argues that one consequence of the media portrayal of polarisation was that these elements of style became reified and amplified in the self-images of group members.

By 1965, the working-class youth subcultures of the mods and rockers had come to be the central focus for what Davis (1990) calls the 'youth spectacle'. This was primarily a result of reports of seaside Bank Holiday clashes between mods and rockers during 1964, setting in motion a spiral of media-conveyed and amplified moral panic. The mods and rockers were widely cast in the role of folk devils, and became the focus for the expression of many anxieties in the parent society and culture (S. Cohen, 1972).[3]

As with earlier images of post-war juvenile delinquency and the rock'n'roll/teddy boy riots of the 1950s, the mods and rockers were associated with mob violence, viewed as a manifestation of a new mindless group orientation and supposedly unprecedented violence amongst certain sectors of contemporary youth. It may be noted that such images of mindless or irrational crowds were hardly new: Le Bon's (1895) work on the crowd used similar imagery. What distinguished them, however, was the way that these disturbances were seen as somehow the product of post-war affluence. Moreover, the association between delinquency and working-class youth subcultures was again reinforced, providing a rationale for the hostile image of youth as a problem of social control. Simultaneously, mods were seen as a manifestation of the youthful, progressive and classless new Britain of the 1960s; a symbol of greater dynamism, mobility and optimism in the future.

By the end of the 1960s, mods and rockers had been replaced as the major folk devils by the skinheads. The skinheads' style was aggressively working-class. They wore big industrial work boots or Doc Martens, jeans (rolled up to reveal this aggressive footwear) or sta-pressed trousers, braces, button-down collared shirts, and hair cut to the skull. They formed local gangs named after a local leader or area, marked their patch with slogans and defended their territory (which included the street corner, the pub and the football ground). They were also violent and concerned with a collective masculine self-conception; masculinity was identified with physical toughness and an unwillingness to back down in the face of trouble.

Their concern with toughness was manifested in several well-publicised skinhead activities: 'Paki-bashing', 'queer bashing' and football hooliganism. According to some commentators, Paki-bashing involved the ritual and aggressive defence of the social and cultural homogeneity of the traditional working-class community against immigrant Pakistanis and other Asians, whose visibility made them obvious outsider scapegoats. Queer bashing (which extended beyond gays and hippies to anyone who was considered to 'look odd') was read as a reaction against the erosion of traditional stereotyped masculinity.

According to Davis (1990), the emergence of the skinheads should be located in the context of rising youth unemployment and inner city decay of the late 1960s. Consequently, more liberal commentators interpreted the phenomenon as a direct and creative response to an increasingly stringent and limiting set of objective material circumstances. However, the appearance of the skinheads marked a downward trend in the image of youth which continued throughout the 1970s and 1980s. And despite their status as folk devils, based largely around their professed involvement in football violence and overt, aggressive racism, the market nevertheless exploited them through skinhead movies, books and bands, so that in the early 1970s there was a thriving skinhead industry both to cater for and create a demand.

The 1970s: punks and nostalgia

During the mid-1970s, a range of styles and groupings, including glamrock, enjoyed fairly widespread allegiance, but none really achieved media prominence until the emergence of the punk subculture in 1976. This has been so vividly and comprehensively documented by the mass media that we need here only present the briefest reminder. Punks wore torn clothing held together with safety pins. They designed asexual creations from plastic dustbin liners, they adapted old school uniforms and used cheap material like lurex or mock leopardskin in their creations. They wrapped chains around their necks as if to symbolise their bondage (Cashmore, 1984). Their hair was shaved close to the head, dyed outrageous colours and later spiked up into multicoloured 'mohicans'. In the early days at least, their integrity was measured by their ability to create their own costume, and therefore persona, which resisted commercial influence. Despite their alleged attack on the uncritical consumption of mass-produced artefacts and style, an industry quickly developed.

Punk music was raucous; it was characterised by (often avowed) musical incompetence and lyrics urging rebellion; New Wave was seen as its more sophisticated version (*Melody Maker*, 28/5/77). It was also seen as a reaction against the adulation of ageing superstars, complex electronic music, musical virtuosity and high prices for concerts. Punks rejected the separation between artist and audience, and punk musicians emphasised their identification with their audiences, often signalled by reciprocal spitting at concerts. (A stereotypical feature of punk rock gigs was that the band members and audience spat at each other, an act which has been interpreted as symbolising their equal status and cohesiveness.)

Punks described themselves as 'anti-social', 'into chaos' and out to shock everyone (Laing, 1978). They denied any explicit political stand, and instead seemed determined to pursue nihilistic and hedonistic lifestyles. Punk was a vague package of criticisms, of which few were constructive (Cashmore, 1984). So, punks were seen as rebelling against families, work, education, morals, religion, the monarchy: every institution that seemed part of the status quo was rejected. In its place, they proposed anarchy. They underlined their refusal to conform and to take on poorly paid, 'dead-end' jobs by making sure they would not be employed (Brake, 1985; Marsh, 1977).

Punk emerged as the major deviant youth subculture of the time. New moral panic was generated, largely as a consequence of media coverage of outrages supposedly perpetrated by the Sex Pistols (Davis, 1990). Newspapers quickly incorporated punk into their headlines and wrote of a menacing new cult which threatened to corrupt the nation's youth. Punk was identified with vulgarity, violence, vileness, venereality and intellectual vacancy (to illustrate this point, Cashmore cites a line from the Sex Pistols song 'Pretty Vacant' (1977): 'we're vacant and we don't care'). The media coverage in turn enlarged punk's appeal to young people with little interest in conformity, no investment in society, and who were unemployed.

Gradually, punks aligned themselves with the Rock against Racism movement and the Anti-Nazi League. They thus became enemies of the second wave of skinheads who reappeared in the latter part of the 1970s, partly due to their active recruitment by the British National and the National Front Parties. Punks' alignment with the Rock against Racism movement introduced social comment and political criticism into their music. This alignment was perhaps not surprising. Hebdige, for example, draws strong parallels between Rastafarians and punks: they came from the same housing estates, were educated on the same irrelevant curricula, and felt a similar sense of alienation and antagonism towards the existing social order. There were also a number of punk-reggae clubs and discos which appeared on the scene in the last years of the 1970s. It is worth noting that during the late 1970s there was a general sense of a worsening economy, rising unemployment, poorer living standards, deteriorating race relations and hence the collapse of the optimism of the 1950s and 1960s. Punk was readily interpreted as a symbol of Britain in decline; and the more progressive and optimistic image of youth disappeared (Davis, 1990).

Punk became less widespread in the 1980s, although a second generation of punks continued to assert the vitality of punk and its relevance at a time of severe depression for youth. Cashmore (1984) argues that the longevity of punk (and Rasta) attests to their lasting significance and the way that they articulated genuine and deeply held sentiments, and gave vent to the bitterness, resentment and sometimes fury of youth in the 1970s and 1980s. During this latter period, punk and punk music went through several transformations: crass, hardcore and skateboard punk, thrash punk and crusty punks.

Alongside punk and a second wave of skinheads, the late 1970s witnessed the revival of a number of earlier youth subcultures. Teddy boys reappeared in 1977, emerging in opposition to the punks. In the following year, coinciding with the release of the film *Quadrophenia*, there was a mod revival in which young people began dressing in the traditional mod style and riding motor scooters decorated with multiple lamps and chromed side panels. These revivals were interpreted as an attempt to recreate the heady, swinging and anti-authoritarian spirit of the 1960s. None of these revivals were long-lasting or significant (Cashmore, 1984).

The 1980s: post-punk subcultures

Some commentators have argued that youth subculture in the 1980s ceased to exist, and that once rebellious and deviant youth had become conformist, conservative and apathetic. Certainly, it seems that (Acid House aside) youth subcultures in the 1980s have not achieved the same notoriety, pervasiveness, or folk devil status of the earlier subcultures. Nonetheless, a number of different distinct subcultures did emerge in the 1980s. For example, there were followers of bands associated with the two-tone movement like The Specials, early Madness, The Jam and The Beat. To varying degrees the two-tone bands were critical of aspects of society, including inequality, violence, unemployment and specific institutions like marriage and mental asylums. The most salient feature of the movement was, however, its anti-racist stance: many of the bands had black and white members, and two-tone concerts were often organised in conjunction with political campaigns against racism.

In the early 1980s (or late 1970s), the image of punk was largely superseded by that of the relatively 'safe' New Romantics who listened to bands like Spandau Ballet, Japan and Simple Minds. They were interpreted as a synthesis of earlier subcultures, especially glamrock, together with an attempt at an alternative lifestyle and bohemian attitude to work reminiscent of the early hippies. They were utterly committed to being unique and went to extreme lengths in their efforts to accomplish this through coloured and spiked hair, outlandish fabrics, wide trousers, flamboyant frilly blouses and jester-pointed shoes. Cashmore (1984) describes New Romantics as the most utterly narcissistic and self-indulgent youth subculture; its adherents had no focus beyond the individual. Instead they divorced themselves from the drab monotony of the working day, and withdrew from socially significant issues. They were, he says, sealing themselves into a make-believe world populated by beautiful people who were unconcerned by material affairs, and who structured their lives around looking good and listening to music. Cashmore interprets this subculture as a response to the crisis of the recession in the later

1970s and early 1980s; since society seemed to have little future, it made sense to live only for the moment, to concentrate solely on oneself and the art of self-attention. New Romantics, however, did not last long and by 1981 the culture had largely disappeared.

A visually stark contrast to the New Romantics were followers of heavy metal, a sanitised version of the rockers from the 1960s. They wore denim clothes covered in studs and appliqués, and their hair was long and wild. In the late 1970s heavy metal seemed to acquire a new popularity. Heavy metal attracted predominantly white working-class followers, devotees of the kind of electric guitar-based rock that grew out of the late 1960s and early 1970s exemplified by Led Zeppelin, but adopted by a whole succession of bands since then: AC/DC, Black Sabbath, Iron Maiden, Motorhead and so on.

Later in the 1980s, the gothics emerged in the media spotlight with the chart successes of bands like The Mission, Fields of the Nephilim, and the Sisters of Mercy. The style was predominantly black clothing, offset by heavy jewellery and whitened faces. Typically, goths dyed their hair black and backcombed it to make it appear untamed. The goths' 'gloom and doom' image (Savage, 1987) was reinforced by purported interest in darkness, death, coffins, grave-yards, (early) horror movies, and, inevitably, vampires.

Finally, the 1980s saw the brief appearance of Acid House which did inspire a moral panic, albeit a minor one. The attributes of Acid House were psyche-delia, Acid (the drug), a 'smiley' face logo, beachwear, Lucozade, and fluores-cent paraphernalia. The music fused two earlier forms, both of which were based on sampling existing forms of synthesiser and computer-generated dance music. The moral panic focused on drug use: ecstasy and LSD were (supposedly) consumed during large warehouse parties which, according to the media, verged on sexual orgies. Ecstasy was reported as a 'sex' drug, and media reports focused on the dangers of the sexual violation of drugged girls (Redhead, 1990).

Perhaps the most significant images of youth in the late 1980s and 1990s are more directly related to social and political issues rather than subcultural groups: unemployment, AIDS and sexuality, drugs and hooliganism (and lager louts) have received more attention in the media than subcultural groups. For the present, the 'youth spectacle' does seem to be locked into the more or less routine and institutionalised portrayal of the latest youth fashions and fads. What has persevered, though, is an image of youth as a problem; what has been lost over the decades is the image of youth as a 'progressive' class, and as an asset to the nation.

Sociological interpretations

The main sociological explanation for these kinds of distinctive subcultural groups was developed by researchers in the Centre for Contemporary

Cultural Studies at Birmingham University. It came to be known as New Subcultural Theory (or theories). In order to understand what was new about this perspective, as well its primary emphases, it is useful to consider briefly the earlier functionalist theories developed by American sociologists interested in delinquency, and by British educational sociologists. These studies focused on four key themes which were to become central in New Subcultural Theory, namely, class, delinquency, culture and leisure. These themes are, of course, related to aspects of the youth spectacle we documented above.

Both early and later theorists were critical of the assumption, perpetuated by the mass media and the work of academics like Parsons (1942, 1950), and Coleman (1961), that youth was a homogeneous, unified and classless group with its own distinct culture. Instead, they emphasised the significance of growing up in a society structured by class. Albert Cohen (1955), for example, described how inequalities and disadvantages in the education system were important in shaping the experiences and self-values of young working-class males. Delinquency was then interpreted as a collective, immediate, and practical solution to structurally imposed problems.

The delinquent solution was not, however, simply regarded as a matter of engaging in particular kinds of activities; these activities were part of a *culture* of delinquency which included a set of core values such as toughness, hedonism, immediate excitement and defiance of authority. Disagreement amongst theorists focused on the origins of the values; how were they derived? A. Cohen (1955) argued that delinquent culture represented a rejection and inversion of the essentially middle-class values embedded in the school system. By contrast, others like Miller (1958) and Matza and Sykes (1961) argued that delinquents picked up and emphasised values which were embedded in working-class culture. Cloward and Ohlin (1960) suggested that delinquents shared certain middle-class values, especially those related to hedonistic consumption and material status. Since their access to institutionalised means of realising these values was restricted, they simply turned to illegitimate means of acquisition. These observations indicated that youth subcultures had to be understood in relation to rather than as separate from working- and middle-class values (Matza and Sykes, 1961).

British educational sociologists developed these ideas further; they conducted a series of ethnographic studies in the later 1960s in which they emphasised the role of cultural artefacts and leisure in the delinquent solution. In particular, they observed that having rejected the school culture, anti-academic cultures were centred around a leisure-based culture of pop music, fashion and leisure activities (Sugarman, 1967; Hargreaves, 1967). Class, nevertheless, mediated anti-school responses and culture. For example, it structured young people's access and opportunities within the domain of leisure; therefore, for many working-class male adolescents, delinquent street corner culture provided the only viable solution to their double disadvantage (Downes, 1966).

As a consequence of these developments, the assumption of a homogeneous youth culture was fully rejected in favour of an understanding of the distinct features of working-class youth cultures and their relation to adult working- and middle-class values (Murdock and McCron, 1976).

Like the older theories, New Subcultural theorists' interpretation of the existence and meaning of the working-class youth subcultures focused on the structural conditions which constituted the problem, and the cultural forms which represented the solution. There were, however, important differences between the two approaches. In particular, New Subcultural Theory embraced neo-Marxism[4] and sought to provide a clearer conception of the interrelations between subcultures and class cultures through the notion of hegemony and winning space (see below).

On a structural level, New Subcultural Theory, like the old, acknowledged that structural relations and inequality provide the basic generating force for the formation or existence of subcultures. But they went further than this by locating the structural problem and its subcultural solution in historical and geographical context (S. Cohen, 1980: v). For example, Phil Cohen (1972), argued that the roots of the problems experienced by youth lay in the postwar destruction of the working-class community and its traditional culture. Corrigan (1979) pointed to the historical role played by compulsory state education in attacking working-class culture which, he argued, was re-enacted every day within the hidden political battleground of the school. In his ethnographic study of 'the lads', Willis (1977) similarly drew upon the metaphor of guerilla warfare to characterise their behaviour. These studies demonstrate the beginnings of a theoretical perspective which emphasises *resistance* and opposition to structural problems rather than compensation for them. Moreover, this intellectual shift had two consequences: it removed the individualistic bias of earlier theories, in which individuals were deemed to feel status frustration, alienation and so on; and the emphasis upon structural considerations meant that analysts did not have to take account of whether or not young people recognised that their membership of subcultures was a collective response to socio-structural problems.

The subcultural solution was analysed at the level of culture, but it was first necessary to specify the relationship between social structure and culture. The culture of a society reflects the values and interests of different groups in society, of which class groupings are the most basic. However, groups do not have equal status in society, and neither do the cultural values attached to them. The dominant values in society are middle-class values; they constitute the norms of society and are reflected in institutions like education. To some extent, the working classes endorse these values; in Gramsci's (1971) terms they consent to be dominated by them. This idea is captured in Gramsci's concept of hegemony: rule by agreement or coercion rather than by force. At the same time, and within the dominant system of values, the subordinate classes negotiate space for the coexistence of their own values. The spaces they win may be physical (streets, pubs, etc.) or social (networks of family and friends, work and neighbourhood relations).

Young people are born into and socialised within a particular class culture, but because social conditions change over time, they are also subject to different experiences and influences from their parents. They therefore negotiate space for their own culture (or, more appropriately, *sub*culture) within the parent class culture. The spaces they win include territory like street corners within the locality, time and space for leisure and recreation, and occasions for social interaction (the weekend, the disco, football matches, or standing about doing nothing). In this way, subcultures both 'create and express *autonomy* and *difference* from parents' and 'maintain . . . the *parental identifications* which support them' (P. Cohen, 1972: 26). Clearly, the concepts of hegemony and winning space are more sophisticated than the original ideas that working-class youth subcultures simply inverted dominant values, or took over working-class values.

As well as negotiating a space for working-class youths' collective existence, it was claimed that subcultures also provided a solution to a range of problems faced by young people: unemployment, educational disadvantage, low pay, 'dead-end' jobs and so on. However, it was not claimed that subcultures offered a direct solution to these problems; rather, it was claimed that they offered a solution at a *symbolic* level. According to Clarke *et al.* (1976), subcultures solve at an imaginary level the problems which remain unresolved at the concrete material level, and this is why the solution is necessarily symbolic. Style enables the young working-class person to achieve in image what they cannot achieve in reality. For example, the teddy boys' appropriation of an upper-class style, in the form of Edwardian dress coats, 'covered the gap' between the implicated lifestyle and their largely manual, unskilled, low status real careers and life chances. Subcultural styles then were seen as symbolic resources in the young person's resistance against societal inequalities.

However, specific clothes and possessions of objects do not in themselves make a style. Instead, '[W]hat makes a style is the activity of stylisation – the active organisation of objects with activities and outlooks, which produce an organised group-identity in the form and shape of a coherent and distinctive way of "being-in-the world" ' (Clarke *et al.*, 1976: 54). This in turn requires the active selection and construction of styles from the raw materials often provided by the new youth industries so that they convey particular meanings. Drawing on Barthes (1971), the New Subcultural theorists argued that objects don't have fixed meanings; instead, it is claimed that their cultural meaning derives from their social use. Objects may thus be taken from one context and given new meanings by placing them in different contexts (Clarke, 1976). For example, when the teddy boys took over the Edwardian suit, which was supposed to signify the aristocratic man about town, they imbued it with new meaning. Similarly, industrial work boots (DMs) were traditionally seen as appropriate footwear for unskilled manual labour. The skinheads took them out of this context, placed them in the new stylistic context of short jeans, braces and short hair, wherein they signified working-class hardness and masculinity. This process of recontextualisation has been called 'bricolage' in New Subcultural Theory. It had considerable power to provoke and disturb because it undermined conventional meanings: it challenged the symbolic universe (Hebdige, 1979).

The reordering of objects was not random, but made sense through its fit with the group's focal concerns; that is, they formed a *homology*. This term was applied to subcultures by Willis (1978) in his study of hippies and bikers, to describe the symbolic fit between the values and lifestyles of a group, its subjective experience, and the musical forms used to express or reinforce its central concerns. Similarly, 'the adoption by skinheads of boots and short jeans and shaved hair was "meaningful" in terms of the subculture only because these external manifestations resonated with and articulated skinhead conceptions of masculinity, hardness and working-classness' (Clarke *et al.*, 1976:56). This image, in turn, was related to the skinheads' concern with 'recapturing' or 'recreating' the kind of working-class life or community that had been lost as a result of the social reorganisation of working-class communities. So, adopted objects, dress, appearance, language, styles of interaction and music formed a unity with the group's concerns, experiences and activities; their concerns were crystallised in an expressive form which then defined the group's public identity.

To summarise, according to New Subcultural theorists, subcultures express a fundamental tension between those in power and those condemned to subordinate positions. This tension is expressed in the form of subcultural style (Hebdige, 1979). Subcultures are then interpreted as a form of resistance which is symbolically represented in style. Subcultural style is then read, like a text, as resistance through *ritual*: resistance to subordination. Territoriality, solidarity, aggressive masculinity, stylistic innovation are all attempts by working-class youth to reclaim community, and reassert traditional values while resisting dominant ones. Finally, in addition to symbolising resistance, style communicates a group identity which is often said to be in opposition to another subcultural group. It provokes a reaction and members are often stigmatised. Subcultural styles have become the principal way in which the mass media report or visualise youth. Judges, the police and social workers will use stereotypes based on appearance and dress to label groups and link them with certain characteristic kinds of behaviour.

Criticisms of the CCCS work

The work of the Centre for Contemporary Cultural Studies has not gone unchallenged. First, it has been criticised for neglecting non-white subcultures, subcultures whose membership is largely female, and female members of traditionally male subcultures. The focus in new subcultural theory is almost exclusively on white male working-class youth. But if subcultures offer solutions to problems that arise through the socio-structural position of this section of the population, what of those who are not only subordinated by being young and working class, but also through their ethnicity and gender? Hebdige (1979) did outline Rasta and rudie subcultures as well as the related musical forms, reggae, ska and bluebeat. His interest in them was, however, primarily informed by his argument that white working-class subcultures are responses to black culture and communities. Women too have been regarded as peripheral in New Subcultural Theory and in subcultures (Dorn and South, 1982; McRobbie, 1980). One reason for this has been that the theory focuses on street life rather than on family and domestic life in which females tend to be more involved, and through which they are more constrained and controlled. There have since been efforts to rectify these omissions. Several studies, for example, show how race mediates both the experiences and responses of black youth (for example, Brake, 1985; Cashmore, 1984; Hebdige, 1987). There have also been attempts to examine females' participation in subcultures, especially the teeny bopper culture (McRobbie and Garber, 1976; see also Brake, 1985), and in delinquent gangs (Campbell, 1981)

Second, Redhead (1990) has argued that the New Subcultural theorists displayed an overcommitment to the *authenticity* of the subculture. They overemphasise the extent to which subcultures are internally generated, at street or grassroots level, rather than a result of commercial enterprise. This has been explained as one consequence of 'the understandable zeal to depict the kids as creative agents rather than manipulated dummies' (S. Cohen, 1980: xii)[5].

Nevertheless, there has been some acknowledgement of the role played by the youth culture industries (fashion, music, media and so on). For example, Clarke *et al.* (1976) claim that these industries make available the objects which are used and redefined by subcultures. Hebdige (1979) examines the tension between the creation of new objects and symbols and their translation into marketable commodities which renders them inauthentic. The main thrust of the criticism, however, centres on the *origins* of the subculture. Thus, Stan Cohen has suggested that the major components in punk were developed by commercial entrepreneurs and 'lumpen intellectuals' from art schools and rock journals. The dispute is theoretically significant because if the subcultural form can be regarded as commercial exploitation rather than a 'folk' expression of the street, then its interpretation as working-class youths' creative resistance to their subordination and to dominant culture and its values is called into question.

Third, CCCS workers have been criticised because their explicit political agenda has led them to overlook the negative elements of working-class youth subcultures, and because economic and ideological abstractions have obscured the importance of personal responsibility (Woods, 1977). To make this point clear, it is useful to contrast the new with the older subcultural theories. In the older theories, the delinquents were neither condemned nor admired; they were simply the casualties of a system that didn't work for everyone. The New Subcultural theories began with a more overtly political agenda: to interpret subcultures as resistance to dominant cultural values. So, Hebdige begins with the idea that style is a form of 'Refusal', and an acknowledgement that this was something to celebrate: that 'this Refusal is worth making, that these gestures have a meaning, that the smiles and sneers have some subversive value' (Hebdige, 1979:3).

This commitment to the idea of resistance meant that the subcultures were admired for every aspect or gesture that could be interpreted as a form of resistance. S. Cohen (1980) suggests that it is because of this commitment that much of the theory masks a curious value distortion.

> The subculture is observed and decoded, its creativity celebrated and its political limitations acknowledged – and then the critique of the social order constructed. But while this critique stems from a moral absolutism, the subculture itself is treated in the language of cultural relativism. Those same values of racism, sexism, chauvinism, compulsive masculinity and anti-intellectualism, the slightest traces of which are condemned in bourgeois culture, are treated with a deferential care, an exaggerated contextualisation, when they appear in the subculture. (S. Cohen, 1980:xxvii)

Fourth, the CCCS workers' political agenda was accompanied and enabled by their commitment to particular theoretical perspectives: a combination of neo-Marxism, structuralism and semiotics. This in turn led to the complaint that their analyses tended to be densely theoretical with little empirical data (D. Clarke, 1980; Davis, 1990). There was, then, a tendency towards overtheorisation.

> [T]he new theories about British post war youth cultures are massive exercises of decoding, reading, deciphering and interrogating. These phenomena *must* be saying something to us – if only we could know exactly *what.* So the whole assembly of cultural artefacts, down to the punks' last safety pin, have been scrutinized, taken apart, contextualized and re-contextualized. The conceptual tools of Marxism, structuralism and semiotics, a Left-Bank pantheon of Genet, Lévi-Strauss, Barthes and Althusser have all been wheeled in to aid this hunt for the hidden code. (S. Cohen, 1980:ix. Original emphasis)

Theoretical ascriptions and the meaning of subcultures

We noted in our historical overview of youth subcultures that youth in general, and youth subcultures in particular, were used as metaphors for actual and potential (or feared) social changes in post-war Britain. New

Subcultural Theory takes this further in reading youth subcultures as *embodiments* of those changes (as well as reactions to them). Thus, forces in society are confused with the beliefs of young people. This point is taken to extreme by Cashmore who argues that, although most youth never get involved in subcultures, '[i]n a way, the subculture is an extreme statement of what youth is thinking, feeling and doing. Subcultures are often the vanguard, leading the way vividly and stridently, and articulating what many others want to say' (Cashmore 1984:18).

So, a set of theoretical assumptions and claims comes to be accepted as though they were making statements about the reality of contemporary adolescent lives and experiences. But this commitment to the 'seriousness' of youth subcultures, and the political message they are supposed to convey, meant that other, equally plausible accounts of their existence were discounted. For example, sociologists interpreted punk music as the direct expression of the youthful frustration of the street, high-rise flats and dole in the mid-1970s Labour Britain. But at the time critics argued that young unemployed people identified with punk because they shared its concern with more hedonistic activities, not because they believed it was a movement which could articulate their grievances (Frith, 1978). So, for many, affiliation may have more to do with fun, fashion, conformity and so on. Of course, without empirical data we are in no position to assess any theoretical account of the social and cultural meanings of subcultural groups.

Davis (1990) argues that an overcommitment to a particular theoretical stance has led to a consequent neglect of inconvenient aspects of the empirical domain. Despite their objective of locating each subculture in a sociohistorical context, subcultural theorists often seem to impose a (sometimes convoluted) theoretical explanation upon the empirical phenomena that they set out to analyse. Thus:

> The fundamentally neo-marxist and semiological perspectives of the 'new subcultural theory' too often seem to lead to a situation in which its proponents *start out* with certain theoretical assumptions – most notably and centrally the 'resistance through rituals' thesis that (all) working class youth subcultural phenomena, whether in the realm of style (mods' scooters, punks' safety pins . . .) or of action (riots, hooliganism . . .) can be read as 'symbolic', 'displaced' (. . . etc.) manifestations of the class struggle and the contradictions of capitalism – and *work back* from this to the empirical domain, when it is by no means always clear that the latter can in fact sustain the theoretical demands that are being made of it. (Davis, 1990:13. Original emphasis)

The point, for Davis, is that theory and empirical investigation should be brought into a closer and more mutually beneficial interrelationship.

Another common theoretical approach has been to interpret aspects of a subculture's style as symbols which hid a message. For example, consider the tendency of some punks to wear swastikas. According to Hebdige (1979), on one level this symbol was worn to outrage and shock others. But more important, he claims it is *really* being employed in a meta-language: the wearers are ironically distancing themselves from the usual message that the symbol conveys. For Hebdige, wearing a swastika illustrates how symbols are taken from their natural context, exploited for empty effect, displayed through mockery, distancing, irony, parody and inversion. Such a reading is, says Cohen, imaginative. But on what basis can we choose between this interpretation, and any other plausible meaning, such as simple conformity, blind ignorance or actual racist sympathies? Hebdige appeals to the stereotyped image of punk as anti-racist to justify his 'ironic' interpretation, and yet we are not told how the wearers themselves 'manage the complicated business of distancing and irony' (Cohen, 1980:xvii). Also, there is the danger that relying too heavily on the symbolic meanings of actions and adornments can lead to peculiar theoretical descriptions of social acts. To illustrate this, Cohen draws attention to Hebdige's assessment of the symbolic significance of skinhead attacks on Pakistanis, in which he claims 'Every time the boot went in, a contradiction was concealed, glossed over or made to disappear' (Hebdige, 1979:58). The contradiction referred to here concerns skinheads' perception of, and reaction to, the threat to white, working-class culture as a result of the black presence in traditional working-class areas, while maintaining an apparently incompatible alliance and partial identification with West Indian immigrants and culture (reggae, ska and rude boys). So, 'Paki-bashing' (violent attacks on members of the Asian community) is interpreted at a symbolic level as a way of dealing with the internal conflict generated from a reaction against and affiliation to aspects of an immigrant culture. Cohen's point is that the language of symbolism may sometimes help by giving meaning to the 'otherwise meaningless', but its help is limited when skinhead attacks on Pakistani immigrants are couched in these terms (Cohen, 1980:xviii; see also Cashmore, 1984).

The absence of members' accounts

Many of the criticisms we have outlined point to a need to address the general issue of the relationship between the individual member and the subculture. They also suggest a need for empirical data in the form of members' accounts of their wider experiences, their reasons for affiliation with a subculture, and the subjective meaning attributed to the subculture. Nevertheless, the purpose and function of such account-gathering are unclear. Amongst the critical commentaries, at least two uses are suggested. First, members' accounts could be used to verify the appropriateness of the sociological interpretation. Second, they could be used to fill in an obvious gap in the theoretical literature: the absence of members' own biographical accounts.

The first role given to accounts relates to the issues of consciousness and intent. Cohen argues that while it would be unreasonable to expect every punk, gothic and skinhead to be fully aware of what his or her style signified, it seems that the symbolic language employed implies a knowing subject, who is at least dimly aware of what the symbols are supposed to mean. In other words, interpreting subcultures with reference to structural problems implies that, at some level at least, members were using them to respond to what they perceived to be structural problems. The implication is that if at least some members' accounts of what the subculture meant matched the sociological accounts, then these latter analytic descriptions would be warranted. However, other theorists disagree about the utility of collecting members' accounts because it is likely that the analysts' and members' accounts would not match: as Hebdige says of his analysis 'it is highly unlikely . . . that the members of any subcultures described in this book would recognise themselves reflected here' (Hebdige, 1979:139). Cohen suggests that theoretical approaches do not take seriously enough the relevance of the subculture to its members: 'The nagging sense here is that these lives, selves and identities do not always coincide with what they are supposed to stand for' (S. Cohen, 1980:xviii).

Perhaps there is an obvious reason for the neglect of members' own accounts and interpretations. Reading the theoretical literature, it is clear that the theorists' obvious admiration for the subcultures is infused with a mild contempt for the actual members. For example, throughout the literature, the people who affiliate with subcultures are referred to as 'kids'. This characterisation carries negative and patronising connotations, which imply that the category incumbents are not themselves taken very seriously. Moreover, it is a label that many people of fifteen and older would not readily accept. Apart from this, it is taken for granted that working-class youth are inarticulate. Take, for example, S. Cohen's comment that, even if one were to re-examine post-war British subcultures, one would have 'just the same (rather poor) sources of information from the same (often inarticulate) informants' (S. Cohen, 1980:ii). Similarly, Hebdige (1979:148), contrasting middle-class countercultures with working-class subcultures, argues that 'the revolt of middle class youth tends to be more articulate, more confident, more directly expressed and is, therefore, as far as we are concerned, more easily "read"'. Opposition in working-class subcultures is, by contrast, 'displaced into symbolic forms of resistance' (op. cit.:148). The implication is that working-class youth are inarticulate and therefore cannot directly express their views.

The analytic approach adopted by the New Subcultural theorists ensures that members of subcultures are effectively silenced before they have even been allowed to speak about their lives; the knowledge about them is not written in their own terms. So

> I sometimes have a sense of working-class kids suffering an awful triple fate.
> First, their actual current prospects are grim enough; then their predicament is
> used, shaped and turned to financial profit by the same interests which created it;

and then – the final irony – they find themselves patronised in the latest vocabulary imported from the Left Bank. (S. Cohen, 1980:xxviii)

The second role for members' own accounts is to cast light on biographical details: how the subculture is actually lived out by its members, and what membership means. In short, what is the nature of the relationship between the individual and the subculture?

Brake (1985) has paid some attention to this issue. Working within the New Subcultural Theory framework, he considers the functional significance of subcultures from the potential member's perspective. Specifically, he identifies five functions which subcultural group membership may serve.

First, subcultures offer solutions to problems which arise through an individual's position in the socioeconomic structure but which are collectively experienced (and at the same time perceived as personal). The style of the subculture symbolises resistance to subordination, challenges the dominant social order, and covers the gap between an individual's low status position in the labour force (or lack of achievement and sense of failure at school) and the position to which they aspire. Resistance, and hence the solution, do not actually do anything about problems like unemployment, educational disadvantage, low pay and so on, instead it provides a magic or symbolic solution. As a solution, subcultures are likely to attract those who feel little investment in or commitment to the system and hence the 'rebellious unconventionality', anti-authority, raw, violent image of subcultures (or street culture) become attractive.

Second, subcultures offer a culture and a collective identity which differs from identities ascribed through school, work and class. The culture includes the attributes of subcultures like style, lifestyle, music, image, values and ideology. These are said to provide a set of 'symbolic resources' which individuals can draw upon, or adopt, in order to project a particular image and hence achieve a different identity, thereby challenging the dominant social order. This in turn enables individuals to escape effectively their ascribed identities, and therefore (psychologically at least) to escape the problems which the ascribed categories entail.

Third, this identity or group membership enables the young person to experience an alternative form of social reality. This is because subcultures win 'cultural space' in which values, behaviour and lifestyles are accommodated which differ from the dominant values. In Brake's dramaturgical terms, they provide alternative scripts, in rebellion from adult authority. The world is perceived and interpreted through subcultural values, beliefs and so on. Building on the spatial metaphor, subcultures offer a 'free area' to relax with one's peers outside the scrutiny and demands of the adult world. The alternative script is performed outside the socialising forces of family, work, school (and marriage). It makes a statement about young people's difference from adult expectations, so that they are more free to develop and explore who they are. This is why their image is often deliberately rebellious or delinquent. Moreover, it dramatically emphasises their difference and individuality even though the latter is contained in a collectivity. The attraction of a subculture is its rebelliousness, hedonism, and the escape it offers from the restrictions of masculinity and femininity.

Related to the above is the fourth, more pragmatic function: subcultures offer a meaningful way of life during leisure. Through them one finds like-minded companions with whom to do things out of school, work, or domestic duties, or while unemployed. This may include going to football matches, clubs, gigs, or just hanging around.

Finally, subcultures offer to the individual solutions to certain existential dilemmas. This last function seems to tie up with ideas – both academic and common sense – about the nature and tasks of adolescence. These include a need to redefine 'who I am' in the face of changing roles and expectations. Moreover, adolescence and early adulthood are regarded as a period for reshaping values and ideas and exploring one's relationship to the world. Thus, subcultures are characterised as offering to working-class youth an equivalent to the moratorium which middle-class youth were said to seek in universities. In other words, they offer a temporal and geographical space, which can be used to test out questions about the world and their relationship to it. Identities and ideas can be experimented with, and possibilities for social change considered (Brake, 1985). This aspect of subcultures also explains why they can be given up, rejected as adolescent in favour of a more appropriate identity as social circumstances change, or as young people move towards alternative identities, say in marriage. For those who feel misunderstood, or that they do not fit, or feel rejected, for a while at least 'the scripts being composed in subcultures become highly attractive' (Brake, 1985:191).

Brake therefore extends the analysis of youth subcultures by shifting the focus to look at subcultures as solutions to problems from the individual's perspective (or from the perspective of the potential recruit). He is, however, working within the framework of New Subcultural Theory. Hence, he takes for granted the claims of that theory, for example, that the style *does* symbolise resistance to the oppressive social order, and that the individual recognises this. But this leads us back to the problem addressed earlier: it assumes that the sociologists' interpretations of the social significance of the subculture are at least similar to the perceptions of any potential or actual member.

We have returned, then, to the two main problems with New Subcultural Theory: its automatic assumption that the dimensions of a subcultural style manifest a form of resistance to structural inequalities; and the absence of any attempt to address members' own perceptions, opinions and attitudes, in short, their own accounts of their existence.

However, Brake's work also reveals other conceptual problems in New Subcultural Theory. For example, there seems to be some conceptual confusion between sub*cultures* and subcultural *groups* or categories. The term 'subculture' is occasionally used to refer to a constellation of cultural elements – style, values, lifestyle – which are grounded in, but separate from, both working-class and dominant cultures. However, the term is also used to refer to a collection of people – a group – who share similar concerns and experiences. Obviously, the group and its cultural form must somehow be related, but the nature of this relationship is unclear. Sometimes the impression is conveyed that cultural forms already exist and are merely 'taken over' by groups, so that 'Culture . . . may be seen as containing a source of signs or potential meaning structures which actors inherit and respond to' (Brake, 1985:8). Thus we are presented with a picture of a 'floating' culture with a life of its own, the elements of which exist in some form independent of their manifestation in people's activities and interaction. On the other hand, however, subcultures may be defined as 'meaning systems, modes of expression or lifestyles *developed by groups* in subordinate structural positions in response to dominant meaning systems, and which reflect their attempt to solve structural contradictions arising from the wider societal context' (Brake, *op. cit.*:8; our emphasis).

Here we are given the impression that it is groups of people who create cultural configurations, implying that the group must in some sense come first. Consequently we are unclear as to whether subcultural forms are the products of individuals' activities, or a predetermined, culturally available template for individual behaviour. To a certain extent, Brake does acknowledge the ambiguities in the use of the term subculture. For example, he notes that there are two complementary aspects of subculture: the structural issue of what constitutes membership of the category, which involves analysing social relations, and the hermeneutic aspect, which involves the analysis of the culture and what it means. The main point here, though, is that the term 'subculture' is used to refer to a collectivity (or symbolic collectivity) *and* a culture. But the main theoretical focus has been on the cultural dimensions of subcultures; there is little attention paid to members' involvement in actual social groups.

A related ambiguity pervades the conceptualisation of the relationship between subcultures and identity. On the one hand, it is suggested that identifying with a subculture entails using its values and imagery to alter one's own self-image (Murdock, 1974), to resolve existential dilemmas, and to emphasise personal difference and individuality. This suggests that being a punk (or whatever) is a central aspect of an individual's personal identity. Moreover, the implication is that subcultures do not constitute a group *one joins*, but instead constitute a *reference group*. The identity thus generated is an *individual* identity, not one that is seemingly related to membership of a group and based in interactions with other members.

On the other hand, Brake (1985) draws on a dramaturgical metaphor; he suggests that being a punk (etc.) is a matter of playing a role, and that this is learned through social interaction with significant others. Role playing involves the appropriate adoption of the image, demeanour (expression, gait and posture), and argot (the special vocabulary or jargon). It also requires the acquisition of performance skills: the ability to project the image with sincerity. The emphasis on learning through social interaction provides a stronger sense of the concrete and of involvement with like-minded others, but the implications of role playing for self-conception and identity are not made clear. What is missing from the sociological literature is any clear conceptualisation of the relationship between self, identity and membership of a subculture.

Moreover, whether affiliation with a subculture is conceptualised in terms of change in self-identity or the adoption of a role, theorists display an over-committed image of subcultural affiliation. That is, it is implied that being a punk is all you are and, as Kitwood (1980:278) observed, 'it can be misleading to characterise [the lives of members of subcultures] solely on that basis'. For example, any individual performs many roles. Even if, say, the punk role is the most important or salient one, the person will still be required to play an occupational or claimant role, or the role of daughter, sister, female and so on. In addition, there is no attempt to account for different degrees of commitment to the subculture, nor to address the possibility that apart from the adoption of a specific style and its code, any specific member may be a model of conventionality in other respects. These criticisms point, of course, to a need to collect biographical accounts of involvement, using an approach which is informed by a clearer understanding of self, identity and multiple social roles.

In social psychology, for example, a number of theorists have found it useful to distinguish between different aspects of the self-concept, social and personal identity. Social identity is based upon group membership and social roles, and personal identity includes a person's idiosyncratic traits and unique qualities (for example, Gergen, 1971). This conceptualisation would imply the status of subcultural identity as a social identity which is distinct from personal identity, and suggests one way of accounting for the ways that members are also individuals. Conceptualising subcultural affiliation in terms of social identity has a further advantage: insofar as it is tied to membership of a group, and groups are part of the social structure of society, it also provides a way of integrating individuals with society. Our subsequent analyses, however, show that there are problems with this notion of social identity; in particular, how it is regarded as separate from personal identity and a product of group membership. Nonetheless these ideas about individuality and social identity constitute a useful starting point in considering the kinds of issues we need to address.

In this chapter we have tried to identify several themes which run through theoretical sociological analyses of subcultures. Most obviously, there is a predominant assumption that subcultural forms equate with resistance to specific social structural conditions. Second, there is a deeply theoretical analysis of this resistance, and how it is manifest in the style of particular subcultures. Throughout our review we have tried to lodge our concerns with this body of work. Consider the idea that subcultures embody and instantiate a form of social resistance. It seems unclear to us whether or not this is a feature of the lives of the members themselves, or a theoretical ascription which simply echoes the political assumptions of a particular theoretical stance. A related concern is that there seems to be little regard for the utility of empirical research, and thus these kinds of highly theoretical analyses are produced in isolation from the actual behaviour of those individuals whose collective practices these theories are meant to illuminate. Clearly what is needed is an empirical attempt to take heed of members' own accounts: their own perceptions, reports, stories and anecdotes. And of course, this in turn forces us to consider the nature of the medium through which those accounts are produced. It seems methodologically imperative to identify what kind of medium natural language is before we produce analyses based on examination of peoples' accounts. We return to this issue in a later chapter.

However, there is a further range of fundamental conceptual issues which we need to address, and we tried to raise some of these by looking at Brake's assessment of the functions of subcultural membership. In particular, we need to be clear about the relationship between the individual, the subcultural group, and wider society. We also need to clarify the nature, status and meaning of social groups. We noted above that one way of understanding their interrelationship has been through the concept of social identity and group affiliation. Consequently, these issues are primary foci in our subsequent analyses. The conceptual relevance to the sociological literature as well as the marked absence of empirical data make our work highly relevant to that literature. Our focus on identity and on language, however, also makes this work relevant to wider debates in the social sciences regarding the self and society. It is a consideration of these issues to which we now turn.

Notes

1. By youth subcultures we are referring to highly visible, named groups of young people who are apparently characterised by their style and hairstyle, music preferences and beliefs: punks, gothics, rockers, hippies and skinheads, for example. We do not provide a more precise definition of these phenomena; we appeal in the first instance to readers' common-sense knowledge of these groups. Later, we shall see how members of the groups themselves characterise the meaning and constitution of subcultural categories.
2. Due to the limitations of space, we are not going to outline details of these latter subcultures; they have, anyway, been of less concern to sociologists.
3. Stan Cohen has examined these purported clashes in detail and in particular the way that they were reported and the (over)reactions to what were actually a few minor incidents. The events themselves were more to do with the inadequacy of local

facilities and rumours that local shopkeepers and publicans would not allow into their establishments any young person who could be identified as a mod or rocker; that is, they were to do with divisions between locals and the weekend trippers. They were amplified through the way they were characterised in the press, presented as 'battles' between the two groups thus crystallising the two groups' identities; transforming what were disparate small groups into national subcultures.

4. This turn towards more overtly conflictual theoretical perspectives may have been stimulated by the context in which New Subcultural theorists were writing (S. Cohen, 1980). During the 1970s Britain witnessed the dissolution of the myths of classlessness, embourgeoisement, consumerism and pluralism; there were early warnings of economic recession; there was high youth unemployment, and recognisable political resistance was weak. This context was woven into New Subcultural theories, and the 'problem' of the working-class adolescent came to be seen in terms of bitter conflict and resistance. The image of the delinquent changed from a 'frustrated social climber' to cultural innovator and critic (Cohen, 1980:iv).

5. Frith (1983) discusses the historical roots of the implication that any product which is commercially produced must be denuded of authenticity. This view derives partly from elitist derision of the 'Americanisation' of popular culture, its wide appeal, and mass production (which implied its inferiority), and the assumption that the masses consumed passively and that, therefore, mass culture was a form of the 'opium of the people' (a view that was popular in the 1950s).

Chapter 2

INDIVIDUALS AND SOCIETY
The linguistic turn in the study of identity

In the last chapter we reviewed the sociological literature on youth sub-cultures. We also identified a series of important issues which tend to be neglected in this literature: for example, the nature of social identity, the nature of the subcultural group, and the relationship between the individual, social group and wider society. An understanding of these issues is crucial if we are to contribute to an understanding of youth subcultures. They therefore constitute a central concern in this book, both conceptually as well as through our analytic focus. Moreover, the centrality of these issues ensures the relevance of our work to a second body of literature, that concerning the nature of the relationship between individuals and society. A review of this literature will show how these issues embody debates which have in recent years assumed a central prominence in a variety of social scientific enterprises.

In sociology, the issue of the relationship between individuals and society is primarily expressed in relation to two sets of concerns, social determinism and social change, both of which relate to the question of whether society exists independently of the individuals who make up society. These concerns arise because, with the exception of microsociology, most sociology is concerned with social influences that shape our lives (for example, Giddens, 1993). These include culture, social institutions (such as the family, education, the media, religion and work) as well as the 'structures of power' through which society is stratified (for example, class, race, organisations, the government and state). Defined in terms of social structures, society appears to have a firmness or solidity comparable to objects in the material environment. Because of this, society seems external to us: we live *in* society, and society exerts social constraints over our actions and sets limits to what we can do as individuals. But accepting the independent existence of society appears to deny human agency, suggesting instead that we are socially determined. This in turn seems to deny human freedom and autonomy. The problem becomes more acute when we consider the issue of social change: if society is independent of us, what is it that brings about these changes? Are they the result of social forces beyond our control? If so, then this surely denies us a role as creative human agents, actively controlling the conditions of our own lives and experiences.

Certainly, we ascribe agency to classes, institutions and governments as though they were entities; we talk about societies having needs and purposes; and we attribute social and psychological characteristics to social groups. But there is a sense in which this is absurd; surely these concepts only make sense when applied to individual human beings? Moreover, capitalist societies are based on a division of labour, but it is individuals who labour; it is individuals who make up families; and it is because there are individuals who are deemed in need of educating that the education system exists. The point is that society *is* only many individuals behaving in regular ways in relation to one another. That is, individuals *are* society, but how can this be reconciled with the apparently independent existence of society?

Within psychology, the individual–society debate has been felt most acutely in social psychology, since it is that area of psychology which is supposed to be about the more social aspects of individuals' mental life and behaviour. Social psychology is defined as an attempt 'to figure out how our social lives work' (Sabini, 1992:1) through its investigation of 'the manner in which the behaviour, feelings, and thoughts of one individual are influenced and determined by the behaviour and/or characteristics of others' (Baron *et al.*, 1974:3). Thus social psychology studies a variety of group and social influences including conformity, group performance, and intergroup relations, conflict and prejudice; it studies interpersonal relationships, and social attitudes, and it addresses social motives such as altruism, justice, bargaining and negotiation.

Nevertheless, social psychology has been shaped by its institutional and intellectual relationship with psychology, conventionally regarded as the study of individuals' mental life. As a consequence, the issue of the relationship between individuals and society is manifested primarily in the concern over the individualistic nature of social psychological theory and research. But this has not always been the case: several recent examinations of the history of the discipline have lamented the decline of the *social* psychological approaches represented by Wundt's (1900–20) folk psychology, McDougall's (1920) concept of the group mind, Le Bon's (1895) crowd psychology and Freud's (1921) psychology of the masses (Farr, 1990; Graumann, 1988).

The transformation to a discipline concerned with individuals' mental processes has been explained by reference to a variety of influences. First, there is the influence of particular social psychologists such as Floyd Allport (1924; for example, Farr, 1990; Graumann 1988) who argued against the idea of the social group and the distinctive reality of collective phenomena. For Allport, individuals are the primary social reality. Second, Parker (1989) has pointed to political struggles and manoeuvres within the American Psychological Association which ensured the prominence of experimentation which, by its very nature, focuses on individuals' responses. Third, it has been suggested that the individualistic focus is partly a result of the efforts to differentiate the social psychology practised in psychology and sociology departments (Parker, 1989). Finally, Gergen (1987) discusses the rise of behaviourism and the subsequent cognitive revolution in psychology. The change from behaviourism to cognition as the dominant paradigm can also be understood with reference to the issue of *agency*. Behaviourism apparently denied human agency by focusing upon the importance of environmental stimuli. Behaviourist psychologists refused to give a role to human minds; these were consequently represented as a 'black box' in between stimulus and response. Cognitivist psychologists, by contrast, gave primacy to individual agency and thinking, and assumed that mental processes and dispositions determine our behaviour.

But of course, our thought processes do not exist in a social vacuum. Society, culture, and the formal and informal groups to which we belong, all influence thinking, behaviour and feelings. In addition, numerous experiments have demonstrated that people make different kinds of decisions and judgements, and they behave differently when they are in the company of others. Clearly, psychological processes are not independent of the social context; if we want to understand fully how they work, we need to take account of these social factors. It is in the context of the cognitivist revolution that social psychologists have set about trying to resocialise the discipline.

Thus, pressure to produce cognitive or mentalistic explanations of social phenomena has meant that rather than being concerned with the relationship between individual and society *per se*, social psychology's attention to 'the social' has in large part been driven more by critiques of the inherent individualism in the discipline. Consequently, attempts to 'resocialise' social psychology emphasise how internal processes are influenced by the social context. One aspect of resocialisation has been the development of a European perspective by Tajfel, Moscovici and others in the 1970s. They reintroduced to social psychology the study of the social group and its relation to individual members.

To summarise, the issue of the relationship between the individual and society, and its variant, the relationship between the individual and the social group, are central to both sociology and social psychology. Do societies have an existence separate from the individuals that comprise them? Is it reasonable to think of individuals as having an existence separate from the society they inhabit? Do individuals create societies, and have free will in determining the course of their actions within society? Or are individuals determined or constrained by the societies in which they live? In sociology, the issue is most closely related to social change; for social psychology, the dilemma arises mainly in the context of attempts to divest the discipline of the individualism that has plagued its modern form this century by reintroducing the social context and the social group and thereby 'resocialising' the discipline.

Theorising the relationship between individuals and society

To some extent, the dilemmas raised in the previous section have been avoided by the emergence of a disciplinary division of labour in the social sciences: sociology studies society, and psychology studies individuals. It seems to be an accepted (if largely unarticulated) assumption that the inter-relationships between the individual and the social will become clear once each discipline has thoroughly researched its particular subject matter.

However, for many social scientists, this is not a satisfactory way to proceed; and they have actively questioned how individuals and society are related. Sometimes their answers have taken the form of processes which are said to underlie the relationship, and which integrate aspects of the social with the individual: examples of such processes include internalisation, interaction and socialisation (see Henriques *et al.*, 1984). Sometimes these processes have been built into theories which focus either on societal processes (in macro-sociology) or on the nature of the self, self-concept or mind (in microsociology and social psychology). In this section we outline four broad ways of conceptualising this relationship.

A macrosociological perspective

Social theorists such as Marx, Simmel, Weber and Durkheim all assumed that individuals are isolated or alienated from society (Burkitt, 1991). By comparing traditional (feudal) and modern (capitalist) societies, they sought an explanation for this condition in the breakdown of the kinds of relationships through which individuals had previously been integrated with others and with society, and from which they had derived their identity. For example, Marx shows how, in feudal times, people depended on identifiable persons, such as the feudal king or landlord who possessed power and owned property. In modern societies, individuals depend on an impersonal, anonymous system (the state, the bourgeoisie) which is therefore seen as external to them. Moreover, in pre-capitalist societies, individuals derived their identities from their place in close knit communities, but in modern societies the division of labour, and the small part played by each individual in the overall task of production, have meant that our identity is tied to our private existence, rather than our public lives.

Durkheim and Weber add an ethical dimension to their analyses. Durkheim, for example, claims that the breakdown of personal dependencies and the division of labour within an impersonal system have predicated the absence of collective values. Instead, a multitude of moral positions generates moral uncertainty, or a condition of anomie, wherein it becomes impossible for individuals to choose any system of values to guide their actions. In modern society, collective consciousness is replaced by 'the doctrine of individualism, which places the highest value on the rights of the individual for freedom of thought and action' (Burkitt, 1991:11). For Weber, the Protestant Ethic (for him the basis of capitalism) has meant that the identity of persons is structured as much by discipline and self-control as by their place in the community of other individuals. The consequence is the existential loneliness of the individual divorced from the roots of social life and social being.

The macrosociological perspective focuses on changes in the organisation of society, and indicates how these have determined our current ontology or sense of personal being. And it is these changes which social theorists have emphasised in explaining why society seems to have an independent existence, external to the individuals that comprise it. However, it is worth stating that in addition to *explaining* individuals' isolation from society, early sociological theorists, such as Durkheim and Weber, also reinforced the division, by implying that it is an inevitable condition of capitalist social organisation and essential to contemporary human life (Burkitt, 1991).

Symbolic interactionism and role theories

Symbolic interactionism developed from the work of G. H. Mead and his students. It has two key assumptions: first, that the self as an object (me) is a product and reflection of society; second, that there is an aspect of self ('I') which is an active, self-reflective process which is a prime determinant of behaviour. Therefore, the self is both socially determined and agentic. The concept of role was crucial to symbolic interactionism, for it seemed at the time that 'no other single concept would seem to offer more possibilities for exploration of the relation between persons and societies' (Holland, 1977:81).

In particular, the notion of roles enabled theorists to conceptualise a reciprocal relationship between the organisation of self and society which was manifested in three aspects of the self: content, structure and dynamics. They proposed that each social role performed bestows on the person a role identity. A person's set of social role identities comprises the content of self, and therefore reflects society. The structural aspect of self also reflects society in terms of the ways that the set of role identities are organised. For example, some researchers propose that role identities are hierarchically organised in terms of the value assigned to each role which may reflect, albeit loosely, society's relative valuation of roles (McCall, 1987). Finally, the dynamic aspect of self embodies a different kind of reciprocity: the mutual shaping of self and society. This is seen, for example, in the ways we attempt to 'live up' to our roles and persuade others to accept our embodiment of them (McCall, 1987; Park, 1927). These 'identity projects' are accomplished through a variety of intrapersonal processes like selective perception, biased judgement and selective memory (Greenwald, 1980) and interpersonal processes which concern various tactics of impression management (Jones and Pittman, 1982; Schlenker, 1980; Snyder, 1979; Tedeschi, 1981). The core problem of identity negotiation, however, is striving to live up to one's structured set of role identities and of managing the role strain that goes with playing multiple roles (McCall, 1987; see McCall and Simmons, 1982).

Role theory is clearly based on a different view of the nature of society and individual being to those adopted in the macrosocial theories. So, society is variously conceptualised as a structured network of social roles (for example, Heiss, 1981); as a network of social relationships (for example, Stryker, 1980); or as a network of organisations. This perspective on society can be understood partly as a reaction against the more pervasive sociological emphasis on macrostructures and processes. However, in role theory the individual is conceptualised merely as a set of roles invoked in a transitory and situation-specific way. This view of our ontology has been regarded as unsatisfactory. Wiley and Alexander (1987), for example, suggest that there is an underlying real self, a constellation of dispositional traits derived only partly from social roles.

In summary, role theories conceptualise the self as a product or reflection of society; the concept of social roles positions individuals within social relationships that make up society. Identity produces particular kinds of action, or role performances which, in turn, are situated within a social milieu and presumably alter or shape the social context. The image of self within role theory is a fluid, dynamic agentic one in which negotiation and 'mutual shaping' between self and others who make up society are central.

Social cognition

The dominant framework within social psychology is known as social cognition. Its focus is on the psychological or cognitive processes which constitute thinking, experience and which lead to action. But these psychological processes are regarded as social products. Within the social cognition framework, the individual is treated as a 'perceiver' or 'information processor' who interprets and accumulates information provided by the social context (Eiser, 1986). Thus 'people do not just receive external information; they also process it and become the architects of their own social environment (Markus and Zajonc, 1985)' (Leyens and Codol, 1988:91). Social cognitivists examine, for example, the process of categorisation which enables people to deal with the vast amount of information provided by their senses. They also focus on the products of this process; these products are variously known as schemata, cognitive representations, categories and scripts. It is assumed within this approach that the basic products and processes are the same whether the perceived environment is physical or social, or whether we are attending to our self or other people. All social categories are initially cognitive categories (Leyens and Codol, 1988).

In social cognition theory and research, schemata tend to be the dominant concepts. A schema is simply a cognitive structure, stored in memory, that can influence the encoding, storage and recall of information (Eiser, 1986). It is an organised representation of a given aspect of the environment (Leyens and Codol, 1988). Closely related to the notion of schemata is the theory of cognitive scripts (Abelson, 1981; Schank and Abelson, 1977). Essentially, scripts are schemata which comprise sequences of related behavioural events; they are a way of organising our 'world knowledge' or understanding of events and situations. The structure of this world knowledge is represented in terms of sets of action rules, which are a way of understanding how we know (and remember) how to behave in particular social settings.

Cognitive processes are defined as *individuals'* processes; consequently, social cognition approaches have been criticised for being individualistic. It is also claimed that within this framework the social world is treated merely as information to be processed, which hardly amounts to a proper appreciation of society and its organisation (Tajfel, 1981).

In defence of the field against these accusations, Leyens and Codol (1988) argue that cognition may be qualified as social in three ways. It is argued, first, that all cognition has a social origin, insofar as it is created or reinforced through social interaction and it is linked with socialisation. Moreover, studies have shown that cultural and social factors affect information processing.[1] Second, all cognition has a social object. For example, social schemata may be representations of types of people, the self, or social roles. (In contrast to the sociological approach discussed above, the primacy accorded to cognition changes the status of roles, for example, from things people do or perform in relationships or social networks, to things that exist in people's heads). Third, social cognition approaches deal with cognitions that are socially shared, and therefore common to different members in a given society or group; that is, cognition is an individual's mental reconstruction of their shared physical and social environment. Nevertheless, in social cognition primacy is given to the individual agent or perceiver, and therefore the implications of the fact that schemata may be shared in common by different individuals is not explored properly (Eiser, 1986). For example, our social life involves many forms of communication and influence through which information and meanings are collectively shared. Social cognition research takes no account of these essentially interactive processes. Consequently, some social psychologists have adopted instead a derivative of the schemata approach, namely, Moscovici's theory of social representations (for example Farr and Moscovici, 1984; see also Eiser, 1986; Leyens and Codol, 1988 and Morgan and Schwalbe, 1990 for further discussion of this particular point, and Litton and Potter, 1985, for a contrary view).

In summary, social cognitivists address the individual and society relationship with reference to individuals as information processors whose processes act on and are modified by the environment and who thereby accumulate structures of knowledge and experience which in turn guide their perception and understanding of the world.

The Social Identity approach

Within social psychology, the Social Identity approach[2] is a more explicit attempt to address the relationship between individuals and society. It was therefore the framework within which the research we describe in this book was originally conceived. The Social Identity approach gives primacy to the social group. It asks how social groups and categories become psychological entities and influence individual self-conception and behaviour. The resolution of the individual–society relationship is thus sought through an understanding of the psychological reality of social groups and the social identity that is derived from group membership. Moreover, the Social Identity approach overcomes individualism through two related and novel conceptual features.

Social identity theory conceptualises self-definition or self-perception and behaviour as lying along a continuum which runs from a purely individual form to a purely group form. At one extreme of this continuum, self-perception, behaviour and thinking are a purely individual matter; at the other extreme, these activities are determined by our social location in groups and social categories. This then allows us to deal with some of the dilemmas we discussed earlier in this chapter. For example: if we accept that individuals are products of society, are we not then denying our own individuality and uniqueness? Moreover, if our behaviour is governed by the social positions we occupy, does this deny a role for individual expression in our behaviour? The individual–group continuum enables us to think of the self as *both* unique and as comprised of social roles or social identities and, bearing in mind that this is a *continuum*, as sometimes reflecting both individuality and social identity simultaneously. Similarly, our behaviour can be thought of as reflecting either our unique dispositions, or we may be acting in terms of social roles or as members of groups (alternatively our behaviour may reflect some compromise between the two). Moreover, conceptualising personal and group-related phenomena in this way avoids giving overall precedence to either dispositions or groups/society in the determination of self and behaviour.

Second, the Social Identity approach conceptualises groups as having both a psychological and a social reality. So, society comprises real social categories (gender, race, nationality, class and so on) which stand in power and status relations to one another. Consequently, they do not exist in isolation, but acquire their meaning and functional significance in relation to other categories. Society is therefore structured according to contrasting sets of social categories (and this is reflected in the structure of the self-concept). This structure precedes individuals who are born into a particular and pre-existing society. In this way, society bestows self-conception, and hence defines at least partially who we are. It is argued that belonging to a group confers social identity or a shared and collective representation of who one is and how one should behave (Hogg and Abrams, 1988). In other words, real social categories are internalised as cognitive structures in the self-concept (Tajfel, 1981). So social identity is therefore 'the individual's knowledge that he [sic] belongs to certain social groups together with some emotional and value significance to him of the group membership' (Tajfel, 1972:31). As a social reality, the specification of the emergence, existence and nature of particular social groups is thought to be the task of sociologists, economists, historians and political scientists. The social psychologist's task is to specify the psychological processes and products involved in creating a psychological reality from a social reality.

So, social identity provides a way of thinking of society as 'in' the individual. The central tenet of this approach is that belonging to a group is a distinct psychological state. Self-categorisation theorists (for example Turner et al., 1987) have, moreover, developed a theory of the nature of the self-concept and how social identities are made salient and influence our self-perception and behaviour such that we act as members of groups to bring the group into objective existence. A psychological group is a social reality to the extent that a number of individuals share and, in relevant circumstances, act in terms of the same social identification. It then becomes possible to see how individuals are active producers of society and changes in society. A further aspect of the Social Identity approach is therefore concerned with different strategies that may be adopted by group members under different conditions to bring about change in the social category in relation to its contrasting category and hence change society.

To summarise, through the concept of social identity, society and social structure are utterly implicated in our identity. Moreover, the specification of the psychological processes which generate the situation-specific psychological reality of groups enables Social Identity theorists to conceptualise a dynamic and reciprocal relationship between individuals and society. Nevertheless, the more recent theoretical and empirical emphasis in this approach relies on a model of the person as an information-processor who perceives or observes the social world (for example, Oakes et al., 1994; see Wetherell and Potter, 1992, and Chapter 10). This emphasis is often difficult to reconcile with theorists' claims that it represents a thoroughly integrated account of the individual and the social.

Changing the subject

So far, we have addressed four broad approaches to the relationship between individuals and society. Macrosociology focuses on capitalist societies and how they have produced isolated individuals; symbolic interactionism focuses on the roles we play in relationships that make up society. In social psychology, the social cognition approach focuses on how society is implicated in our mental processes and products; and the Social Identity approach shares the concern with individuals' mental life but focuses in particular on the psychological group which has a social reality.

Although these are very different ways of addressing the relationship between individuals and society, they have two features in common. First, it is assumed that individuals and society are separate entities or orders of phenomena; that is, in different ways each approach assumes a *dualism* between individuals and society. Second, they share an image of human beings as self-contained unitary individuals whose uniqueness lies deep inside themselves.[3]

> It is a vision captured in the idea of the person as a *monad* – that is, a solitary individual divided from other human beings by deep walls and barriers: a self-contained being whose social bonds are not primary in its existence, but only of secondary importance. This understanding of people as monads creates one of the central problems of the social sciences, a problem that has become known as the division between society and the individual. Alongside this dichotomy is another . . . the real self or the person we feel ourselves to be deep down inside, and the self we present to others, in the roles we adopt or the identities we assume. That is, we often believe we present a 'face' to others, and hide our true feelings inside. There is thus a division between our feelings and our ability to express them in public. (Burkitt, 1991:1 emphasis added)

It may seem common sense that there there is a separation between individuals and the society in which they live; and it may seem to be intuitively true that each individual is a unique, self-contained entity with idiosyncratic thoughts and feelings. However, there are good reasons to question the adequacy of these assumptions as the bases for theoretical and empirical investigations. In the next section we will draw on three sources of evidence: anthropological studies of other cultures; historical studies of Western civilisation; and Foucault's genealogical studies of punishment and sexuality.

Anthropological and historical evidence

The monadic view of ourselves, as separate persons who experience an outer world, is thoroughly ingrained in both scientific and everyday discourse so that it is difficult to think of how things could be otherwise (Pollner, 1987; Widdicombe, 1992). Nevertheless, from his anthropological study of the concept of the person, Geertz concludes that:

> The Western conception of the person as a bounded, unique, more or less integrated motivational and cognitive universe, a dynamic centre of awareness, emotion, judgement, and action organised into a distinctive whole and set contrastively against a social and natural background is, however incorrigible it may seem to us, a rather peculiar idea within the context of the world's cultures. (Geertz, 1979:229)

One of the studies reported by Geertz (1979) is a study by Leenhardt of the concept of the person amongst the Canaque of New Caledonia. Although the

Canaque can represent, analyse and describe the body surface, they have no term for the body as such. Consequently, they are unable to distinguish the body from nature, or to conceive of it as the site of a self or ego, and they are unaware of the body as something they possess. They do, however, have a concept, *Kamo* or living thing (which can also refer to plants and animals) and this can become invested in a particular relationship to constitute a personage. The personage exists only in and through social relationships and the regard it receives from others. These various relational identities cannot be collected into a single person because the Canaque don't experience themselves as an enclosed and bounded individual standing apart from their relationships. Thus, there is a diffuse sense of self or ego, and the loss or disturbance of a relationship may precipitate an existential crisis in which the individual is threatened with non-being and acting *bwiri* or randomly. Since Leenhardt's research, Westerners introduced to the Canaque the concept of the body as a relatively autonomous, biological entity, and the locus of organic and psychological processes. This then allowed the Canaque to collect relational identities together to define themselves as a person.

The cultural specificity of the person as a self-contained and independent individual is coming to be increasingly recognised (Hayes, 1993; Moghaddam *et al.*, 1993). Moreover, historical analyses of the concept of self show that our current understanding is a product of the modern era (that is, post-seventeenth century). Logan (1987) and Elias (1978, 1982) show that individualism began to emerge in the late Middle Ages. Prior to this, selves were probably defined more through group identity than unique individual traits.

In the Middle Ages, the self emerged as an autonomous subject, an *I* who acted in the world. Medieval biographies were generally descriptions of archetypal moral virtues, not unique personalities, and the even rarer autobiographies seldom dealt with inner life, recounting instead the person's activities. During the Renaissance (1400 onwards) and the Reformation, the autonomous *I* became more self-assertive (for elite males). This was manifested in the view of self as an agent in the world who affected society. The important thing was to have effects on the world. As a result of this, Logan suggests that artistic endeavour increased, along with individual enterprise. The origins of the Protestant Ethic can also be traced to this period.

The seventeenth-century Age of Reason, and the eighteenth-century Enlightenment saw the development of science and scientific method. At this point, the self began to be known not just in terms of its effects on the world, but also in terms of its competence in reasoning, knowing and dealing with the world. It is here that we begin to see the emergence of an understanding of self as something inner and personal. This culminated in the nineteenth-century shift from a focus on 'I as subject' to 'I as a self-aware object', and the beginnings of the idea of individual personality and an idiosyncratic inner life. Romantic writers began taking the self as the object of their interest and writing about themselves, their reactions to the world, and the effect of the world on them and their innermost feelings. Over time, there was a gradual shift from 'how I reason about and affect the world' to a sense of self as shaped by the world.

The most recent (twentieth-century) development in the sense of self was reflected in the rise of existential philosophy and humanistic psychology, in which the self was seen as an alienated object. The self-as-object became a kind of lost object, so deeply inner that it is like an essence that we believe is there, if only we could find it. Thus we live in an age in which we are driven to self-knowledge, in which the real self is me. Since I must seek the real inner me to get in touch with myself, I (the subject) is merely a tool in the search for self.

Elias (1978, 1982) argues that changes in the structure of society were responsible for the transformation of the self concept: in particular, the increasing centralisation of the state under the aristocracy. Alongside this change was the predominance of more abstract and regular rules that governed the behaviour of those living in court society. Throughout the period of the Renaissance (which lasted until the end of the seventeenth century), there was a gradual shift from a reliance on external rules and punishments to control people's behaviour towards a situation in which the more abstract rules that governed conduct became internalised within individuals as self-controls.

Foucault's studies of power, discipline and sexuality

Foucault (1977) relates these changes in the concept of the self to a new form of power, *discipline* as opposed to direct sovereign power, which emerged alongside a constellation of social, economic and political changes. Discipline works in conjunction with what he calls three *modes of objectification:* dividing practices, scientific inquiry and subjectification. And the consequence of these processes was that people became objectified: their individuality became an object of knowledge and a site for exercising power. He derived these conclusions from his study of the 'ancestry' of the concept of individuality which through his genealogical method he traced in two specific sociohistorical developments: changes in the penal system, and increasing concern with sexuality (see Sheridan, 1980, for a summary of these works).

In *Discipline and Punish*, Foucault examines how the prison became the predominant means of dealing with crime around the turn of the eighteenth century. The prison physically divided the subclass of criminals from the non-criminal working classes. It also divided them socially, because the criminal or delinquent came to be seen as a particular category of person. (Here we see the operation of *dividing practices.*) Categorical divisions then provided a focus or an object to study for the newly emerging human sciences. These modes of *scientific inquiry* transformed social categories into types of persons.

Within prisons, this transformation was enabled through the disciplinary practices which were used to reform the criminal. An important feature of discipline is that it operates in the most mundane aspects of our lives and it is largely a matter of inducing *self*-control. According to Foucault, discipline works through three techniques of hierarchical observation or surveillance, normalising judgement and examinations. Surveillance is brought about through architectural design which makes it easy to watch what individuals are doing, and through a hierarchical system of observers, from fellow prisoners through a hierarchy of prison wardens. This generates a feeling that one is constantly being watched, or could be observed at any time. This fear of being seen doing things that others would disapprove of induces self-control or self-regulation, and it is reinforced through punishment for any slight deviation from correct behaviour. So, in observing individuals' behaviour, one is applying a normalising judgement on it, that is, assessing their behaviour and checking its deviation from a standard or norm and in comparison to other individuals' behaviour. In this way, discipline exercises a coercive, centralised normality on people.

Surveillance and normalising judgements come together in the third disciplinary technique, the examination. Through examinations, individuals can be classified, differentiated and judged, and they thereby become a case, an object of knowledge. Once people had become objects of knowledge, they became a site for the exercise of power: on the basis of examinations, people can be trained, corrected and normalised. And as a consequence of the use of examinations, certain categories of person can be excluded from areas of activity; for example, the development of IQ testing led to streaming in classrooms, ensuring (eventually) that those who performed poorly on intelligence tests received a qualitatively different education to those who had excelled.

The processes of surveillance, normalising judgements and examinations worked together to produce the concept of the individual. But it is important to note that this process was primarily textual: these constructive processes were accomplished and administered through *written discourse*. Nowadays, of course, there are reports and files on everyone. One has only to think in a contemporary context of the knowledge that is accumulated on each person: school reports, medical histories, dental records, employment records, credit records, etc.. Foucault notes that whereas it used to be the case that only the great and famous were the subject of written documents, in the age of modernity the reverse tends to be the case (Sheridan, 1980). That is, the lower the status of the individual, the more written records there are: for example, children's health, behaviour and abilities are more extensively documented than adults'; the medical records compiled on the sick are greater than those of healthy people; more is written on prisoners' case histories than law-abiding citizens and so on.

Discipline spread throughout the new institutions: schools, hospitals, psychiatric clinics, the army base. But it also spread beyond the institutions. According to Foucault (1977), with the advent of the Industrial Revolution, the bourgeoisie moved out into the suburbs and built estates for the workers. From the employers' point of view, the workers were a mass who lived in close proximity but about whom they were ignorant. The fear and suspicion associated with ignorance led the middle classes to view the working classes as being rebellious and volatile, with an inherent tendency towards criminality. Since it was believed that potential delinquents were working class, there was an excuse for policing the whole population. So, surveillance of the population spread outside institutions, and at the same time, provided a legitimate subject matter for a variety of emerging human sciences, such as statistics, sociology, psychiatry and social work (and the extension of Foucault's second mode of objectification: *scientific inquiry*).

In summary, as a result of techniques of disciplinary power, people became individualised and objectified as cases. They became objects of knowledge and objects for exercising power; the human sciences became possible and, in turn, further increased knowledge of individuals. An important point is that discourse was the *site* in which disciplinary power and knowledge came together: in case reports, scientific writings, exam results, etc. This is why Foucault emphasises the centrality of discourse in the creation of individuality. He developed these themes further in his study of sexuality as an object of concern.

In the introduction to the *History of Sexuality (Volume 1,* 1981), Foucault shows that although we generally regard the Victorian era as one in which people were sexually repressed, in fact there was a proliferation of discourses about sex and sexuality became an object of concern. Governments needed knowledge of the birth and death rates, life expectancy, fertility and so on, in order to increase or decrease the birth rate as required to balance available resources with industry's need for an expanding workforce. Anything that departed from reproductive sex between married couples was of particular concern, and therefore the focus of much knowledge construction or discourse production. A science of sexualities developed, and this in turn produced a multitude of perversions, along with concern over children's sexuality and female hysteria. The object of concern shifted from the sexual act to the nature of the perpetrator. For example, previously sodomy had been regarded as a crime and a sin, and its perpetrators were simply treated as criminals. But in the nineteenth century, the homosexual became a member of a species with a distinct case history, a particular type of childhood, mode of life, and even anatomy; and all kinds of corrective technologies were applied to homosexuality, from cold baths to hypnosis. Sexualities were subject to surveillance by families, doctors, teachers and psychiatrists, producing medical, psychiatric and school reports.

But how could something as seemingly private as sexuality become the object of scientific inquiry and knowledge? According to Foucault, the human sciences extended the practice of confession which was a well-established means of producing truth in the Church.[4] It became the first part of a two-stage process in which the person first confesses or offers experience, dreams and so on in raw, uninterpreted form in which their meaning or significance is implicit, and the truth about the person contained therein is hidden. Second, an analyst interprets the content of the confession so that it can be scientifically validated and the truth revealed. Moreover, the dual process of confession–interpretation was thought to have a therapeutic effect; the truth spoken over time could heal. Because of its association with healing, confession spread beyond a concern with sexuality; indeed, it has become so all-pervasive that we no longer see it as the effect of power but as liberating.

> [The confession] plays a part in law, medicine, education, family relationships and sexual relations, in ordinary, everyday matters and in the most solemn rites; one confesses one's crimes, one confesses one's sins, one confesses one's thoughts and desires, one confesses to one's past and to one's dreams, one confesses to one's childhood, one confesses one's illnesses and troubles; one sets about telling, with the greatest precision, what is most difficult to tell; one confesses in public and in private, to one's parents, to one's teachers, to one's doctor, to those one loves; one confesses to oneself, in pleasure and in pain, things that it would be impossible to tell anyone else, the things people write books about. . . . Western man has become a confessing animal. (Foucault, 1981:59)

These processes constitute the third mode of objectification, *subjectification*. Here we are subjects in two senses of the word: the subject of self-inquiry and self-knowledge, and subjected to a search for knowledge of our hidden selves.

To summarise, Foucault's work is primarily about the power that is exercised over life (of individual's bodies and the life of the population). In the exercise of power, people became individualised, self-contained and self-regulating, and they become objects to be studied. Moreover, our belief in the liberating and healing properties of confession has meant that we are driven by a desire for self-knowledge, or our hidden selves (cf. Logan, 1987). Foucault thus identifies the emergence of modern individuality in the interplay of what he calls power-knowledge, and the proliferation of discourses, in connection with dividing practices, the emergence of the human sciences, and subjectification. Foucault provides a perspective on self and individuality which has become popular because of his emphasis on the role of power which is largely neglected elsewhere. Moreover, his work is important in showing how our individuality is constructed in the most local, mundane activities of our everyday lives.

Burkitt (1991) notes three ramifications of this kind of perspective. First, it has led to the critical examination of social psychology as a discipline (for example, Parker, 1989). Thus, Foucault's genealogical approach and his ideas have been used as a basis for examining the role of psychology in creating and refining modern individuality. Rose (1989a), for example, examines in detail how psychology and social psychology have partly created and supported the image of the isolated, rational, self-regulating individual that is needed in the calculating world of capitalism (for a brief overview, see Rose, 1989b, 1990). Second, it has led to a similar deconstruction of psychology's subject, that is, the model of individuality assumed in psychology (Henriques *et al.*, 1984; Sampson, 1986, 1989, 1990; see also the collection of chapters in Parker and Shotter, 1990). The third ramification is that it opens the possibility that the social sciences may be instrumental in creating *new* visions of subjectivity or our experience of ourselves (see Henriques *et al*, 1984; Hollway, 1989; Parker, 1992; Rose, 1989b). A central theme of these critiques, then, is the need to redefine the discipline of psychology, and change its subject matter.

To summarise: first, we changed the nature of our concern from 'How are individuals and society related?' to 'How can we overcome the dualistic approach which automatically treats individuals and society as discrete entities?' Second, we have questioned the primacy of the monad, the self-contained individual, by showing that the concept is an historical, cultural and sociopolitical construction. Third, we have seen that language is centrally important in the construction of selves. But where do we go from here? What conceptual tools are at our disposal for understanding the integration of selves and society through language? What should the focus of our inquiry be?

Overcoming dualism: towards an alternative subject for the social sciences

In this section we will consider a number of attempts to redefine the subject matter of the social sciences. In this way, we arrive at a central theme of this book: the possibility of replacing the categories of self or individual and society with a focus on language use.

Mead's theory of social selves

First, we can return to G. H. Mead (1934) for an early but influential attempt to provide a truly social understanding of the nature of self and individuality. For Mead, society, and therefore our social origin, was comprised of other selves in a social environment. These selves are locked into patterns of communicative social activity. So society is a social process, an ever changing and emergent organisation of activities which is always in the process of meaningful reconstruction. These social processes logically antedate the individual self and are the basis for individual selves and minds.

A central theme in Mead's work was the interplay of actions in which humans are engaged in a process of mutual adjustment through social communication and cooperative interaction. Initially, the acts to which Mead refers are gestures. In interaction, others treat the infant as an object whose acts are responses to the caregiver's act, and stimuli for further responses. As the infant becomes aware that its actions are responsible for changes in the conduct of other individuals, it is forced into a 'subjective attitude' (Mead, 1910). That is, an attitude of self-reflection in order to design actions that are better attuned to others' actions and will call out desired responses in others.

Self-consciousness or the mind emerges when people begin to sense that there is a meaning to activity. Meaning is derived from the part played by an act or gesture in social interaction and communication. Actions are interpreted and given meaning in relation to the kinds of gestures they make possible in the others' behaviour. Social interaction and mutual adjustment are also the basis for the emergence of the self. This is because central in the emergence of self-consciousness is an awareness of ourselves as objects to which people are responsive, and ourselves as subjects who must reflect upon the objective self in order to produce responses. This is how Mead derived his distinction between 'I' the subject and 'me' the object.

Language eventually becomes the primary medium for mutual adjustment and social communication, and hence for the emergence of the self and the subjective attitude. The functional significance of language is due to its status as a truly objective or impersonal (Morss, 1985) system of communication. Other people use language as the medium through which they communicate their responses, thus giving us an objective sense of the way in which we have affected them and, through this, an objective sense of our own self which is internalised to form our subjective attitudes. It is only in language that such a general, impersonal standpoint can be communicated, against which individuals can react to their own selves and organise their responses accordingly. Language is the most developed form of symbolic interchange; it is through language that individuals can converse and orient their activities in a more complex fashion; and through language that the attitudes of the whole group can be communicated.

Moreover, self-consciousness, having been established through language, reflects the meanings, morals and values contained in discourse. So Mead argued that one aspect of me is a monitor and censor of actions, thought and speech, a running current of awareness which attends over the mind and its imagery; it criticises, approves, suggests and plans the next stage of conduct in accordance with the 'I'. Mead conceptualised this process as a conversation with a *generalised other*.

Burkitt (1991) argues that Mead's theoretical perspective overcomes dualism because he does not demarcate a personal and social realm; we are always in social relations and hence always social beings. Society and individuals evolve in tandem from the very beginning; they are not separate subsystems which can only interpenetrate or interact. This is because we actively participate in mutual adjustment and the social organisation that arises from this through communication. We are not merely *observers* or *perceivers* of a scene which unfolds before our eyes, as suggested in social cognitive perspectives in social psychology. Moreover, it is not the 'activation' of a particular form of self-perception or a role that enables us to act in the world. From the beginning it is in communication, particularly through language, that individuals become self-conscious and gain control over their own responses *within social activity*.

Interpersonal relations and the moral order

Here, we are concerned with Goffman's dramaturgical model and Garfinkel's ethnomethodology. It is, however, important to be clear from the outset that neither Garfinkel nor Goffman set out to produce a theory of social selves; neither produced a theory of social action; nor did they attempt to conceptualise a resolution to the individual–society debate. Instead, Goffman's primary concern was with face-to-face interaction as the domain of study and in particular with the strategies of self-presentation and the roles we play in social interaction. Self-presentation is significant partly because it is often in our interests to manage the impressions that others form of us, and partly because sustaining identities is important in maintaining social interaction. Nevertheless, although Goffman acknowledged these motives for self-presentation, he was more concerned with how we put on a successful performance and the resources we use. So, he was interested in the set of procedures that are part of our background, cultural knowledge and which informs the ways in which people manage the face-to-face domain. These procedures he regarded as trans-situational. To bring an occasion to life requires us to select, mobilise and arrange in fine detail ways of presenting ourselves to others which, in turn, 'render our behaviour understandably relevant to what the other can come to perceive is going on' (Goffman, 1983:51). Our behaviour can then be designed so as to enable other people to see in it evidence of our broader cultural knowledge, memberships and identities (see Drew and Wootton, 1988).

It is important to note that for Goffman the world of social interaction was a moral one, in which the 'technical mechanisms' of interaction were only of sociological significance insofar as they were vehicles for participants' moral enterprises (Drew and Wootton, 1988). At the centre of this essentially moral world of interaction is the individual: a revered object as revealed in the analysis of the ways in which the individual is treated by both self and others. It is also a vulnerable object which can be stigmatised or desecrated. Goffman's interest in the 'abnormal' was a way of understanding the normal ways, the props, used to maintain a sense of individuals' integrity.

Garfinkel, one of the central figures behind the sociological approach known as ethnomethodology, similarly advocated the study of interaction. He was concerned with the way that the social order is constructed and maintained in a skilful yet taken-for-granted way by members of a society or social group, through procedures or skills known as 'ethno' (folk) methods. These ethnomethods comprise the tacit or background normative conventions which can be used by members to construct, account for, and give meaning to the everyday activity of the social world. The central principle is that the activities through which members manage and produce their organised and everyday affairs stem from the same procedures through which they account for their actions. This is because competence in constructing accounts is contained in our implicit and explicit understanding of the social world and our own actions within it. Social scientists must then try to identify and describe these methods if they are to understand the ways in which people make sense of their everyday social interactions.

It is worth noting that although Garfinkel did not produce an explicit theory of social selves, his work was premised on a concept of the person as a competent member of society rather than as a 'judgemental and cultural dope'. The term 'judgemental dope' was used in an explicit rejection of Parsons' claim that the social norms of a society are simply internalised, absorbed by the individual who then behaves accordingly: as a cultural dope. Garfinkel argued that this conception of the individual's relation to social norms denied the reflexivity of the person, and the way in which social norms must be continually reproduced (see Heritage, 1984:110–20). For Garfinkel, socialisation is viewed as a process in which actors acquire and/or are treated as having acquired, a body of normatively organised knowledge in terms of which they treat their own and one another's everyday conduct as accountable. Motivation for 'perceivedly normal' conduct is furnished by the actor's reflexive awareness of the differential accountability of alternative courses of conduct. It is not, as for Parsons, established by a past history of rewards and punishments which create enduring dispositions to act in normatively prescribed ways for a given situation.

Goffman and Garfinkel, then, provide one way of overcoming dualism by focusing on interaction and the kinds of background knowledge and skills through which interaction, and hence the social and moral order, are maintained. Nevertheless, in the absence of a theory of social selves, some commentators have regarded the sole focus on interaction and its technicalities as an unsatisfactory resolution to the individual–society debate (for example, Burkitt, 1991). In addition, Burkitt (1991) is critical of the way that the focus on the social construction of the social world, its meaning and objects, overlooks the historical and cultural specificity of the social order. Moreover, background expectancies are assumed not analysed in terms of their origins, nor how they are anchored in 'the *practical reality of people's socially structured experience*' (*op. cit.*:69; original emphasis). The problem, for Burkitt, is essentially the absence of a conceptualisation of the reality of society conceived in terms of macrosocial structures.

The ethogenic approach

Harré's ethogenic approach draws upon each of the perspectives we've considered so far in constructing a theory of social selves. Central to Harré's work is a distinction between two very different orders of reality: the expressive order and the practical order. Marx, he argues, is the prime philosopher of the practical aspects of social activity, while Veblen is the best guide to the expressive order (Harré, 1979). The practical order includes physical features of the environment along with the world of work and production, and non-conscious, unpremeditated reflex responses of human beings. In this order, physical objects are located in space and organised according to causal relations. The practical order is dominated by the expressive domain on which Harré concentrates and in which selves and society are constituted.

> I take the array of persons as a primary human reality. I take the conversations in which those persons are engaged as completing the primary structure, bringing into being social and psychological reality. Conversation is to be thought of as creating a social world just as causality generates a physical one. (Harré, 1983:64–5)

Harré distinguishes between social and personal being which are both achieved within the expressive order. Individuals' social being is largely dependent on the presentation of self in public, the parts or roles that an individual plays in social life, and the way the person accounts for him or herself. In turn, social being is wholly dependent on the social scripts of rules, resources and conventions, and the activity and conversation that take place in the social scenario of everyday situations. Thus, people will have different aspects to their social identities depending on the different situations in which they are involved, and these are referred to as personas.

Personal being is characterised as an inner sense of being, and differs from the social image we project. Harré's personal being, or subjectivity, is based on the beliefs a person holds about their own self existing as a certain type of social and moral actor. So that theories and beliefs about what it is to be a person in society, and about the type of person one actually is, are at the centre of the experience of one's own self. Personal being, as a set of theories and beliefs, implies that a person is a being who has learned a theory, in terms of which his or her experience is ordered (Harré, 1983:20).

Finally, individuals' characters are distinct from both persona and personal being. They are developed in everyday situations and are based on the moral judgements that others make of a person's actions which are in turn related to the values of the local moral order. A person's character is closely bound up with their moral career which is related to the winning and losing of honour and respect within the expressive order. Characters are therefore similar to that aspect of Mead's 'me' which monitors moral aspects of the self and is derived from the objective attitudes of the generalised other.

An important aspect of Harré's work is his attention to the issue of agency and here he draws upon ethnomethodology. Like Garfinkel, Harré did not want to see people as judgemental dopes whose actions are 'caused' in a mechanical way by an external force (environmental, cultural or historical) working on them. Instead, he regards human agents as responsible and auto-nomous individuals who use accounting practices, rules and conventions to construct their everyday activities and give meaning to them. They are also held to account by others for actions they undertake and are thereby turned into morally responsible agents. Individuals are knowledgeable and self-aware about the things that they do. They rely on the information they have about people and settings in which they are involved, and through this infor-mation they structure their actions in a moral way. Accountability and need for respect and admiration of fellow actors are the basic motivation for people to act socially in all places and times.

Social construction, poststructuralism, and the 'death of the unified subject'

The final set of conceptual developments we shall address share in common the premise that selves are socially constructed in discourse. For example, Shotter and Gergen argue that:

> the primary medium within which identities are created and have their currency is not just linguistic but textual: persons are largely ascribed identities according to the manner of their embedding within a discourse – in their own or in the discourses of others. In this way cultural texts furnish their 'inhabitants' with the resources for the formation of selves; they lay out an array of enabling poten-tials, while simultaneously establishing a set of constraining boundaries beyond which selves cannot be easily made. (Shotter and Gergen, 1989:ix)

Therefore, it is argued that the focus of our intellectual and empirical endeav-ours should be on the text or discourse within which or through which selves and identities are socially constructed. Moreover, a concern with *texts* of identity is described as part of 'a struggle with a single dominant text: the centrality and sovereignty of the individual, and the problems to which it gives rise' (Shotter and Gergen, *op. cit.*:ix). These approaches, which we shall refer to as postmodern, consider the 'death of the subject' to be a matter of moral and political and not just academic concern.

There are, however, a burgeoning variety of ways in which the conceptual death of the subject has been accomplished. We shall describe just two ap-proaches here.

Let us consider first the social construction approaches of Gergen and Shotter. Gergen (1987) argues that in order to overcome dualism we need to move towards relational theories of selves. This requires abandoning forms of inquiry in which the individual person is the subject of inquiry; it also means finding a way of talking of motives, beliefs, understandings, plans and so on as products of social interchange, and not as if they were properties of individual selves. But in order to do this, he says, we need a new relational vocabulary: 'It is as if we have at our disposal a rich language for characterising rooks, pawns, and bishops but have yet to discover the game of chess' (Gergen, 1987:63). Moreover:

> In order to make the conceptual leap new metaphors are required. It is my suspicion that the most useful metaphor may prove to be that of the text. In the same way that individual words cannot be understood outside of a linguistic context, the understanding of individuals requires comprehension of social context. Text comprehension may thus stand parallel to comprehension of the more wholistic units of which individuals are localised manifestations.

Alongside the metaphor of the text, Shotter (1989) and Gergen (1985; 1989) propose that metaphors of persons in conversation, in relationships and engaged in joint activities may prove to be useful.

More recently, Shotter (1993) characterises the social world as an inherently moral world, structured through what he calls a 'relational ethics' or an 'ethics of communication'. The moral order is created in joint activities which are shaped by and achieved through what he calls the 'social ecology' of inter-dependencies between people which comprises taken-for-granted common-sense understanding. Joint activity produces a social world of meanings and accounting practices which determines consciousness, the structure of the personality and the future actions of social beings. Moreover, within this social ecology of joint activity and interdependence, the self is formed as people are called to account. According to Shotter, we owe our constitution as autonomous beings to our embedding in joint activities and accounting practices that demand of us that we act as free and responsible agents. Thus, Shotter proposes that the moral order requires interpretation if we are to understand the ways in which individuals are enabled as agents in the social world.

These approaches embody two apparently disparate ways of conceptualising language. On the one hand, there is an emphasis on the metaphor of the text. On the other hand, the emphasis on communication and accounting to people suggests a different view; language as the medium of conversations. Poststructuralist approaches, by contrast, refer to discourses as the focus of theoretical and empirical concern. In the next and subsequent chapters, we provide details of this approach, in this chapter we merely want to note that this focus has given rise to a view of selves or individuals as *positions in discourses* through which individuals are ascribed identities. Thus, within these approaches, the term identity rather than self is often used. For example:

> Identity as a dynamic aspect of social relationships is forged and reproduced through the agency/structure dyad, and is inscribed within unequal power relationships. In other words, identity is not one thing for any individual; rather, each individual is both located in, and opts for a number of differing, and at times conflictual, identities, depending on the social, political, economic and ideological aspects of their situation – 'identity emerges as a kind of unsettled

space . . . between a number of intersecting discourses' (Hall, 1991:10). This conception of identity thus precludes the notion of an authentic, a true or a 'real' self. Rather, it may be a place from which an individual can express multiple and often contradictory aspects of ourselves. (Bhavnani and Phoenix, 1994:9)

This approach is appealing because the poststructuralist concept of discourse promises a link between individuals and macrosocial structures (cf. Burkitt's criticisms of Garfinkel and Goffman above). This is because discourses are regarded as products and reflections of social, economic and political factors, and power relations (e.g. Gavey, 1989; Parker, 1992). The identities they confer upon individuals are therefore thoroughly political. In addition, different positions in discourses are said to vary in terms of the power they offer individuals.

In the last chapter we considered the sociological literature on youth subcultures. In this, we have touched upon social theories, symbolic interactionism, and two broad approaches in social psychology, as well as a variety of perspectives which elevate the significance of language. Clearly, these approaches are diverse but we have nevertheless tried to identify common themes which cut through these otherwise disparate bodies of work. The unifying themes concern issues of individuals and society, of identity and the social group. So, in the last chapter we argued that an understanding of the interrelationship between individual, subcultural groups and society ought to be central in understanding youth subcultures; yet these issues are inadequately addressed in the literature on these phenomena. By contrast, macrosocial theories, role theory, social cognition and Social Identity Theory share a common concern with individuals and society, their integration and reciprocity. Finally, the dualistic assumptions built into these more traditional approaches have in part stimulated the turn to language. This conceptual turn has provided us with the basis for an approach through which to address further themes in the sociological literature on youth subcultures which we thought to be problematic. For example, we were critical of the reliance on theoretical interpretation instead of empirical research; and the almost automatic assumption that youth subcultures were intrinsically a form of social resistance. But before we consider how language can constitute the basis for an empirical approach, it is useful to summarise the main points of our argument so far.

In this chapter we have focused specifically on the assumption that individuals and society are two separate and ontologically discrete orders of things; and that the individual is a bounded, cognitive universe. We have tried to show that both these conceptions are social constructions which arose as a consequence of specific historical and political developments. These traditional assumptions about identities, individuals and society are not then objective features of the social world, and unyielding constraints on social research. Once we recognise their constructive and contingent nature we are liberated from them, and can begin to look for new perspectives on individuality and the relation between individuals and social collectivities.

Earlier, we sketched some previous attempts to re-fashion research on the individual and social collectivities. There are three overriding points we wish to draw together from the work of writers such as G. H. Mead, Harré, Foucault and Shotter. First, there is a focus on the constructed nature of selves and social identity. Second, there is an emphasis on the importance of language in all its forms and uses, in this process of construction. Third, our attention is drawn to the relationships between members of collectivities as the site in which selves and identities are produced and fashioned. This in turn points to the importance of discourse, because language use is the medium through which social relationships are developed and maintained. At the same time, though largely implicit in our discussion so far, is the issue of agency and the basis of human action. In particular, the turn to language has reawakened concern with a variant of social determinism: are we simply discursively constructed, or do we have some degree of choice in our self-construction? There is thus a new set of issues which we must address: the relationship between self or identity and action.

We have, then, the basis for a new conceptual framework for a perspective on self, social identity and subcultures which is clearly very different from the image of the actor playing the subcultural role. Moreover, the emphasis on the construction of self or identity in interaction facilitates a more concrete understanding of subcultural groups. What we need to do next is to translate those conceptual concerns into an empirical research programme. Therefore, we need to address how we can accommodate a concern with language, relationships and the construction of identity into a viable methodology, and this will be the topic of our next chapter, in which we consider some recent methodological arguments in the social sciences. Our discussion of these debates will allow us to fashion an appropriate strategy for empirical research, while at the same time permitting us to consider the relationship between identity and action.

Notes

1. For example, Bruner and Goodman (1947) showed that when asked to estimate the size of coins, poor children will estimate the coins to be bigger than the rich children will. When cardboard discs are used instead of coins, the two groups are not different. The difference observed is due to the social origin of the subjects and to the value they attribute to coins (see also Tajfel, 1969, 1981).
2. This approach embodies two separate but related theories: a theory of intergroup relations, conflict and social change (known as Social Identity Theory, Tajfel, 1978; Tajfel and Turner, 1979) and a theory of how individuals can act as group members and hence bring the group into objective existence (this is the Self-Categorisation Theory of Turner, 1985; Turner et al., 1987).

3. To some extent, role theories evade this image because they do not contain an explicit concept of the person who manages the roles. Nevertheless, criticisms of role theory and subsequent modifications seek to rectify this absence through the addition of an underlying real self with unique dispositions (see Stryker, 1987; Wiley and Alexander, 1987).

4. Though as Derek Edwards points out (personal communication), the idea of confession as a means to truth has come under attack in a series of notorious and well-publicised trials and acquittals. For example, the Guildford Four and the Birmingham Six were released after serving long prison sentences on the basis of uncorroborated confessions. Thus, we already have a notion of confessional evidence as socially produced. This notion is further manifest in discussions of the ways that child abuse testimony is interactionally produced.

Chapter 3

TALK, TEXTS AND ACTION
Some methodological issues

We have now reached the stage where we need to discuss the kind of analysis we are going to use in the following empirical studies of young people's accounts of their lives as members of subcultures. This requires us first to state our general assumptions about language and language use, and then to discuss the varying analytic stances that are informed by these presuppositions. Once we have done that we will discuss how our approach helps us in our investigation of the kinds of issues we have raised in the previous two chapters. To do this, we consider some themes about the nature of social identity and language, and about the relationship between identity and action. But first we need to describe some of the main influences which have shaped our understanding of language.

The action orientation of language

For many years within some areas of social psychology and sociolinguistics, language has been treated largely as a passive medium. For example, a long-standing field of research in social psychology has been to investigate language as a screen onto which are projected psychological and social psychological characteristics of speakers (Giles and St. Clair, 1979; Robinson, 1972); others have tended to see language as simply mirroring social processes (for example, Chaikra, 1982). And in sociology the traditional approach has been to treat

> speech as either as a source of 'hidden' realities – such as values, attitudes and beliefs – waiting for the sociologist to uncover them, or as the reporting of members' perceptions of social facts, to be verified or falsified by 'scientific' procedures. (R. Turner, 1974:213)

What is common to such approaches is that they fail to attach proper significance to the *dynamic* properties of language use; properties which have been revealed through a range of philosophical and sociological writings. In his later writings, for example, Wittgenstein (1953) rejected theories which portray language as a medium which merely reflects or describes the world, and emphasised instead the importance of language *use*. He urged that we consider language as a series of tools which acquire their purpose and function from the social and cultural milieux in which they are used.

Although very different from Wittgenstein's philosophical method, Austin's (1962) work also underscored the dynamic properties of ordinary language and their importance to everyday social life. His work focused on instances of specific types of sentences. He began by distinguishing between two types of utterances: constative utterances, which report some aspect of the world; and performative utterances, which perform a specific action. An example of a performative is 'I suggest you do this', where saying these words is to perform the action of suggesting. Other examples are promises, warnings, declarations and so on. He termed such utterances, speech acts. Austin subsequently rejected the distinction between performative and constative utterances: his investigations convinced him that all utterances could be treated as performative and constative. He concluded that any use of language, regardless of what else it might be doing, was a series of actions.

Sociological interest in language use was stimulated by ethnomethodological writings. Pioneered by Harold Garfinkel (1967) the fundamental tenet of ethnomethodology is that the sense of social action is accomplished through the participants' use of tacit, practical reasoning skills and competencies. As so much of social life is mediated through spoken and written communication, the study of language was placed at the very heart of ethnomethodology's sociological enterprise. Sacks' (1992) studies of the organisation of conversation are also important. Although diverging in many important respects from Garfinkel's conception of the proper topic and methods of sociological research, Sacks' studies of conversational organisation embodied many principles which underpinned ethnomethodological research. In particular, his studies described the tacit communicative competencies which underpinned the production of orderly conversational interaction. But Sacks' analyses also described the kinds of work which utterances do: he emphasised the importance of describing both the kinds of interactional tasks for which turns at talk have been produced, and the ways in which utterances are designed with respect to the sequences of turns in which they occur.

Finally, discourse analysis is an analytic method which grew out of the sociological study of scientific knowledge (Gilbert and Mulkay, 1984), but which developed principally in social psychology (Potter and Wetherell, 1987; Parker, 1992). Unlike conversation analysts, discourse analysts examine all forms of verbal and textual materials: spoken and written accounts, letters, scientific journals, newspaper reports and so on. The object of empirical study is to describe the way that such texts are constructed, and to explore the functions served by specific constructions at both the interpersonal and societal level.

However, the situation in social psychology is slightly confusing because there are at least two distinct strands of work which are both known as discourse analysis. We should not be surprised that there is confusion surrounding the term 'discourse analysis': there are many types of work which have this title. For example, there is a tradition of work in sociolinguistics which draws upon linguistics and speech act theory (for example, Brown and Yule, 1983). However, the confusion we point to is not between types of discourse analysis practised by researchers from *different* disciplines; we are concerned about two types of work both of which have currency in contemporary social psychology. It is useful to describe them briefly.

The first major appearance of the term 'discourse analysis' came with the publication of Potter and Wetherell's (1987) *Discourse and Social Psychology: Beyond Attitudes and Behaviour*. In this book the authors introduced social psychologists to research on social texts. They also set out to establish an empirical research programme which would provide a resource for researchers wishing to study social texts. Finally, they wanted to demonstrate the ways that fundamental theoretical notions in social psychology (attribution, social representations, attitudes and categories) could be addressed through the examination of language use, both spoken and written. Indeed, they argued that 'the *failure* to accommodate to discourse damages their theoretical and empirical adequacy' (*op. cit.*:1). Hence, a second point of divergence from conversation analysis is that this kind of discourse analysis tends to be more topic-focused; that is, made explicitly relevant to an issue which is a concern for both social researchers and participants.

The authors' empirical programme stemmed from the following points:

1. Language use has an action orientation: people do things with it.
2. Language is constructed and constructive.
3. Any state of affairs can be described in a number of different ways.
4. Therefore there will be variability in accounts.
5. There is no foolproof way to deal with variation and sift through and find the 'best' and 'most informative' accounts.
6. Consequently, the purpose of analysis should be to study the ways that language is used flexibly and constructively.

This work challenges orthodox social psychology in a number of ways. Social psychologists rely heavily on the information provided to them by the subjects in their experiments and studies: accounts, reports, descriptions and so on. Conventionally, these discursive reports are treated simply as 'stand-ins' for the state of affairs being studied: people's accounts are regarded as (potentially) accurate versions of events in the world, or as (potentially) transparent representations of inner mental states and processes, such as attitudes, opinions, attributions, and so on. But Potter and Wetherell's claims about variability and the constructive nature of language set a question mark over the adequacy of these assumptions and the experimental methods which enshrined them. As an alternative they advocate the investigation of language use, and the construction, function and rhetorical organisation of accounts. These features of their empirical research programme forced attention on the action orientation of language. But they did not neglect the content of accounts; instead, they drew upon Gilbert and Mulkay's (1984) notion of linguistic repertoires. These are coherent systems of meaning, expressed in figures of speech, metaphors and recurrent descriptive patterns through which individuals can construct specific kinds of versions of the world in certain ways. The analytic goal then is to see how people themselves work out and address 'attributions', 'personal identity', 'group membership', 'social categorisation' and so on in discourse. The analyst is thus liberated from working with data produced in the artificial setting of the experimental laboratory, and can instead investigate how these issues permeate the use and organisation of spoken and written language in real-life settings (and interviews) and texts (we use the word 'text' here to refer to written documents, for example, newspaper reports).

Discourse and Social Psychology was an introduction to critical arguments about social psychology's methods and assumptions, and it established the direction for future empirical work which tried to take account of the action orientation of language use. A more sustained empirical demonstration of certain features of this approach is Edwards and Potter's (1992) *Discursive Psychology*. In this project, they drew more heavily upon conversation analytic research, and emphasised rhetorical strategies rather than the broader linguistic repertoires which formed a key feature of the analytic programme laid out by Potter and Wetherell (1987). More substantively, this book questions many of the cognitivist assumptions in psychological studies of processes of attribution and memory. They argue that any naturalistic study of attribution and memory (that is, studies of real-life events) must in the first instance address the pragmatic work *accounts* of attributions and memories are designed to do. So instead of treating accounts as representations of inner mental processes, they show how those discursive attributions and rememberings are irreducibly social products, marshalled for specific interpersonal ends: for example, to warrant the credibility of one's own position in a dispute, and to manage issues of accountability. Indeed, the issue of accountability permeates much of their discussion; they show how in constructing versions of events, or whatever, speakers attend to the accountability and responsibility for the actions and so on portrayed in the accounts. But they also attend to the way that they are accountable as the producer of the report. If, for example, the report produced by a speaker is seen to be motivated or self-interested, then the veracity of the account is undermined. Finally, these features, action, managing interest and accountability, are embodied in a conceptual scheme which they refer to as the 'discursive action model'.

The second strand of discourse analysis within social psychology is associated with the writings of Parker (1990a, 1990b; 1992) and many of the chapters in Burman and Parker (1993a).[1] There are several distinguishing features of this kind of discourse analysis. First, the word 'discourse' is not used to refer to language use generally, but has specific theoretical connotations derived from the work of French social theorists and poststructuralist philosophers, such as Foucault (see Chapter 2) and Derrida. Second, this approach does not restrict itself to the analysis of instances of talk and writing, rather it examines texts: objects, events or processes which are imbued with meaning and interpretation. All forms of language use can be treated as texts. Third, this type of discourse analysis has the political objective of emancipating ordinary individuals, especially those subordinated through membership of social categories which render them powerless: 'ethnic minorities', 'women', 'the working class' and so on. (For a further discussion of this issue, see Weedon, 1987, and Lather, 1992.)[2]

There are, then, two very different strands of discourse analysis within contemporary social psychology; both could be used in our own analysis of the accounts produced by members of youth subcultures. However, while we share many of the assumptions about language and social action which inform the first strand of work (and indeed we drew upon these ideas in the last chapter), we have some reservations about the latter development of discourse analysis. Our concerns centre around three sets of issues: the conceptual, the methodological and the practical. We will deal with each in turn.[3]

Conceptualising discourses and texts

In this section we shall refer to Parker's (1992) description of discourses.[4] These are coherent sets of meaning and interpretations; and Parker quotes Marin's claim that discourses are 'linguistic sets of a higher order than the sentence . . . and *carried out* or *actualized* in or by means of texts' (Marin, 1983, quoted in Parker, 1992:7; original emphasis). Texts are 'delimited tissues of meaning reproduced in any form that can be given an interpretative gloss' (Parker, 1992:6). So, discourses are realised in, and inhabit, specific textual forms. Thus '[a]ll of the world, when it has become a world understood by us and given meaning by us, can be described as being textual' (Parker, *op. cit*.:6–7). Parker illustrates this by describing how a distinctly Christian discourse is represented in a child's liquid crystal display electronic game, in which the object is to prevent spirits returning to their graves; this is done by operating a male figure, who, brandishing a crucifix, casts the ghosts into flames at the side of the display. Discourse analysts, then, study texts to describe the discourses which inhabit them, and to show how '[D]iscourses facilitate and limit, enable and constrain what can be said (by whom, where, when)' (*op. cit*.:xiii).

The term 'discourse' is a theoretically loaded concept; as we have said, it is in part derived from the writings of French cultural analysts, philosophers and historians, including Derrida, Foucault and Barthes. Moreover, it is a conceptual tool which is charged with an overtly political dimension. This is clear in Parker's claim that language is structured to reflect power relations and inequalities in society. Thus he argues that discourses support some institutions in society, and have ideological effects. There is, then, a link between social structural conditions and discourses, and this has important implications for analytic work. 'The notion that social structure is a precondition for discourse means that discourse analysts must draw on other theoretical work which uncovers the material basis of oppression (capitalism, colonialism, patriarchy)' (*op. cit.*:40). Discourses are thus conceived as systems of meanings which reflect real power relations, and which in turn are a consequence of the material and economic infrastructure of society.

There are two important implications which follow from the sociopolitical definition of discourses. First, if analysts adopt this kind of definition, they are also necessarily adopting specific assumptions about contemporary society and the material basis of social structural conditions. These assumptions are embedded in the concept of a discourse. Thus any empirical work which adopts this terminology is unavoidably trading in a specific form of social political theory.[5] Second, this formulation of 'discourses' (and why we should examine them) suggests that analysts *should* be motivated in their work to make political interventions, or to expose the ideological workings of specific discourses in texts. Indeed, some discourse analysts argue that there is no point trying to do discourse analysis without this overtly political goal. As Parker and Burman say:

> If we do not [make political interventions], we will be assimilated into main-stream empiricist research. We would then find our own work relayed among the repertoires of the discipline, rather than offering, as it should, critical readings of its texts. (Parker and Burman, 1993:170)

However, this is a political and moral position; others may not share it. Yet it has become enshrined in the definition of the central concept of a 'discourse', and infuses descriptions of the kind of work discourse analysts should do. Furthermore, there is an implicit claim that intellectual work should be political work. Again, this is an assumption that other researchers in related disciplines may not subscribe to, however politically informed they may be.

We should make it clear that we do not object to the overtly political character of this methodological prescription because we hold different political opinions. Indeed, it is likely that we actually share many political sentiments. Equally, we find it laudable that these discourse analysts wish to make some active political intervention. What we object to is the way that the entire project has been set up to be *no more* than a political exercise; and a political exercise which rehearses a relatively limited range of political theoretical stances. This for us is worrying because it establishes at the outset a set of limits upon analysis, and upon the kinds of questions it is legitimate and proper for analysts to ask. Additionally, there is an assumption, which permeates discourse analytic writings, that intellectual work which does not pursue a political agenda is either 'naive positivism', or even constitutes an inadvertent support of the status quo. So Burman and Parker are able to claim that discourse analysis which does not function as 'ideology-critique' is in danger of amounting to no more than 'traditional positivist methods *masquerading as* discourse analysis' (Burman and Parker, 1993b:11; emphasis added). And Parker states that we must be careful not to let 'an analytic sensitivity to discourse become *just another thoughtless empirical technique*' (Parker, 1992:123; emphasis added). These kinds of claims do little to encourage those who might be sympathetic to many of the goals of discourse analysis, but who have differing methodological and intellectual principles.

We also have reservations about the study of 'texts'. Recall that texts are any events, objects or processes which are imbued with meaning and subject to interpretation. Discourse analysis is the method for the study of these texts, and the discourse(s) which infuse them. Parker (1992:7) provides an illustrative list of texts. He starts, not surprisingly, with speech, writing and non-verbal behaviour; but goes on to include fashion systems, architecture, stained glass, tarot cards and bus tickets. Anything, then, can be treated as a text, and studied using the methodological steps he outlines.

An initial concern might be that an analytic mentality or methodological approach which can be legitimately exercised in the investigation of anything and everything must be so all-encompassing as to be vacuous. But of course this issue is neatly circumnavigated because these various subjects have been transformed into a series of single, analytic objects: texts. Political speeches, and software instruction manuals, death warrants and crisp packets, centre partings and crazy golf: all are levelled and equal before the discourse analyst. Analysts are thus able to focus their intellectual endeavours while at the same time enjoying the heady luxury of legitimately investigating everything and anything they want to. But what are the grounds for this great levelling? Certainly, bus tickets express meanings, and they can be interpreted: bus drivers and ticket inspectors interpret them all the time. However, just because one *can* perform interpretative work on a bus ticket and one *can* understand a tape recording of people talking to each other does not in itself warrant the ascription of equivalence between these events for analytic purposes.

However, although speech, bus tickets and the displays of electronic games can be treated as texts, empirical research has, so far, focused on language. Indeed, in a recent collection of discourse analytic research papers (Burman and Parker, 1993a), all empirical chapters examined some form of spoken language. In practice, then, discourse analysts primarily study talk produced in a socio-interactional environment.

Analysing discourses and texts

Perhaps our main concern about the second strand of discourse analysis is that empirical studies have a tendency towards ascriptivism: imputing a discourse to texts (or bits of speech and writing) without explicating the basis for that imputation. Consequently, empirical analyses tend to gloss the social functions of language use, rather than describing them. For example, the following extract comes from Marks's (1993) study of a meeting between academic researchers and educationists. The educationists have been concerned about the needs of one particular individual, Mike.

> Sally: [an education welfare officer] and we had this meeting (.) and I found that meeting very frustrating (.) . . . *the situation hadn't been able to be resolved* (.) er (.) the pure fact that the person who actually isn't here today [coughs from a couple of people] who at the time was responsible in the social services department (.) er (.) wasn't able to to to *bring the situation together for Mike* to come to school to feel good about himself (.) and (.) as I do remember quite well, my own frustrations. (Marks, 1993:140–1, original emphasis)

This is what Marks says about this account.

> In this extract Sally refers to a mysterious 'situation' which could not be resolved in a general sense. This turned out to be the problem of Mike's low self-esteem and the failure of another professional from the social services to deal with it. By referring to Mike's presumed emotional difficulties in passive terms as 'the situation' no acknowledgement is given to the possible existence of competing accounts. The repetitious reference to 'the situation' serves to mask rhetorical positions by objectifying the assertion that the problem is Mike's lack of self-esteem and the solution lies in the help of the caring professions.
>
> Mike's life is thus presented as being fragmented. Appeal is implicitly being made to the humanist therapeutic discourse which sees the subject as being unified and integrated. (*op. cit.*:141)

We will use Marks's account of this piece of data as a point of departure for a more general discussion of methodological and analytic issues. However, we have not selected Marks's observations because we think they are weak or insubstantial; on the contrary, we think her paper makes several significant contributions. We are simply using her paper as a basis from which to begin to describe the finer details of the kind of analytic approach we wish to pursue in subsequent chapters.

In the passage we have quoted, Marks makes a number of interesting observations about the kinds of implications or rhetorical functions served by specific features of Sally's account. For example, Marks rightly draws attention to the way in which the use of the phrase 'the situation' may be performing certain kinds of work in the context of the account. And we think Marks is correct to identify the presence of a specific discourse by tracking evidence of it throughout Sally's account.

However, our concern is that this level of analytic investigation rarely encourages the analyst to ground or explicate the basis for specific analytic observations about the data or text being studied. For example, the reader is not told what exactly it is about this bit of speech which substantiates the analytic claim that it is informed by a 'therapeutic discourse'. Indeed, it appears that the main warrant for this assertion does not come from Sally's utterances, but from the analysts' claim that certain fragments of Sally's talk have specific meanings or connotations. For example, Marks claims that Sally's reference to 'a situation' is a reference to Mike's low self-esteem. On the basis of this, and no more, we are then informed that 'Mike's life is thus presented as being fragmented' in Sally's account. And then, finally, we are told that Sally's (apparent) reference to Mike's state of fragmentation is itself (implicitly) appealing to a humanistic therapeutic discourse. So, the analysis of this series of utterances begins with a reference to something Sally actually said; but it is only through a series of unwarranted extrapolations, and without any further reference to any other utterances in Sally's account (apart from yet another unexplicated assertion about a further reference to 'the situation'), that we arrive at the claim that Sally's account appeals to a specific kind of discourse.

The tendency to impute the presence and relevance of discourses to people's utterances does little to inspire confidence in analysts' claims for the materials they study. For in addition to producing analytic claims which are unsubstantiated by the data from which they are purportedly produced, this discourse analytic stance ignores the interactional circumstances of the occasion in which these utterances were originally produced. We will illustrate this point by considering two (related) issues which may be relevant to a section of Sally's account: the way that utterances are designed to perform specific interactional or inferential work relevant to the circumstances at the time, and the kinds of concerns which inform how people refer to persons. These issues can be deeply consequential for the shape and composition of utterances. Consider, for example, the following part of Sally's account: 'the pure fact that the person who actually isn't here today [coughs from a couple of people] who at the time was responsible in the social services department (.) er (.) wasn't able to to to *bring the situation together for Mike*'.

Although space does not permit it, it would be possible to build an analytic case that Sally is here engaged in the conversational action of registering a grievance about this individual on the basis of his or her failure to exercise their professional duties effectively. There are several interesting features of this extract which bear on this claim. An immediate observation is that the first reference to this individual is 'the person who actually isn't here today'. Note that it is not 'the person who *can't* be here today' or 'the person who *couldn't* make it today'. The absence of the person is not reported in such a

way as to account for that absence, or to give any hints at a possible explanation, such as other unavoidable commitments, or unanticipated problems.

Presumably there were a large array of people who were not present at that
meeting. Yet they are not mentioned as being absent. So by referring to this
individual in this way Sally is able to introduce his or her absence as a *notable
absence*. And absences of people become noticeable – and accountable – in
those circumstances in which others have some expectation that they would,
or should, be present. So in the way that Sally describes this individual she is
able to establish that he or she is somehow 'at fault' in their non-attendance.
They are portrayed as having 'failed to attend', rather than as having a legitimate excuse for non-attendance. So, the design of the reference to this individual neatly meshes with the kind of conversational action Sally has
embarked upon; indeed, the inferential work addressed by this reference is
itself a *resource* in the interactional business of building a grievance.

The point is that when examining verbal interaction it is important to take
account of what is being done with the talk.[6] The kind of interactional business people address through their talk is consequential for the design and
shape of the things people say. Interactional considerations have an impact on
the very composition of the utterances people produce; utterances which in
turn become the 'text' for discourse analysts to analyse. But, these kinds of
contingencies, and the way they impinge upon the production of utterances,
are not addressed; it is as if the bits of talk which are studied appear in an
interactional vacuum. And to a degree, this is one of the dangers of treating
instances of talk as text. Talk is produced in the first instance for specific
others, to attend to interactional and interpersonal sensitivities generated in
the course of social interaction. To treat talk as text invites the analyst to
overlook the situated relevance and production of communicative actions.

And here we come to a paradox in the discourse analytic programme.
Discourse analysts tend to shy away from the detailed analysis of talk. There
seems to be a sense that issues of political concern can only be revealed in an
analytic stance that adopts a broader focus than the detailed investigation of
naturally occurring communicative competencies. This is a pity, because
issues such as asymmetries in status, and the exercise of institutional power
may well infuse social life at its most basic level: in the order of conversational interaction. Zimmerman and West's (1975) research, for example,
suggests that there are systematic gender differences in the distribution and
execution of interruption in conversational interaction. Moreover, it is
through precisely these kinds of communicative competencies that people will
exhibit their orientation to the relevance of such inequalities in actual
episodes in their social lives.

Unfortunately, though, discourse analysis is concerned to address political
or moral issues through the analysis of *discourses* in discourse. The adoption
of this kind of theoretical and methodological prescription at the outset of
research can actually divert the analyst's attention from an investigation of

the ways in which people themselves fashion their talk to address social and political issues. Imposing an analytic agenda may obscure the ways in which issues of inequalities and asymmetries may become relevant issues for participants in spates of verbal interaction.

The practical implications of analysing discourse and texts

The latter type of discourse analysis has many laudable aims, many of which stem directly from the concern of its proponents to make political interventions in wider society. But we wonder whether the analytic programme itself actually *thwarts* those ambitions. For example, discourse analysts talk of giving a voice to groups of people who are powerless or marginalised in society. But the work of discourse analysis has been characterised as the analysis of 'discourses' in 'texts'. This in turn encourages not the investigation of peoples' use of language, but the imputation of meaning and significance to specific instances of talk and writing. So although analysts may wish to use discourse analysis to speak on behalf of powerless and marginalised groups, their analytic concerns do not give those groups a voice. Indeed, by studying instances of the use of language to evidence the influence of discourse, discourse analysis actually seems to deny the significance of what people may be saying *and doing* with their talk.

Parker has written: 'You take your first step into discourse research as you take your first step away from language' (Parker, 1992:xi). Although Parker calls this a paradox, it is in fact an accurate description of this version of discourse analysis. Despite its avowedly political character, and its concern for the weak and the powerless, discourse analysis does not provide the analytic resources with which to address the discursive activities of members of those disadvantaged groups, or, for that matter, any other social category. By focusing on 'discourses' as coherent sets of meaning and interpretations, the discourse analyst does indeed turn away from language use as a topic in itself. Instead, it is regarded as a screen onto which the material infrastructure of society has somehow projected discourses to serve ideological functions. Consequently, language is to be treated with caution, for it reflects the operation of insidious and and politically charged forces. Thus we are urged to 'attend to every word with a *suspicious* eye' (*op. cit.*:122; original emphasis). And the use of the concept of the 'text' to refer to the ways in which people use language, transforms the diverse and myriad activities of human agents into neat analytic units. In so doing, it diverts attention from the practical ways in which people themselves assemble and negotiate the meaning and significance of their social actions in and through their talk.

It is in this sense that Parker's statement is accurate, because the first step in discourse research *is* a turn away from language. And it is because of this that

Parker's statement is also a revealing and telling indictment of the weakness of this form of discourse analysis.

In our subsequent empirical chapters we will examine the accounts produced by members of youth subcultures to investigate how language is used to produce and construct social identities, and to characterise the wider experience of being a member of a particular group. In this sense we share many analytic goals with the kind of discourse analysis associated with Edwards and Potter (1992), and to some extent with Potter and Wetherell (1987). (Any further use of the term 'discourse analysis' will refer to this tradition of work unless otherwise stated.) So we are interested in exploring how social identities are made relevant for, and realised through, the fine grain of verbal interaction. But our analysis is perhaps more fine grained and draws more heavily on conversation analysis than Edwards and Potter; at the same time we pay less explicit attention to the rhetorical organisation of the accounts we collected. In the rest of this chapter, we will describe some of the underlying common assumptions between conversation analysis and discourse analysis, and show how these will inform all of the subsequent empirical chapters. This discussion also allows us to show how our concerns mesh with research on language and identity from other perspectives.

The relationship between language and social identity has been the subject of much research in a range of disciplines: social psychology, sociolinguistics and ethnographic studies of communication. However, in the vast majority of cases, the relevant social identities have been defined in terms of wide-ranging political or social issues. For example, there have been studies of the relationship between language and national or regional identities (Khleif, 1979; Le Page and Tabouret-Keller, 1985), language and ethnic identities (Edwards, 1985, Giles and Coupland 1991; Gumperz, 1982) and language and gender (Maltz and Borker, 1982; Tannen, 1990; Zimmerman and West, 1975). Although our research begins with an explicit interest in a similar form of social identity – a subcultural identity – it will become apparent that our approach to the relationship between people's talk and their social identities is very different to that which informs the research in the kinds of studies we have just cited. One way in which we differ is that we do not see social identity as a property of a person which in some way is conceived of as existing independently of language use, and which is merely reflected in their language. Rather, we see identity as something which is produced through, and embedded in, everyday forms of language use.

The focus on everyday language

There has been a tendency to study those aspects of language use which are conspicuous, or esoteric: distinct accents or dialects, or the use of unusual or novel vocabularies. This tendency is especially pronounced in ethnographic studies of communication. Our concern, however, is with the everyday, routine features of language use. We do not seek to identify the production of social identity through analysis of people's use of a special vocabulary, or their adoption of striking accents or dialects. Rather, we wish to discover the ways in which identity work is embedded in the organisation of routine, everyday verbal interaction.

We can clarify some of the issues involved if we consider a study by Abrahams (1974). Abrahams set out to identify some of the characteristics of speech production used by young black people on the streets of the United States. Through the identification of these special linguistic practices Abrahams provides evidence that, at least at the time he did the research, the Afro-Americans in the United States constituted a distinct speech community. From his study of primarily teenage black males talking informally on the streets, Abrahams identified two broad features of their language use: their invention of new words, or innovative use of already established words, to refer to aspects of their lives, interpersonal relations, specific people and happenings and so on; and he also documented their invention and use of phrases and sayings which were more centrally concerned to characterise certain aspects of their interpersonal relations with their peers.

Throughout this interesting account of the speech patterns of young black males there is the implicit claim that their identity *as* young blacks to some degree rests on their use of these distinctive speech patterns. It is this point with which we wish to take issue; not because we consider it to be incorrect, but because it diverts analytic attention away from the extent to which identity may also be established through speech practices which are not conspicuous or colourful: in short, the everyday and routine.

There is a sense in which it is ironic that a focus on the noticeable should be accompanied by a neglect of the routine, because the very appearance of novel language use rests upon communicative skills which are in use all the time. For example, it seems hard to imagine how such colourful forms of verbal behaviour could obtain any sensible character if they were not embedded in a range of tacit and taken for granted interactional competencies: knowing how to ask, recognise and answer a question; knowing how to make an invitation, and accept or refuse one; knowing how to make and reply to jokes, etc. The very use of an exotic vocabulary presupposes precisely the kind of framework of communicative skills and competencies within which such lexical items can have any relevance.

But there is a more important point. Conversation analytic studies have shown that ordinary language use is the site for social action: through their talk, people perform such actions as questions, answers, complaints, justifications, mitigations, invitations, acceptances or refusals and so on. They perform a myriad range of social actions. And it is quite likely that the kinds of exotic words and phrases noted by Abrahams were being used in the production of similar kinds of social actions. We can assume, then, that the significance of those lexical items was, at least to some degree, related to the kinds of social actions being accomplished through the utterances of which those items were component parts. This in turn implies that the kinds of social identities being established through the use of novel or exotic items were to some degree also the product of *everyday* linguistic competencies.

A concern with the organisation and performance of routine communicative skills yields an unexpected benefit. Whereas it is certainly true that the social identities of the young black males may in part result from their use of different vocabulary to that used by their white counterparts, it is extremely unlikely that the same words and phrases would be employed by any other social groups to establish *their* social identities. Indeed, the very point of such an analysis is to demarcate what sets a group apart from another. The findings from such studies, then, are always limited: they refer to a specific social group and, therefore, will have a restricted geographical and historical relevance. However, if we focus on the underlying communicative competencies through which social identities are established, we may be in a position to generate findings with a more general relevance. That is, we are concerned to identify the ways in which everyday tacit communicative skills are employed to establish, maintain or negotiate social identities. But the kinds of discursive practices we wish to chart are not associated with specific social groups or collections of persons; rather, they are part of the culturally available, communicative competencies in which, by virtue of their socialisation, all members of the natural language community are expert. Our analytic claims, then, will be relevant to a wider community of persons than those projects which seek to describe processes of identity production which reside solely in the use of limited and particularised varieties of language use.

We should note, then, that the exclusive focus on the novel or esoteric can obscure the importance of ordinary communicative competencies in the production of social identities. But more than that, it fails also to take note of the relationship between *social actions*, as constituted through turns at talk, and the social identities of the speakers. It is this relationship to which we now turn.

Discursive identities and social actions

There has been much research in sociolinguistics which examines the relationship between language use, social identity and social action. We have already noted that in such projects the analytic focus is on wide-ranging social identities, conceived in terms of issues relating to nationalism, ethnicity and gender. Similarly, the kinds of social actions which are studied are primarily conceived in terms of political actions. For example, there has been interest in the ways in which the Basques and Catalans in Spain, and the Welsh, Scots and Cornish in Britain have all tried to use their native languages to establish or cement ethnic and national boundaries.

It should be apparent by now, however, that our concern with social action, like our interest in social identities, will be focused on a realm of interpersonal actions which do not necessarily reflect or refer to wider political developments. Of course, we do not claim that such wider political or social developments are uninteresting, nor irrelevant to the conduct of verbal interaction; but in the first instance we wish to monitor the way that language and social identities are mobilised with respect to immediate, interpersonal relations. If such discursive practices in turn make explicit reference to, or invoke the relevance of, wider political events, then these too will fall into our analytic remit. But we will not assume the relevance of wider political issues unless we can assert that in their behaviour speakers themselves are orienting to the significance of such issues for the trajectory of their verbal interaction. Similarly, Schegloff asserts that

> For the lively sense we may all share of the relevance of social structure . . .
> needs to be converted into the hard currency . . . of defensible analysis – analysis
> which departs from, and can always be referred to and grounded in, the details of
> actual occurrences of conduct in interaction. (Schegloff, 1991:48)[7]

But there is another point which distinguishes us further from traditional sociolinguistic studies of language, social identity and social action. It is this: we do not merely treat social identities as the *vehicles* for social action, but regard them also as *resources* for social action. To explain this point, we need to discuss briefly the relationship between social identity and categories.

Consider some of the social identities that we have discussed or simply mentioned so far in the first three chapters: punks, gothics, business people, young black males, men, women, daughter, speaker, skinheads and so on. All of these are membership categories: they are culturally available resources in our language for the identification and description of persons, which allow us to make reference to other people or to ourselves. In his early lectures, Sacks (1992) was particularly interested in the kinds of conventions which informed the ways in which people use categories in verbal interaction. He observed a number of 'rules' which underpin such categorising activities. For example, he observed that for practical conversational purposes, a single membership category will constitute an adequate reference for one or more persons. This he termed an 'economy' rule. Sacks also noted that membership categories can be grouped into collections, which he termed membership categorisation devices. So, for example, the device 'family' will include such categories as mother, father, son, daughter, aunt, uncle, etc.

Such categories do not merely provide us with convenient labels which allow us to refer to persons; they also provide a set of inferential resources by which we can come to understand and interpret the behaviour of persons so designated. That is,

> Membership categories may conventionally be seen as having category-bound predicates . . . they are loci for the imputation of conventional expectations, rights and obligations concerning activities (for instance) which it is expectable or proper for an incumbent of a given category to perform. (Watson and Weinberg, 1982:60)

Clearly, the notions of category membership and social identity are crucially linked. Many of the types of social identities we have mentioned in this chapter could also be described as categories. Thus, when we talk of a person's social identity, we are also referring to their membership of a specific category, and this in turn will provide the basis for the legitimate (that is, conventional and warranted) imputation of motives, expectations and rights associated with that category and its incumbents. In short, the assignment of a person to a category ensures that conventional knowledge about the behaviour of people so categorised can be invoked or cited to account for or to explain specific actions of that person.

Categories, then, are 'inference rich'; and participants in interaction display their orientation to the kinds of inferences which may warrantably be drawn about them by virtue of their membership of categories. The following example comes from one of Sacks' lectures (1992:46–7). These fragments are taken from a recorded conversation between a psychiatric social worker 'A' and a suicidal man 'B'.

(1)

A: Is there anything else you can stay interested in?
B: No, not really.
A: What interests did you have before?
B: I was a hair stylist at one time, I did some fashions
      now and then, things like that.

The conversation proceeds for some minutes and then the following sequence occurs.

A: Have you been having sexual problems?
B: All my life.
A: Uh huh. Yeah.
B: Naturally. You probably suspect, as far as the hair stylist
      and uh, either one way or another, they're straight or
      homosexual, something like that,

What is interesting here is the way that B seems to assume that the social worker may infer that he has homosexual tendencies because of his former occupation as a hair stylist, and general interest in fashions. Moreover, he does not reject such inferences as unwarranted: that is, regardless of his actual sexual orientation, he does not question whether it is legitimate or not for his recipient to draw certain inferences from his former incumbency of the occupational category, 'male hairdresser'.[8]

There is, however, a more interesting aspect to this sequence. As Sacks points out, from his later talk it seems that B took it that he was *hinting* at his homosexual tendencies by mentioning his previous occupation as a hairdresser, his interest in fashion and 'things like that'. So, by relying on what is conventionally known about the category, 'male hairdresser', he is able to perform subtle interactional work: allowing a recipient to infer something to which he may wish to draw attention without explicitly doing so. And it is in this sense that social identities are resources for social action: category ascriptions, or what is conventionally known about a category, can be occasioned, invoked, indexed or made relevant so as to accomplish specific inferential tasks which arise in the course of interaction (see also Wooffitt, 1992).

Of course, it is also possible that one might pursue certain interactional ends by describing *other* people so as to make relevant certain features of *their* social identity. For example, Wowk (1984) examines sections of a police interrogation of a man accused of murdering a woman. During this interrogation he confesses to the murder, so his talk is not directed towards maintaining or establishing his innocence, but is directed towards minimising or mitigating his guilt. At various points in the interrogation, the man refers to his victim. Wowk shows how, in describing the woman's activities, the offender constructs her identity as a 'slut' or 'tramp': he says 'she propositioned me'; 'she asked if I would like to get laid', and 'she called me a prick a no good sonofabitch and threw what was left of a bottle of beer at me' (Wowk, 1984:76). Through such descriptions the offender describes how he was provoked by the actions of the victim. But more important, perhaps, is the way that the offender's descriptions occasion the relevance of the victim's *moral* identity: that is, invoking the victim's social identity as a 'slut' in turn makes available a moral frame of reference for the interpretation of her behaviour. By so invoking the impropriety of her conduct, the offender is able to characterise his own subsequent actions as less blameworthy.

Examining procedural knowledge

The kind of data we will be examining are verbal accounts: episodes, stories and anecdotes obtained during informal interviews. What interests us in these accounts, however, is not just their substantive content: in addition to our interest in what people say about their identity, we are keen to explore how they say it. This not because we doubt the words of our respondents; and neither do we seek to ironicise their accounts of their experiences by imposing analytic frameworks which provide alternative explanations to those offered directly by our respondents. Rather, we wish to identify the underlying communicative practices through which identity is negotiated, applied, modified and used in interaction. To explain why we emphasise these underpinning discursive competencies, it is useful to discuss a study by Watson and Weinberg (1982).

Watson and Weinberg conducted interviews with gay men, during which the interviewees discussed and described their homosexuality. Watson and Weinberg's subsequent analysis investigated some of the linguistic and discursive resources through which the respondents' identities as homosexuals were produced in the interaction. They frame their analytic emphasis by reference to a distinction made by Ryle (1949:28ff.) between two types of knowledge: *knowledge that*, which refers to the kind of information which can be acquired through conscious learning, and *knowledge how*, which refers to tacit and common-sense skills. Watson and Weinberg claim that they are not concerned with substantive conceptions of homosexual identity which occur in the interviews (knowledge that), but are interested in the procedural knowledge (knowledge how) which is deployed in building and communicating these substantive conceptions. They suggest that knowledge that presupposes knowledge how; that is, they claim that a procedural knowledge allows us to use substantive notions of a state of affairs for practical ends. So, we cannot be said to 'know' a substantive proposition about something unless we can be seen to use it, amend it, rectify it, modify it and so on. 'In short, procedural knowledge provides for the application of substantive or prepositional knowledge to everyday life contexts, as realised in the performance of actions' (Watson and Weinberg, 1982:56).

So, their interest in knowledge-in-action requires inspection of accounts of homosexual identity not only for substantive content, but also, and primarily, to describe the practical reasoning skills, embedded in language, through which those substantive conceptions are made available throughout the interview. This in turn indicates that the analyst should treat features of the interview as vehicles for the realisation or mobilisation of substantive manifestations of identity.

There is another argument which warrants their particular focus. They claim that by looking at the procedures through which identities are fashioned and constructed they can make more generic kinds of claims. Instead of limiting their analysis to a specific kind of identity, they tease out the interactional, discursive strategies through which identity *per se* is mobilised. They are teasing out not substantive knowledge *that* homosexuals have certain types of attributes, but culturally available knowledge *how* that identity is produced through talk. So by focusing on the organisation and use of procedural knowledge, then, we hope to be able to generate analytic findings which are not limited only to that collection of individuals who may be characterised as members of youth subcultures.

It is clear by now that we do not treat social identity as a realm of mental events which is separable from language, and which is simply expressed in linguistic terms. Rather, we are interested in the ways in which language is constitutive of social identity. In this book, then, we are concerned to identify and describe a range of discursive procedures through which individuals produce, negotiate, modify and use their social identities in social interaction. Primarily, we focus on subcultural social identities: the identities of young people which accrue from their affiliation to subcultural groups such as punks, gothics, rockers, skinheads and so on. We are interested in the ways in which their identities *as* members of specific subcultural groups are produced in verbal accounts, stories and anecdotes produced during recorded informal interviews. Consequently, we concur with the position expressed by Tannen (1990) in the following quote, in which she asks us to consider

> the notion of speakers expressing a social identity. It is common currency among sociolinguists, but . . . do people really 'have' such fixed and monolithic social identities? Furthermore, is it correct to see language use as expressing an identity which is separate from and prior to language? To put the point a little less obscurely, is it not the case that the way I use language is partly *constitutive* of my social identity? To paraphrase Harold Garfinkel, social actors are not sociolinguistic 'dopes'. The way in which they construct and negotiate identities needs to be examined in some depth before we can say much about the relation of language to identity. (Tannen, 1990:86; original emphasis)

We are proposing that identities are produced in and through the organisation of everyday discursive practices. Moreover, we propose that the identities so constructed serve particular socio-interactional functions for the speakers: functions which are available through a detailed investigation of their talk.

There is, however, a final point that we need to address. We emphasise in this and subsequent chapters the importance of attending to the communicative competencies and practices of ordinary conversational interaction. Moreover, we draw on principles of conversation analysis which are derived from studies of naturalistic conversations. But the accounts we analyse are derived from interviews and not, for example, spontaneous conversations that just happened to take place with us, or between members themselves. So, it may be argued that the interview situation furnishes a context which somehow systematically constrains the talk of the participants. But it is not obvious that such a description actually, or always, coincides with participants' understanding of the circumstances. Certainly, there are occasions when respondents did orient to the relevance of their talk as interview talk; in Chapter 4 we discuss one such occasion, the openings of the interviews. The point is that the relevance of talk as 'interview talk' (or any other kind of categorisation of the interaction) should be manifest in the data. A further point is that it seems highly unlikely that people have a special set of communicative competencies which are exclusive to interviews. Therefore, it seems most fruitful to treat interviews as a method of eliciting rather than constraining speakers' accounting practices. So, rather than treat the material we collected as primarily exercises in information gathering (the primary purpose of interview talk), unless our data indicate the contrary, we have analysed the interviews as informal conversations. Therefore, we have treated these interviews as the kind of environment in which peoples' interpretative reasoning practices would be exhibited in their talk (Potter and Mulkay, 1985).[9]

Notes

1. One important text which seems to bridge the two strands of work is Wetherell and Potter's (1992) *Mapping the Language of Racism*.
2. The confusion between these different types of work stems in part from their common title. But it is compounded when the latter strand of discourse analysts try to assimilate the earlier work by referring to it as though it is a useful component of their own project. This unfortunately glosses over substantial divergences between the two strands of work.
3. To focus our discussion we will examine this latter strand of discourse analysis to see how useful it might be for our study of people's verbal accounts, although we realise that analysts in this tradition investigate a range of discursive materials.
4. It should be pointed out that Parker's description is produced hand in hand with a set of methodological requirements for doing discourse analysis. Indeed, the latter group of discourse analysts have been conscientious in trying to describe the practical steps in their work. However, these methodological suggestions are not relevant to our present purposes, and so we shall not discuss them here.
5. This kind of social theoretical work, and this particular strand of Marxism/conflict theory, has been a staple component of traditional sociological theorising and research. However, with the advent of postmodernist reconceptualisations of social life and social theory, 'grand' conflict social theories have had a reduced significance in the discipline. We mention this not to complain that discourse analysis has simply appropriated one set of conceptual assumptions from sociology. We are more concerned that the theoretical tools they draw upon enjoy a diminished significance in sociology. It is odd, then, to find a theoretical tradition which is subject to intense critical speculation in sociology being assimilated into social psychology as a kind of radical departure.
6. See also Potter's (1993) review of Bhavnani's (1991) study of young people's talk about unemployment, racism and politics.
7. Given that lack of attention to social structure has been a significant issue in critiques of conversation analysis and ethnomethodology (see also Chapter 2), it is worth citing further from Schegloff's useful discussion. He attends to

> three sorts of issues mobilized, or remobilized, for me when the talk turns to 'talk and social structure'. However lively our intuitions, in general or with respect of specific details, that it matters that some participants in data we are examining are police, or female, or deciding matters which are specifically constrained by the law or by economic or organizational contingencies, however insistent our sense of the reality and decisive bearing of such features of 'social structure' in the traditional sense, the challenge posed is to find a way to show these claims, and show them from the data in three respects:
>
> 1. that what is so loomingly relevant for us (as competent members of the society or as professional social scientists) was relevant for the parties to the interaction we are

examining, and thereby arguably implicated in their production of the details of that interaction;

2. that what seems inescapably relevant, both to us and to the participants, about the 'context' of the interaction is demonstrably consequential for some specifiable aspect of that interaction; and

3. that an adequate account for some specifiable features of the interaction cannot be fashioned from the details of the talk and other conduct of the participants as the vehicle by which *they* display the relevance of social-structural context for the character of the talk, but rather that this must be otherwise invoked by the analyst, who furthermore has developed defensible arguments for doing so.

In brief, the issue is how to convert insistent intuition, however correct, into empirically detailed analysis. (Schegloff, 1991:65–6; original emphasis).

8. At the time of writing, this conversation is approximately thirty years old. However, the kinds of inferences being made available here are salient even today.

9. It is also perhaps worth noting that we do not look like prototypical market researchers; and although our appearance did not clearly implicate any particular style, we did not look obviously out of place in the festivals we attended.

Chapter 4

CONVERSATIONAL ORGANISATION AND THE MANAGEMENT OF IDENTITY

In this part of the book we focus on the way that identity is woven into the fabric of social interaction. To begin to substantiate this statement empirically, in this chapter we will examine some features of the exchanges between the interviewer and the respondents in our interviews. Our analytic goal will be to describe how it is that both participants in the interview organise their talk to mobilise the relevance of the respondents' identities *as* members of specific subcultural groups. Our emphasis, then, is on the ways in which displays of identity are embedded in talk-in-interaction. To explain some of our analytic observations it will be necessary on occasion to describe some of the systematic properties of language use; to do this we will refer to some conversation analytic studies of the organisation of ordinary conversational interaction. We will also demonstrate the importance of tacit communicative competencies which inform the production of sequences of interaction in which the social identity of the respondent(s) is a salient feature.

In particular, we will examine some properties of the opening sequences in the interviews with our respondents. We have elected to examine these sequences for two reasons. First, they are easily identifiable: in many cases they are the first exchanges recorded on the tape; and if they are not the actual first words on the tape, the interviewer invariably produces a turn such as 'Right' or 'Okay' which marks the shift from 'background' or 'incidental talk' to the beginning of the interview proper. But more important, the opening sequences in the interviews had a crucial significance for the success or otherwise of the research project for which these data were collected. Remember that these interviews were conducted as part of a social psychological investigation of the motivation behind membership of social groups. Specifically, the project was designed to assess the extent to which Social Identity Theory (Tajfel, 1978; 1982) was able to provide a useful explanation for membership of youth subcultures, and an account of the relations between different subcultural groups and between members of the same subculture. To ensure the social psychological validity of the data we derived from the interviews, it was important that the interviewees explicitly declared themselves to be members of a specific subcultural group. Consequently, the first question of the interview was designed to be somewhat vague, and raise at a very general level the issue of how the

76

respondents would describe themselves. It was hoped that such a question might elicit the kind of category identification which was required. If it did not, however, the interviewer would then ask explicitly if the respondent was a member of a subculture.

Although there was an agenda of issues that we wished to raise, we did not conduct the interviews according to a rigorous interview schedule, and therefore the interviews were informal. As the majority of our interviews were conducted at rock festivals or in the street, where it would have been inappropriate to try to establish a formal setting for the interview, it is not surprising that these exchanges evolved into a form of conversation between the respondents and the interviewer.[1]

In this chapter, then, we will be addressing several issues. We will try to show how the properties of conversational interaction inform our data. We will also describe some of the common-sense communicative skills upon which our respondents relied when talking to us. But we will not lose sight of our central aim, which is to show the interactional processes through which identity becomes salient, and towards the end of this chapter we will sketch some analytic themes which will be developed further in Chapter 5. But first, then, we need to discuss some of the properties of conversational interaction which are relevant to our interviews with our respondents. To this end it is necessary to discuss some of the findings from conversation analysis.[2]

Over the past twenty-five years conversation analysts have systematically studied the communicative competencies which underpin mundane, everyday interaction. Such studies have produced a substantial and cumulative body of findings about various dimensions of conversational organisation. (An appreciation of the distinctive methodological approach of conversation analysis can be gained from Atkinson and Heritage, 1984; Drew, 1994; Sacks, 1992.)

Many central features of conversational organisation appear to have recurrent properties which seem to be independent of the individual personalities of specific participants, and which are not caused or determined by the context or setting in which interaction occurs. For example, in conversation, at different points different participants will be speaking. A conversation, then, requires that the participants draw upon their tacit understanding of the procedures whereby the opportunity and right to speak is allocated to specific people. Similarly, it can be observed that a large proportion of conversational interaction proceeds through paired exchanges, such as question–answer sequences. In later sections of this chapter we will be describing in more detail the ways in which some properties of conversational organisation informed the behaviour of the respondents and the interviewer in our interviews.

When we speak, we do not only rely on our tacit knowledge of procedural issues in interaction, such as how we distribute turns to speak. There is also a wider range of culturally available, taken-for-granted tacit knowledge upon which we draw as interpretative resources to make sense of the actions of others, and which inform our own actions and behaviour (Garfinkel, 1967;

Sacks, 1992). This domain of knowledge is described as tacit because it is not a set of constraining 'rules' of interaction or norms of behaviour which we could consciously articulate, or upon which we can reflect. Instead, this practical knowledge is embedded in the very weave of social life, and thereby becomes invisible and unnoticeable. Our analysis will demonstrate the extent to which this realm of practical knowledge informs the exchanges in our interviews.

To focus our discussion we will examine the following sequence, which comes from an interview with two female punks.

(1) 2P:F:T2SB[3] [CM] ('I' is the interviewer, 'R' is the respondent.)

		((*Tape starts*))
1	I:	about your sty:le
2		(.3)
3	I:	and who you are
4		(.4)
5	I:	how would you describe yourselves
6	R1:	huhh huhh hhagh punk rockers
7	R2:	punk rockers yeah huhh huhh
8	I:	How long have you been punk rockers,
9	R2:	three:– ah've been three years
10	R1:	yeah three

Unfortunately, the tape starts just at the end of the interviewer's introductory question so we have no clear record of what exactly was said. However, the interviewer had a stock question with which the interviews were started, and the kind of first turn which was used is illustrated in the following fragments.

(2) 1P:F:T1SA [KHS]

		((*Tape starts*))
1	I:	CAn you tell me something about your sty:le
2		and (.) °y'know°
3		(.)
4	R:	⌈°uhm°
5	I:	⌊the way you're dressed

(3) 2G:F:T1SB [KHS]

		((*Tape starts*))
1	I:	°right° (.) SO as: a said I'm doing stuff
2		on style and appearance can you tell me
3		something about yourselves th- (.3) the way
4		you look

(4) 2G:F:T1SB [KHS]

		((*Tape starts*))
1	I:	the traffic
2	R1:	yeah
3		(.6)
4	I:	So (.2) how would you describe yourself=your
5		style and everything,

Obviously we cannot be certain of what the interviewer said in extract (1), and it is far from ideal to have to speculate, but on the evidence of recordings which are complete, it is *possible* that the missing part of the interviewer's first turn contained an initial statement like the one from extract (3): 'SO as: a said I'm doing stuff on style and appearance' (lines 1 and 2). But it is very *likely* that the interviewer's missing turns contained the first part of a question, such as 'can you tell me about . . .' or 'can you tell me something about . . .'.

We can make some observations on the recorded parts of the interviewer's first turn in extract (1), and the respondent's subsequent turn. The recorded part of the interviewer's first turn has three components: she asks about the speakers' 'style', asks 'who they are', and then asks how they would describe themselves. At the end of this component one of the respondents produces her first contribution, which, apart from the short spate of laughter at the start of the turn, consists entirely of the nomination of the subcultural identity of the speaker and her companion: 'punk rockers'.

Given that our stated objective of this chapter is to show how identity is managed and negotiated interactionally, it may seem perverse to begin with a sequence as mundane as the first two turns in extract (1). Indeed, it may seem somewhat strange to claim that there are *any* processes of identity management occurring in this initial exchange. But there is complex interpretative work being accomplished in these first two turns. A first point is that the interviewer has said something, and then the respondent said something: they took turns to speak. Furthermore, this turn exchange occurred very smoothly: there was no gap between the successive turns; similarly, there was no spate of overlapping talk. So, then, the two speakers have been able to draw upon their tacit understanding of the procedures for executing turn exchange to produce a coherent two-turn sequence.[4] (These conversational skills are referred to as 'tacit' because they are not the kinds of rules or norms of behaviour which we could consciously articulate, or on which we would reflect in everyday life. Instead, they inhabit the very fabric of social life, and are invisible and unnoticeable.) The procedures by which participants organise the coherent turn-by-turn development of an exchange have been well documented (Sacks, Schegloff and Jefferson, 1974), and the details of those procedures need not concern us here. What we want to address is the issue of the coherence between the two turns.

Much of the coherence of conversational exchanges rests upon the ways that speakers produce consecutive utterances that constitute pairs of actions: greeting–greeting, question–answer, request–acceptance/refusal, etc. Although it was Sacks who first discussed the properties of pairs of conversational actions in his early lectures (published as Sacks, 1992), it was Schegloff and Sacks (1973) who provided a more formal account of the recurrent structural properties of the organisation of paired actions. They proposed the concept of the adjacency pair, which is a sequence of two utterances which are adjacent, produced by different speakers, ordered as a first part and second part, and 'typed', so that a first part requires a particular second part, or range of second parts (for example, questions are typed with answers, invitations are typed with acceptances or refusals, etc.). However, the structural property of paired actions does not entail that these are necessarily produced as successive actions which occur next to each other: it is not a statement of empirical invariance. Neither is the concept used to indicate an empirical generalisation, for example, that in a specified number of cases second parts immediately follow first parts. Rather, the importance of the concept is that it underlines the *normative* character of paired actions; that is, the production of a first part proposes that a relevant second part can be expected. In other words, a second part is made conditionally relevant by the production of a first part (Schegloff, 1972). Therefore, one method by which a participant in an exchange can display that his or her turn coheres with, and is relevant to, a prior utterance, is to ensure that the action constituted by that turn is an appropriate action to produce after the action constituted by the prior turn: a question should be followed by an answer, a greeting followed by a return greeting, an invitation by an acceptance or a refusal and so on.

Of course, conversation does not always cohere smoothly; occasionally, misunderstanding and confusion arise. However, it is noticeable that for at least a proportion of such conversational difficulties the root lies in the misalignment between first-pair parts and second-pair parts. For example, consider extract (5), which comes from an exchange between a mother and her son about a Parent Teachers' Association meeting.

(5) (From Tersaki, 1976: 45)

Mother:	Do you know who's going to that meeting?
Russ:	Who.
Mother:	I don't kno:w!
Russ:	Oh::h Prob'ly Mr Murphy an' Dad said
	prob'ly Mrs Timpte an' some o' the teachers.

In this extract Mother's question 'Do you know who's going to that meeting?' can be heard as performing one of two actions: as a genuine *request* for information about who is attending the meeting, or as a *pre-announcement* of some news concerning the people who will be attending the meeting. Each of these first actions projects the relevance of specific kind of second: a request for information projects the relevance of information-giving (or an account as to why it can't be provided); and a pre-announcement ensures that the next turn should be one that returns the floor to the producer of the pre-announcement. In this case, Russ returns the floor to his mother with a question, thereby displaying that he treats her utterance as a pre-announcement. And Mother's next turn displays that, on this occasion, Russ got it wrong: he produced the inappropriate second-pair part.

Extract (5) not only provides an example of the way in which the concept of adjacency pairs and their properties can inform our understanding of a sequence of conversation in which some misunderstanding occurs; it also illustrates an important methodological principle which is central to conversation analytic research.

Conversation analysis seeks to describe the way that sequences of turns cohere into orderly patterns of turn exchange. However, unlike many methodological approaches to the study of language use, there is no attempt to explain this coherence in terms of a limited and theoretically derived set of categories of turn types. Rather, the goal of analysis is to see how *participants themselves* analyse and 'classify' the kind of business that a turn in dialogue is attending to. That is, in conversation analysis, the goal is not to try to *impose* an order on the relationship between successive turns: it tries instead to describe how *speakers themselves* arrive at an interpretation and understanding of how a turn is appropriately placed in a specific sequence of turns. Consequently, the first step in analysis of any sequence is to see how a next speaker interprets the prior turn. With respect to extract (5), Russ's first turn in this sequence is informed by, and is a public display of, the interpretation he made of his mother's prior turn. Similarly, Mother's second turn in the exchange exhibits her understanding that Russ has arrived at an incorrect assessment of the kind of business her first turn was designed to address. So, the kinds of interpretative and reasoning procedures that conversation analysis seeks to identify are thus displayed in the turn-by-turn unfolding of interaction.[5]

With these points in mind, let us return to the sequence of exchanges in extract (1).

(1) 2P:F:T2SB [CM]

		((*Tape starts*))
1	I:	about your sty:le
2		(.3)
3	I:	and who you are
4		(.4)
5	I:	how would you describe yourselves
6	R1:	huhh huhh hhagh punk rockers

7	R2:	punk rockers yeah huhh huhh
8	I:	How long have you been punk rockers,
9	R2:	three:– ah've been three years
10	R1:	yeah three

We can see that utterances in the first two turns appear to be a pair of consecutively produced actions. Initially, we might characterise this as a question–answer pair (although later we will argue that we can provide a more informative description of these turns). The first respondent's first turn consists of a subcultural identification of herself and her companion. Her answer thereby displays her reasoning about the kind of action constituted by the interviewer's prior turn.

If this interpretation was incorrect, and the interviewer's first turn was designed to facilitate an entirely different kind of utterance from the respondent, the interviewer would be able to initiate correction in her subsequent turn. So, for example, had the interviewer's first utterance been designed to elicit a literal description of the speakers' style – say, an account of what they were wearing at that moment – the respondent's subsequent answer ('punk rockers') would have displayed to the interviewer that she had misunderstood the prior turn. At which point there would be a chance for the interviewer to produce a clarification and rephrase the question another way. But the interviewer instead provides a further question, 'How long have you been punk rockers,' (line 8), which in no way challenges the relevance of the respondent's prior turn. Indeed, it is directed to, and predicated upon, a feature of the speakers' lives as members of that subculture to which the first respondent had assigned herself and her friend in the prior turn. Therefore we have evidence, indigenous to the trajectory of the interaction, that the interviewer's first utterance was indeed designed to elicit an identification of the kind produced by the respondent.

But it is not obvious that the interviewer's first turn *was* designed to elicit this kind of category identification. Remember that there were (at least) three components in the interviewer's first turn: a request for the speakers to say something about their style, a request for them to say who they were and then a request that they describe themselves. So, the question that the respondent addresses is far from unambiguous. It could have been interpreted in a number of ways. For example, that kind of utterance could have been taken literally and treated as a request for the respondents to describe what they were wearing at that moment.

(6) 1 Non-Punk:M:T9SB [KHS]

		((*Tape starts*))
1	I:	'KAY can you te ((*tape glitch*)) thing about
2		yourself your sty:le and that

```
3                   (1.2)
4          R:       well, it's jus the way (ah loo(k)) lots
5                   of leather loads of chains and things
6                   I like (.) (my) red 'air
7                   (.)
8          R:       it's ⌐really good (.4) it'll probably be
9          I:       └°mm hm°
10         R:       purple next week (.) ↑Hah
```

Equally, the respondent could have provided an announcement of her identity, but fashioned this in terms of a range of personal characteristics other
than her subcultural affiliation. For example, in the following extract the
respondent describes herself as unemployed, and formulates a description of
where she lives.

(7) 2 Non-Punks:F:TS1A [KHS]

```
                    ((Tape starts))
1          R1:      ahm (.) Debbie, >ahm unemployed, and
2                   ah live in: (.) Newcastle
```

Finally, the respondent could have made an explicit topic of the ambiguity of
the question.

(8) 2P:MF:T8SA [CM]

```
                    ((Tape starts))
1          I:       okay, hh how you you describe yourselves
2                   'n your style and that
3                   (1)
4          R:       I could answer that
5                   (in a lot of ways) -(k)hhuh huhh
```

Indeed, given the range of ways that the opening question could have been
interpreted, we might begin to consider how it was that the respondent in
extract (1) seemed to be able to arrive at the interpretation that she did. What
kinds of interpretative resources did the respondent draw on to come to see
that the interviewer's opening utterance ensured that a formulation of her
identity *as* a member of a specific subculture was a relevant next action?

There are two related kinds of common-sense tacit knowledge which inform the respondent's interpretation of the interviewer's first utterance.
Throughout this chapter we have referred to the exchanges with our respondents as interviews (albeit interviews conducted informally and conver-
sationally). However, there are grounds for arguing that our respondents
also shared an understanding and definition of the exchange as a form of

interview (as distinct from a spontaneous conversation with people they just happened to meet). We were, after all, strangers, equipped with micro-phones and recording technology, who approached them in the street and asked if we could talk to them. Such an approach, as a method of engin-eering a verbal exchange, is much more resonant of market research inter-views conducted on the street, than of ordinary conversational interaction. And, on occasions, the respondents' orientation to the interview format of the occasion became manifest explicitly in their talk. Once the people we approached agreed to talk to us we took them to a quiet spot (that we had decided upon earlier) to allow us to conduct the interview with the minimum amount of distraction. We also had to arrange the positions of microphones, ensure the tape recorder was working, and attend to various other technical considerations before we could begin. It was during this period, prior to the start of the interview proper, that many of the respondents spontaneously remarked that they had never been interviewed before (or recounted that they had previously been interviewed).

Of course, the respondent's orientation to the kind of dialogue on which they were embarking would not merely have provided a label, or 'definition of the situation'. Such an understanding also furnishes a set of interpretative resources with which to come to an understanding of the subsequent events; that is, because the circumstances could be characterised as an interview, the common-sense, taken-for-granted properties of interview interaction were therefore available to be drawn upon to inform the respondent's understand-ing of the moment-by-moment development of the interaction.

Perhaps one of the most obvious features of interviews is that, right at the beginning, it is customary that the interviewer elicit an identification of the interviewee. This is particularly true of market research interviews: anyone who has been approached for a market research interview on the street, or who has been telephoned at home, will recall that the researcher's first task is to assess whether the respondent is the type of person whose opinion is relevant to the nature of the research project being undertaken: 'house-holder'; 'user of specific household consumables'; 'small business owner'; 'be-tween twenty-five and thirty-five years of age'; 'female/male', etc.

Recall also that the interviewer's first utterance on the tape was easily identifiable *as* the first question in the interview. The switch from the period of pre-interview general chat (which followed our initial approach to the respondent(s)) to the beginning of the interview was signalled in two ways. First, we had to arrange the technical apparatus we were using, such as micro-phones and tape recorders. Second, on occasions the shift to the interview proper was marked by the interviewer's use of an item such as 'right' and 'okay' to preface the first question. (For instances of this verbal marking of the onset of the interview, see extracts 6 and 8.)

There is also a sense in which the outpourings of popular culture may have contributed to the tacit understanding that an appropriate (or necessary) action at the start of formal interaction is the elicitation of an identification of the respondent/interviewee. For example, anyone who has watched a television drama which depicts events involved in a courtroom cross-examination will be aware that the first question addressed to the witness is of the kind 'Are you [name] of [address]?'. (Whether or not this is how business is actually transacted in courtrooms is irrelevant: as more people watch television and visit the cinema than attend courtroom proceedings, it is the visual media portrayal of such events which will impinge upon public perception.)

So, then, our respondents in extract (1) had the resources of our culture to assist them to come to an understanding of the kinds of actions that are salient or likely at the start of spates of interaction that can be seen to be, or characterised as, 'interview talk', as opposed to, say, conversation; that is, they had a culturally available understanding of the kind of action that they were being invited to perform as a response to the interviewer's first utterance in the interview. And the first respondent's subsequent action – 'huhh huhh hhagh punk rockers' – exhibits an understanding that the interviewer's prior utterance was an invitation to provide an identification.

However, this does not explain how the respondent came to see that it was a characterisation of her identity as a member of a specific *subculture* that was appropriate. That is, there are a range of categories which could have been invoked in her description: she could have identified herself as a female, as a person of a certain age, as an English person (or whatever), as a Catholic (or whatever), as a resident of London (or wherever) and so on. So how did she arrive at the conclusion that a report of her identity as a punk was relevant at this point in the exchange?

It is important to bear in mind that the rather unusual and direct methods by which we solicited people's permission to conduct an interview would have also produced a puzzle for our respondents. Remember that we simply walked up to people we had never previously met, nor to whom we had even spoken, and asked if we could talk to them. So one immediately relevant issue for our respondents was, 'why me?': how could the respondents make sense of our decision to approach them, rather than anyone else.

We can arrive at one obvious answer to this puzzle via a consideration of the appearance of the people we approached: all the respondents looked strikingly different to other people in the street at the time. We selected specific individuals because they were dressed in such a way that it seemed likely, at least to us, that they would claim to be members of a subcultural group. So we were drawing upon our common-sense knowledge of subcultures to inform our selection of specific individuals for interview. And of course, that same common-sense knowledge was available to respondents to come to an understanding as to why they had been selected: they could infer that our reason for approaching them was related to the way that their appearance made available the inference that they were members of a specific subcultural group. So that, in extract (1), when the interviewer's first question

constituted an invitation to formulate an identity, the respondents were able
to infer the kind of identity which was being made salient.

Just because the respondent was able to recognise the appropriateness of a
certain type of action does not mean that she was in any way committed to
producing that action. We are not making deterministic claims about sequences of actions. What we are trying to point to are the ways that the
sequential properties of language inform and enable specific interactional
enterprises. And with regard to extract (1) it was through the production of
the first part of an invitation sequence that the respondent's identity as a punk
was made salient; and it was through the production of the appropriate
second-pair part that the respondent's identity as a punk became mobilised
and brought explicitly into the exchange.

In the next extract, however, we can begin to see some of the communicative resources through which respondents interactionally resist the mobilisation of a subcultural identity.

(9) 1R:M:T5SB [RRF]

```
                 ((Tape starts))
1        I:      how would you descri:be (.) yourself
2                and appearance and so on
3                (.)
4        R:      describe my appearance,
5        I:      yeah
6                (1)
7        R:      su- su- slightly longer than average hair
                 (Respondent goes on to provide an account of his
                 appearance)
```

In this extract the speaker does not provide an immediate answer to the
interviewer's first question, but instead asks a further question 'describe my
appearance'. This is treated by the interviewer as an attempt by the respondent to clarify or confirm his understanding of the kind of action he is being
invited to do by the prior turn. The respondent's clarification utterance is
greeted with a simple confirmation by the interviewer, after which the respondent begins to produce a literal description of his appearance, starting
with the length of his hair.

Compare the opening sequence in extract (9) with the opening sequence
in extract (1). In extract (1) the respondent produced an answer immediately after the interviewer's opening utterance; and this turn exhibited her
orientation to the invitation to offer a category membership constituted by
the prior turn. Furthermore, the place in which that category ascription was
produced in extract (1) was a turn which constituted the second-pair part
to the invitation to offer a category label. But in extract (9) the speaker

initiates a clarification sequence through which he is able to provide a formulation of the kind of response the prior turn was designed to elicit: that is, he characterises the prior turn as requesting a literal description. This in turn ensures that the respondent is able to avoid providing a formulation of his subcultural identity in a sequential position where the provision of such an identification is a salient activity.

This may appear to be an ambitious observation, for it seems to ascribe to the respondent's first turn a far more strategic purpose than an initial inspection of the data may suggest. But there are two sorts of evidence to support this claim. There is a source of evidence which is endogenous to the rest of that exchange. Consider the sequence after the respondent begins to give a literal description of his appearance.

(9) 1R:M:T5SB [RRF]

```
                 ((Tape starts))
1      I:        how would you descri:be (.) yourself
2                and your appearance and so on
3                (.)
4      R:        describe my appearance,
5      I:        yeah
6                (1)
7      R:        su- su- slightly longer than average hair
8                (.)
9      I:        °mm hm°
10               (.3)
11     R:        ah pr- prefer to wear (.) denim than
12               (.2)
13     R:        denim and leather than anything else (s)
14               (.3)
15     I:        would you call yourself a ↑rocker
16               (.4)
17     R:        yeah (i)f someone asked me what ah was
18               (.)
19     I:        °mm hm°
20               ah su- s:(pp)ose that's what ah'd say
```

Note that after the respondent has provide a description of his appearance the interviewer produces a question which blandly asks if the speaker is a member of a certain category. Note that his response, although affirmative, is heavily conditional: he does not answer immediately, and when he does, he characterises his acceptance of that label as an action he would do only in circumstances in which he is being asked to comment on the appropriateness of a category label. In short, he produces an answer which formulates his acceptance of that label as something which would happen in a situation like the one in which he found himself *at that moment he was speaking*. Thus he makes his answer relative to specific circumstances.

But there is corroborative evidence that distinctly strategic actions can be accomplished through the production of turns in sequential positions in which a certain type of turn has been made relevant by the production of a certain kind of first-pair part.

Some of the earliest analytic themes developed by Harvey Sacks in his work on conversational interaction were generated from his analysis of recordings of calls to the Los Angeles Suicide Prevention Center. He had observed that, in the majority of cases, if the Center's personnel gave their names at the beginning of the conversation, the callers would give their names in reply. Sacks noticed, however, that in one call the caller (B) seemed to be having trouble with the agent's name.

(10) From Sacks 1992:3

A: this is Mr. Smith, may I help you
B: I can't hear you
A: This is Mr <u>Smith</u>
B: Sm<u>i</u>th.

Sacks also observed that for the rest of the conversation the caller remained reluctant to disclose his identity. Sacks began to explore this call to determine 'where, in the course of the conversation could you tell that somebody would not give their name' (Sacks, 1992:3). With this question, Sacks examined the caller's utterance 'I can't hear you'. He argued that saying 'I can't hear you' is one way of displaying 'not hearing'. Such an action entails that the person not heard should repeat their prior utterance. Thus, doing 'not hearing' establishes the relevance and onset of a short clarificatory sequence. What Sacks also noted was that, basically, there are specific places in conversations where it is appropriate for things like greetings and name exchanges to be done. Specifically, they get done right at the start. (And there is a sense in which such exchanges like greetings *should* be done at the start of interactions: if they are introduced later into a conversation, people tend to do some special work to warrant the provision of such actions in a strange place. For example, it is not unusual for people who have been talking for a while, for example on a plane, or at a dinner party, to say something like 'I'm sorry, I didn't introduce myself earlier, my name is . . .', or, 'by the way my name is . . .'. Items like 'by the way' are displacement markers. They display the speaker's understanding that whatever activity they preface is not being done in the place where it should be done.) Sacks came to the conclusion that by doing 'not hearing', the caller is avoiding giving a name in that place in the conversation where name giving is expected. Moreover, initiating a clarification sequence moves the conversation on a few places so that it is increasingly unlikely that there will be another appropriate place for the agent to elicit the caller's name. So, in this case, doing 'not hearing' seemed to be one way, one method, of doing 'not giving a name'.

With regards to extract (9) then, it may be the case that the initiation of a clarification sequence not only secures the respondent the right to provide a literal description of his style, but is a method by which the respondent can avoid providing an appropriate category identification in a place in the interaction in which such a self-ascription is both salient and warranted by the interviewer's prior turn. In the next chapter we explore this argument further, and try to describe some of the interactional and inferential consequences of resisting a category ascription. But first we wish to address some broader methodological issues.

In this chapter we have examined in detail some of the properties of the opening sequences of our interviews with members of youth subcultures. Identity negotiation, and the resistance of category ascription, are subtle processes and thus require a detailed examination of the talk through which they are accomplished. But there are other benefits to be gained from the technical appreciation of the organisation of turns at talk.

In Chapter 2 we noted that many researchers have turned to language in the study of identity as a way of exploring and resolving conceptual problems of the emphasis on isolated individuals and monadic selves. A number of these 'linguistic turns' argued for the utility of the metaphor of persons in conversation; for example, Shotter (1989) and Harré (1987; 1989). They argue that this metaphor emphasises the centrality of language and, given that conversations take place between people, it highlights the significance of selves in relationships and joint activities. Unfortunately, though, the utility of this metaphor is generally not realised in practice. Instead, their arguments are warranted through an examination of the existence of grammatical terms, in particular, pronouns. For these reasons, then, their perspective remains largely at the conceptual or metaphorical level and does not try to address the practical business of identity work which is accomplished through verbal interaction. This is an unfortunate oversight given that, for many sociologists, conversation is taken to be the primordial site of social life.[6]

However, through the detailed analysis of actual instances of conversational interaction we are able to provide a practical and contextualised grounding for the metaphor of selves in conversation; that is, whatever the *conceptual* utility of the conversational metaphor, conversations are *actual activities*, the details of which are available for analytic attention. The study of turn-by-turn sequences provides a way of seeing how selves and identities are actually *produced* in conversation. We propose that the analytic approach we have adopted provides the beginnings of a way of understanding the production of selves in conversation, and that the back-and-forth flow of interaction between interviewer and respondents constitutes the basis of joint activity through which identities are produced (and resisted).

This in turn can inform our understanding of the importance of 'shared meanings' in the production of identity. Individuals do not define the meaning of selves, activities and events in isolation; instead they depend on shared understanding. Therefore, these are *social* products. The analysis of interaction can provide a way of studying shared understanding and, hence, a practical appreciation of what Heritage (1984) calls the 'architecture of intersubjectivity'. He argues that because conversations are organised and implemented on a turn-by-turn basis, 'a context of publicly displayed and continuously up-dated intersubjective understandings is systematically sustained' (*op. cit.*:259). The turn-by-turn character of talk allows – and requires – displays of the participants' understanding and interpretations. These displays are embedded in the kinds of next turns participants produce. (So, for example, in extract (5) Russ's first turn displays his understanding that his mother's prior turn was a pre-announcement of some news, rather than a genuine request for information.) Linked conversational actions, produced in turn-by-turn sequences, are the basic building blocks of intersubjectivity. Such understandings are publicly displayed; in the first instance for the benefit of co-participants. But if the interaction is recorded and transcribed, these public displays of understanding are also available for subsequent analytic inspection. And by studying the turn-by-turn development of talk, the analyst has the opportunity to study the emergence and influence of knowledge held in common by participants in specific sequences of interaction.

Of course the study of next turns does not provide straightforward access to participants' understandings of prior talk. A speaker's analysis of prior talk is often *indirectly* exhibited in her own turn (for example, 'accepting' is an indirect way of displaying an understanding that the prior turn constituted an 'invitation'). Furthermore, next utterances often characterise the talk in a way that is relevant to the projects of the next speaker (Heritage and Watson, 1979) which may not coincide with the prior speaker's project. And, finally, participants in interaction may try to influence the trajectory of any spate of interaction by failing to pursue a course of action implicated or made relevant by a prior turn. So, there is more to intersubjectivity and interaction than shared understanding: speakers also *transform* meanings in the course of conversational interaction. It is an analytic imperative, then, that we regard the emergent features and properties of conversational interaction as *joint* products. And insofar as social identities are emergent features of verbal interaction, we should treat these as socially produced.

Our analytic approach can, then, contribute an empirical appreciation of central concepts in some linguistic turns in the social sciences; for example, we can show how identities are joint products which depend upon intersubjective understandings. But this is not the only way of understanding selves, identity and language embodied in the linguistic turn. In the last chapter we discussed that kind of discourse analysis associated with the work of Parker (1992) and Burman and Parker (1993a). In this analytic tradition, a discourse is seen as a coherent web of meanings; and persons are ascribed identities according to the ways they are positioned or embedded in relevant discourses (Henriques *et al.*, 1984; Parker, 1992; Wetherell and Potter, 1992; see also Chapter 2). One consequence of this approach is that discourses (and, presumably, actual instances of language use) are reified as abstract entities; we have no sense of a living spoken language. Discourses are treated as somehow lurking behind actual language use, and the search for their significance leads the analyst away from an appreciation of the actual properties of a dynamic spoken language. Equally, there is no scope for the investigation of the ways that people use their communicative competencies in the production of their identities, and those of other people in interaction. Potter *et al.* (1990) make similar points: they draw an analogy between Parker's notion of discourses and the geology of tectonic plates which clash, grind, circulate or slip over each other while massive but unseen forces work beneath them. Abstract discourses similarly are seen to work on other abstract discourses, and while this conceptualisation can provide a useful historical perspective, what is excluded is 'the actual working of discourse as a constitutive part of social practices situated in *specific* contexts' (*op. cit.*:209).

There is a related point: the postmodern conception of social identities as subjects' positions in discourses tends towards social determinism. Discourses are seen as potent causal agents which produce subjects and objects (Wetherell and Potter, 1992) and individuals are thus taken to be socially determined through discourse (see Henriques *et al.*, 1984; Hollway, 1989). But by taking into account the way that participants interact, and in so doing, accept and resist categorical identifications, we move away from a sterile account of individuals entrapped in coherent webs of meaning.

Thus, the primary benefit of a detailed analysis of turn-by-turn sequences in interaction is that it reveals *how* identities are produced in joint action and through negotiated understandings. Clearly, this kind of conversation analytic stance has much to offer the concepts and theoretical perspectives which constitute the linguistic turn in the study of identity. However, conversation analysis is *not* a theory of social selves and identity, but the study of talk-in-interaction. When it is harnessed to a conceptual shift in ways of understanding social identity, the study of verbal exchanges has an important, practical contribution to make to our understanding of selves and identity. This practical contribution is further explored in our next chapter.

Notes

1. It might be objected that we are overlooking a salient difference between the exchanges in our interviews and ordinary conversational interaction: in the latter

case, any participant can ask a question; whereas in the former, the provision of questions is conventionally the responsibility of one party. But our respondents were able to ask some types of questions: so, although they did not ask questions which initiated topics, or shifted the focus of the interaction, they were able to ask for clarification. And in Chapter 5 we provide an analysis of some properties of one type of question posed by the respondents immediately after the interviewer's initial question.

2. Of course, the study of language use has not been the sole province of conversation analysis: other approaches include linguistically informed discourse analysis (Sinclair and Coulthard, 1975; Brown and Yule, 1983); speech act theory (Austin, 1962; Searle, 1969); the study of conversational maxims (Grice, 1975); the ethnography of speaking (Bauman and Sherzer, 1974; Gumperz, 1982; Gumperz and Hymes, 1972); the social psychology of language use (Giles and Coupland, 1991); and we must not forget that much of Goffman's later writings were dedicated to the examination of verbal interaction (1974; 1981).

We do not have the space here to explain in detail why we have elected to pursue a conversation analytic approach, and not any of these alternative methodologies. If readers are interested in debates on the utility of conversation analysis in comparison with other approaches, they are referred to the following sources: Atkinson and Drew, 1979, Chapter 1 (on ethnography); Lee, 1991 (on ethnographic and anthropological studies of language and culture); Levinson, 1983, Chapter 6 (on the differences between conversation analysis and that branch of discourse analysis informed by linguistics and speech act theory); Potter and Wetherell, 1987, Chapter 4 (on the importance of conversation analytic research for the social psychological study of accounts); and Schegloff, 1988, 1992 (on Goffman and Searle respectively).

3. All extracts from the interviews we conducted are coded. This system is used to record the number of speakers, their subcultural affiliation, (Punk, Rocker, Hippy, Gothic), their gender, and a reference to identify the location of the specific fragment on the original tapes. The letters in square brackets are references to the place where the interview was conducted, and are explained in the Appendix.

4. It may be thought that it is obvious and self-evident that turn-taking progresses in the following way: one person says something, the next person says something. And so you get the Interviewer – Respondent, Interviewer – Respondent pattern which we see in our data. However, it simply does not follow that just because we have an A – B, A – B sequence here, the procedures for organising turn exchange are simple or obvious. If it was the case that turns simply passed from one to another, then in a four-party conversation, we would expect A to speak, then B, then C, then D and then A again and so on. And that just does not happen, except perhaps in formal debates in which normal procedures for conversational exchange have been formally suspended and turns to speak are allocated in advance (Sacks et al., 1974).

Further indication of the complex business involved in turn-taking comes from a consideration of the *place* in which the first respondent in extract (1) began to speak. The reader might like to consider how it was she came to see that it was appropriate for her to begin to speak after the interviewer's turn had reached its third component, and not after the first or the second components, both of which were followed by short gaps which could have been interpreted as constituting the end of that turn.

5. It is for this reason that conversation analysts place great emphasis upon the examination of *sequences* of interaction, rather than, say, the detailed analysis of utterances which have been extracted from the sequential context in which they occurred.
6. This is not to say that there are no non-conversational shared activities within which identities become relevant, nor that conversation is divorced from other non-verbal practices.

Chapter 5

SOME PROCEDURES FOR RESISTING CATEGORY ASCRIPTION

In the last chapter we showed how the interviewer's first question in the interview could be interpreted as an invitation to the respondents to describe themselves in terms of their subcultural affiliation. So, we considered common-sense knowledge about the organisation of interviews in general, and the kind of information which is conventionally sought in the first few exchanges. We also argued that the respondents could infer that we had chosen to approach them by virtue of their alternative or subcultural appearance. Finally, we pointed to the way that the interviewer's first question was designed to elicit a subcultural self-identification.

Of course, respondents were not compelled to describe themselves in terms of a subcultural membership; for example, we looked at one interview (extract 1 below) in which the speaker initiated a clarification sequence instead of providing any self-identification.

(1) 1R:M:T5SB [RRF]

		((*Tape starts*))
1	I:	how would you descri:be (.) yourself
2		and your appearance and so on
3		(.)
4	R:	describe my appearance,
5	I:	yeah
6		(1)
7	R:	su- su- slightly longer than average hair
		((*goes on to describe appearance*))

We suggested that the initiation of a clarification sequence may be a method by which the respondent can avoid giving a subcultural self-identification at that point in the interview. In this chapter we want to develop this argument. We will describe other instances in which clarification sequences are produced immediately after the interviewer's first question in the interview. We examine these clarification initiations to see how they are designed to establish the relevance of a different kind of self-description to that projected by the interviewer's first question. We then discuss some of the inferential implications of this strategy, and consider some other discursive strategies by which respondents can resist giving a subcultural self-identification.

Underlying the analytic observations is the claim that social identities in talk are inextricably related to the management of specific interactional episodes: in this case, the opening sequences in informal interviews. This empirical approach to the analysis of social identity in action is very different to, and much less cumbersome than, theoretical explanations offered in the conventional social psychological literature. We return to this argument at the end of the chapter.

We noted in the previous chapter that a large amount of conversational interaction is conducted through paired exchanges. However, the simple production of the first part of an adjacency pair does not necessarily legislate that the second part will follow immediately. Before the provision of the expected second part there may be *insertion sequences* (Schegloff, 1972), often composed of embedded and nested adjacency pairs, during which matters relevant to the first part are addressed before the second part is produced. Thus one obtains patterns of, for example, questions and answers of the following form:

(2) (Taken from Sacks' unpublished lectures; lecture 3, 1972:23)

A:	Hello			
B:	Is Fred there?			**Q1**
A:	Who is calling?		**Q2**	
B:	Is he there?	**Q3**		
A:	Yes	**A3**		
B:	This is Joe Henderson		**A2**	
A:	Just a moment			**A1**

Let us consider some of the properties of extract (1). A first point to make is that the respondent's answer to the interviewer's first turn is not produced immediately after that turn. Instead, it is produced (in line 7) after a short insertion sequence. The insertion sequence in extract (1) is

1	I:	how would you descri:be (.) yourself		**Q1**
2		and your appearance and so on		
3		(.)		
4	R:	describe my appearance,	**ins.**	**Q2**
5	I:	yeah	**ins.**	**A2**
6		(1)		
7	R:	su- su- slightly longer than average hair		**A1**
		((*goes on to describe appearance*))		

A further example of this phenomenon is illustrated in the following extract.

(3) 1P:F:T7SA [KR]

```
                ((Tape starts))
1       I:      RIght how would you describe your sty:le,
2               (.6)
3       R:      how would I describe ┌the style        ins.   Q
4       I:                           └yeah             ins.   A
5               (.4)
6       R:      well (.4) it's:: (.) different it's
7               usually dirty and
                ((continues))
```

The first parts of these insertion sequences in extracts (1) and (3) ('describe my appearance,' and 'how would I describe the style') have the character of a 'question-seeking-clarification/confirmation'. (And in both cases the interviewer's minimal affirmative responses display that this is indeed how she treats them.) So instead of producing the relevant conversational action – a self-identification provided in terms of a subcultural category – the respondents have produced an entirely different kind of action. But more important, perhaps, are the sequential implications which follow from the production of these insertion sequences: through these actions the respondents are able to recharacterise the business of that part of the interview. So that, instead of being question–answer sequences in which the respondents formulate a description of their identities, the subsequent utterances now focus on other concerns: descriptions of (superficial) appearances.

There are other ways of resisting a subcultural self-identification. Respondents can, in various ways, simply question the legitimacy of the interviewer's first question. For example, in the following extract, the first respondent formulates her negative attitude to the prior question, and thereby resists providing any kind of self-identification.

(4) 3:no specific group:F:T3SA [FP]

```
                ((Tape starts: respondents talking to each other about
                Princess Anne for approximately 12 seconds.))
1       I:      can you tell me something about your style and the way
2               you look,
3               (.7)
4       I:      how would you descri:be yourselves
5               (.7)
6       R1:     °huhh°
7               (.7)
```

```
8      R1:    I dunno >I hate those sorts of quest┌ions uhm
9      R2:                                         └yeah horrible
10            isn't it
```

The first respondent's utterance, 'I hate those sorts of questions', constitutes a complaint about having to provide a characterisation of herself. Her reluctance to answer the question has therefore become an explicit feature of the exchange. Although an overt complaint about the interviewer's question does not necessarily index an imminent breakdown of the interview, it certainly constitutes a 'trouble' in the exchange. This is a marked departure from routine conversation in which participants rely on various interactional practices to minimise the likelihood of explicit conflict or disagreement (for example, see Schegloff *et al.*, 1977, remarks on the preference for self-correction in the organisation of repair in conversation). Explicit rejections of questions, then, can jeopardise the smooth flow of the interview, and can undermine the relationship between interviewer and interviewee.

The production of an insertion sequence which seeks clarification, however, does not question the propriety or salience of the prior turn. Yet it does permit the speaker to establish a spate of talk in which the likelihood that they will be expected to produce a subcultural self-identification is minimised. In this sense, the production of an insertion sequence is a delicate strategy: it allows the respondents to avoid giving a subcultural identification in such a way that their resistance does not become an explicit focus of the exchange.

An interesting property of these insertion sequences concerns the way in which they have been designed to mirror or echo lexical components from the interviewer's prior turn. So, in extract (1) the interviewer's prior turn is 'how would you descri:be (.) yourself and your appearance and so on'. With the appropriate pronoun change the respondent's subsequent turn repeats the words 'describe (yourself and) your appearance'. And in extract (3) the respondent's recycling of components from the interviewer's prior turn is extensive: the only changes are the deletion of the exclamative ('RIght,') which prefaces her first turn proper, and the change from the possessive pronoun ('your sty:le,') to the definite article ('the style').

However, these insertions are not exact echoes. Take extract (1): although certain parts of the interviewer's prior turn have been selected for repetition, other parts have been ignored. So we find that the component 'describe *yourself*' has not been recycled as 'describe *myself*' but 'describe my appearance'. In this sense, the respondent's turn in line 4 formulates a *version* of the interviewer's prior utterance.

This phenomenon is similar to that identified by Heritage and Watson (1979). They explored the ways in which participants in news interviews formulated versions of other people's prior talk, and the interactional tasks accomplished through such formulations. They identified two methods used by participants to construct utterances which draw on aspects of immediately prior talk: as gists, or summaries, or as upshots, or consequences. Their analysis reveals that these devices allow speakers to constitute reflexively the character of the preceding talk. Gists and upshots are used in three main ways: they are are used to preserve, transform or delete aspects of the prior talk. These three operations are illustrated in the following extract. This is taken from a face-to-face interview with a winner of a 'Slimmer of the Year' competition, which was broadcast on the radio.

(IE = interviewee; IR = interviewer.) (Heritage and Watson, 1979:132)

```
 1    IE:    You have a shell that for so long
 2           protects you but sometimes
 3           things creep through the shell
 4           and then you become really aware
 5           of how awful you feel. I never
 6           ever felt my age or looked my age
 7           I was always older – people took me
 8           for older. And when I was at college
 9           I think I looked a matronly fifty.
10           And I was completely alone one weekend
11           and I got to this stage where I
12           almost jumped in the river.
13           I just felt life wasn't worth it any
14           more – it hadn't anything to offer
15           and if this was living
16           I'd had enough.
17    IR:    You really were prepared to commit
18           suicide because you were
19           a big fatty
20    IE:    Yes because I – I just didn't
21           see anything in life that I had
22           to look forward to . . .
```

The interviewer's phrase 'a big fatty' preserves the essential aspects of the interviewee's prior utterances – her weight problem. At the same time, this issue is transformed in the way it is portrayed: 'a big fatty' resonates with children's insults, and neither invokes nor addresses the seriousness of the problem. Indeed, the interviewer's recharacterisation of the problem in these terms deletes the more damaging consequences of obesity which the interviewee discusses.

Let us consider in detail the way in which the first respondent in extract (5) constructs her subsequent turn by building on, or 'borrowing', components from the interviewer's prior utterance.

(5) 2G:F:T1SB [KHS]

```
              ((Tape starts))
1      I:     °right° (.) SO as: a said I'm doing stuff
2             on style and appearance can you tell me
3             something about yourselves th- (.3) the way
4             you look
5             (1.6)
6      R1:    >w-wu-wh't d'you< mean li:ke,
7             (.3)
8      R1:    what do you mean (.) about ourselves
9             's a bit general huhh
```

The interviewer introduces various aspects of self or personal identity in her initial turn: she mentions, first, style and appearance, and then goes on to formulate an explicit invitation to the respondents to talk on 'something about [them]selves' and 'the way [they] look'. So there are (at least) three aspects of self and identity which the respondents could focus upon. (And indeed, the options open to them at this point are increased if we consider the way that they could design turns to address a combination of these characteristics.)[1]

Moreover, the interviewer's first utterance is designed to facilitate the likelihood that the respondents will come to see that they are being asked about their personal style as members of a specific subculture. Consider the request for the respondents to say something about 'the way you look'. Although such a formulation by itself is ambiguous, the respondents can inspect the interviewer's claim that she is 'doing stuff on style and appearance' as a way of interpreting what the interviewer is seeking with the phrase 'the way you look'. And in the previous chapter we described some of the culturally available, tacit knowledge through which the respondents can come to infer that their selection for interview was related to their visibility as members of a specific subculture. So there are interpretative resources, both intrinsic and extrinsic to the actual exchange, which warrant the respondents' interpretation that the interviewer is inviting them to speak as goths, rather than, say, as women, students, or whatever.

However, despite these interpretative resources, the first respondent's subsequent turn (in lines 6 to 9) does not provide a self-identification, but instead initiates a clarification sequence. Moreover, the component of the interviewer's turn which the respondent attempts to clarify is 'about ourselves'. '[W]hat do you mean (.) about ourselves' is strongly resonant of reported speech: the somewhat disjointed syntax, and the prior phrase 'what do you mean', display that the speaker is not simply using the same vocabulary as the interviewer, but is recycling specific features of the prior turn.

But it is not the case that the respondent simply ignores sections of the interviewer's prior turn, and repeats other parts. Rather, the component of the prior turn she recycles to initiate clarification is amended in her subsequent use of it. So that, whereas the interviewer asks the respondents to say '*something* about yourselves' the respondent seeks clarification only of 'about yourselves'. Her construction of what the interviewer said therefore deletes the word 'something'.

This is not a trivial omission. 'Something' may seem a vague way of specifying what the interviewer wants. But it is produced after the interviewer has referred to style and appearance. Given that context, it is likely that the phrase 'something about yourself' will be heard as a request for information relevant to these characteristics. Consequently, it constitutes an invitation to the respondent to produce a self-identification in terms of her membership of a subcultural group.

In her first turn, then, the respondent performs an action other than the kind made salient by the prior utterance. In seeking a clarification of the prior utterance she focuses on, and incorporates into her own turn, only one component of that utterance, thereby ignoring or deleting other components. The components which she does not recycle in her own turn are those which mark the prior utterance as being directed to personal identity, and subcultural identity in particular.

Through the introduction of this clarification sequence, the respondent is able to avoid performing the kind of self-identification made relevant by the prior turn; but it is not the case that she is avoiding self-categorisation altogether. Rather than stating explicitly the relevance (or irrelevance) of a particular categorical identity, she is making available certain inferences about her identity via the design of her utterance. So she does not address the prior question as a member of a subcultural category; instead, her utterance is designed to display that she is addressing the question as any normal person would. By producing a turn in which she does not address those parts of the prior turn which make relevant, and invite her to confirm, a particular kind of categorical self, she makes available the inference that that kind of identity is not relevant to her. In this sense, her first turn in this exchange thereby invokes, and makes salient for that stage in the interaction, her identity as an ordinary person. Through her utterance, she is doing 'being ordinary'.

It was Harvey Sacks who first observed that an individual's status as an ordinary person could be treated as an achievement which is, at least in part, constructed and maintained through discursive practices. In one of his lectures (published as Sacks, 1984) he argues that

> Whatever you may think about what it is to be an ordinary person in the world, an initial shift is not to think of 'an ordinary person' as some person, but as somebody having as one's job, as one's constant preoccupation, doing 'being ordinary'. It is not that somebody *is* ordinary; it is perhaps that that is what one's business is, and it takes work, as any other business does. If you extend the analogy of what you obviously think of as work . . . then you will be able to see

that all sorts of nominalized things, *for example, personal characteristics* and the like, are jobs that are done, that took some kind of effort, training, and so on.

So I am not . . . talking about an ordinary person as this or that person, or some average; that is, as a non exceptional person on some statistical basis, *but as something that is the way somebody constitutes oneself, and in effect, a job that persons . . . may be coordinatively engaged in to achieve that each of them . . . are ordinary persons.* (Sacks, 1984:414–5; final italics added)

To illustrate Sacks' remarks, we can consider two studies which investigate the ways that language, and in particular, description, can be employed so as to exhibit and to accomplish the ordinary character of the speaker. Jefferson's (1984) study of reports of events such as shootings, hijackings, accidents and so on, examines a phenomenon first noticed by Sacks. In their subsequent accounts of their experiences, witnesses to these extraordinary events often employ a format Jefferson identifies as 'At first I thought . . . but then I realized'. A well-known example is the way that witnesses to the shooting of J. F. Kennedy reported a loud bang, which they first thought to be a car backfiring, but which they then realised was gunfire. Jefferson's analysis begins with the observation that in the first part of the device ('At first I thought . . .') speakers proffer their incorrect conclusions from an initial assessment of the events they observed. Her examination of these 'first thought' formulations suggested that witnesses were assembling unexceptional versions of extraordinary events to present themselves as having had the kind of initial assumptions about the event that any normal person may have arrived at.

Wooffitt's (1988; 1992) study of accounts produced by people who claim to have had paranormal or supernatural experiences develops similar themes. Focusing on the ways in which speakers describe features of their experiences to occasion the relevance of specific social identities, he provides a detailed analysis of the following part of an account, in which a woman is describing her first perceptions of an anomalous noise in her house.

(6) (From Wooffitt 1992:74)

```
1     every time I walked into
2     the sitting room, (.3) er:m. (.7)
3     right by the window (.3)
4     and the same place always
5     I heard a lovely (.3) s:ound
6     like de↑de↓dede↑dedede↓dededah
7     just a happy (.) little tu:ne (.5)
8     a:nd >of course<
9     I tore apart ma window
10    I tore apart the window frame
11    I >did Everything<
12    to find out what the hell's causing that
```

Wooffitt argues that the speaker's description of her reactions are designed to portray her normality in extraordinary circumstances. For example, the speaker claims that she searched for the cause of the noise. This is a perfectly reasonable reaction to the sudden appearance of weird noises; indeed, it is easy to imagine that the occurrence of such an anomaly which did not precipitate a search for a cause would itself be a reportable matter. The search itself is described to portray the normality of the speaker's thoughts and actions in these circumstances: that she conducted the search with urgency ('I tore apart'; lines 9 and 10), and that it was exhaustive (I did >Everything<'; line 11). As ordinary people do not immediately come to the conclusion that every odd event is the product of supernatural forces, her normality is further warranted in the way she reveals that she looked for a *physical* cause of the noise. Wooffitt's analysis therefore reveals the ways in which the speaker described her reactions to the onset of a series of anomalous noises so as to make relevant, for the circumstances she describes, her membership of the class of ordinary people.

In the studies by Jefferson and Wooffitt, the speakers' ordinary identities are occasioned through their descriptions of their assumptions about, or physical responses to, states of affairs in the world which they claim to have witnessed. In the exchange in extract (5), however, the respondent invokes her ordinary identity in the way in which she designs her turn to display a specific interpretation of the prior turn.[2] She produces a request for clarification, which would be produced by any normal, unexceptional person who could not infer what it was about *them* in particular that had motivated the interviewer to approach them, and ask a question concerning style, appearance and so on.

The following extracts provide further instances of the ways in which respondents selectively recycle or echo parts of the interviewer's prior utterance, thereby accomplishing in the design of their turns their own normality and ordinariness.

(7) 1P:M:T6SB [KR]

```
                    ((Tape starts))
1       I:          OKaY
2                   (.6)
3       R:          (                          )=
4       I:          =M mmn
5                   (.5)
6       I:          SO(hh)-
7                   ((tape glitch))
8       I:          d'you describe your style then
9                   (.)
10      I:          tell me something
11                  about yourself.
```

```
12                (.3)
13      R:        TEll you something ab↑out myself?
14                (.4)
15      R:        like what, huh ah huhh aHU(gh)-UH
```

(8) 2G:F:T1SA [KHS]

```
                  ((Tape starts))
1       I:        okay c'n you tell me (.) how you
2                 descri:be yourselves=y'know what (y-)
3                 (.3)
4       I:        what the sty:le's all about
5                 (1)
6       R1:       wu:ll (.5) I du(h)nno:(hh) ah mean
7                 (.7)
8       R1:       what do you mean by descri:be our- (.) ourselves
```

In extract (7) the respondent's first turn in the interview consists first of an echoic component ('TEll you something ab↑out myself?') a query marker ('like what,') and a short spate of laughter. The echoic component is a mirror of a part of the interviewer's prior turn, with amendments to the relevant pronouns. The echoic component in extract (8), by contrast, displays more selection: the respondent recycles 'describe yourselves', rather than any other components. In both cases, however, the respondents do not echo the interviewer's reference to their style: those parts of the prior turn which most strongly implicate the relevance of the respondents' subcultural category affiliations are ignored. The respondents thereby portray themselves as not-seeing-the-relevance-for-them of the category implicative reference to style.

But why are respondents providing the kind of answer that someone might give if it was not clear what kind of categorical identity that was being made relevant?

They are, first, resisting a way of being *seen*. Doing 'being ordinary', or at least, through their actions portraying themselves as not belonging to a specific category or group, is a method by which respondents can counter what must be a routine feature of their everyday lives: that by virtue of an inspection of their dress and appearance, other people assume that it is possible to see what kind of person they are. Regardless of whether such an inference is true or not, another's assumptions about a person's categorical affiliations – one's social identity – mean that whatever is known about that category can be invoked as being relevant to that person, whether as a set of resources for interpreting and accounting for past or present conduct, or as a set of knowledge to inform predictions about likely future behaviour (Sacks, 1979; 1992). And there is a sense in which this is a form of social control: by virtue of a category membership (either attributed by others or offered by the individual), a person's own behaviour can be glossed, interpreted and characterised in terms of what is known and expected about that category. It is therefore always potentially the case that the sense or purpose of a person's actions, beliefs, opinions and so on, may be understood by virtue of what is known commonly about the category to which the individual can be seen to be affiliated. It is this ever present potential state of affairs which the respondents' first utterances are designed to resist. By portraying themselves as 'not seeing the category relevance of the interviewer's first turn', the respondents are rejecting the validity of (what they can infer to be) the basis on which they were selected for interview; they are resisting the categorical affiliation which the interviewer's first turn tacitly asks them to confirm.

But there is another point. The production of an insertion sequence allows the respondents to display one instance of their ordinariness: but this action is not produced randomly in the account, but *in their first turns in the exchange*. So that when the interviewer subsequently asks explicitly if they belong to a specific category, their acceptance of that label merely constitutes *one further dimension* of their identity. So instead of being a criterial identity – a central component of their social selves – the subcultural identity is produced as merely one of (at least) two relevant identities. Through their talk, then, the respondents display that they do not, in the first instance, see themselves as being punks, or gothics, while not definitely denying the *potential* relevance of a subcultural identity. And this is a useful resource, for it is possible that in some contexts the respondents would affirm their categorical identity as members of a specific subculture. In some of the interviews we conducted, the respondents did indeed go on to accept the category term offered by the interviewer, having earlier provided the kind of resistance that we have explicated in cases (5), (7) and (8). Indeed, there is a sense in which an outright denial of a subcultural affiliation could warrant assertions of deliberate mischief, disingenuousness, or simple perversity. After all, the kinds of dress and appearance of the respondents invite a certain kind of categorical ascription. So the respondents' talk displays their sensitivity to the delicate issue of undermining the criterial relevance of their subcultural identity, while at the same time minimising the likelihood that a categorical denial of the relevance of their subcultural affiliation could warrant unfavourable conclusions about themselves and their behaviour.

Moreover, the production of an insertion sequence is not the only way in which an ordinary identity can be occasioned by respondents to undermine the relevance of a subcultural identity. For example,

(9) 1 non-Punk:F:T3SA [KR]

```
           ((Tape starts))
1     I:    how would you de((tape glitch))
2           your style and that
```

```
3                (.3)
4        R:      Me::.
5        I:      yeah
6                (.8)
7        R:      well I haven't got (None of) that
8                I (jus feel like) a human being really you know
9                jus: am (.) what I am
10               (.5)
11       R:      'n (ah) happy about it
12               as well >(k)huH: huhh huhh hhuhh<
13               (.3)
14       I:      °would yo⌐u°
15       R:          └'s about it really
16               (.)
17       R:      I dunno I wouldn't
18               (.)
19       R:      wouldn't give a
20               (.)
21       R:      na::me to myself or anything
22       I:      °would you° ⌐(ca-)
23       R:                  └(bu(t))
24       I:      would you call yourself a punk at all.
25               (1.4)
26       R:      >WE(ll) NEh No< 'cos I don't like ↑labels.
27               ah jus: (sor(t)a) ss ahm jus: a human being
28               really ('n) like everyone else but a bit
29               different ah suppose
30               (.)
31       R:      a bit khhuhh huhh h⌐hh
32       I:                         └mm hm
```

After the interviewer's first turn, which is partially obscured by a technical problem, there is a short insertion sequence ('Me::.' – 'yeah'), and the respondent's answer begins in line 7. There are two components to this answer. First, the respondent addresses the issue of his style. But he does not treat the interviewer's reference to style as implicating the relevance of a subcultural identity; rather his utterance 'well I haven't got (None of) that' displays that he treats the reference to style as a personal possession, or characteristic, like, for example, flair.

It is not the case, however, that the respondent avoids the issue of self-identification altogether, for after this mildly self-depreciating remark, he does provide a description of himself: 'I (jus feel like) a human being really'. His self-characterisation as 'a human being' is markedly different from the kind of identification made relevant by the interviewer's initial turn. So, as in extracts (6) and (7), the respondent displays his ordinariness in the manner in which he designs a turn to display a specific kind of interpretation of a component of the interviewer's initial utterance; but this is augmented when he identifies himself as a 'human being', a category which is, in a literal sense, applicable to anyone.

The respondent's turn reaches a possible completion point after his summary '[I] jus: am (.) what I am (.5) 'n (ah) happy about it as well' and the short spate of laughter. Indeed, the interviewer's attempt to begin another question in line 14 indicates that she interpreted the respondent's laughter as marking the end of his turn. The first part of the turn that the interviewer attempts to initiate is 'would you', a component which indicates that the turn was going to be a question or a request. But before that turn can be completed, or even extended beyond the turn initial component, the respondent begins to speak again. He commences this next spate of talk as though it is a continuation of his prior turn; that is, he provides a summary of what he said before, but he then goes on to reject explicitly the personal applicability of 'labels'. But note that when the interviewer eventually produces her next turn ('would you call yourself a punk at all.'), this is exactly the kind of action her turn is designed to invite the respondent to perform (and he rejects it). It would seem, then, that the respondent had anticipated what kind of verbal action the interviewer was going to produce from an inspection purely of the turn initial component 'would you'; and that he had restarted his turn to display that the kind of self-identification her turn was designed to achieve was not relevant to him. The structure of his turn even echoes the turn initial component of the interviewer's turn in line 14: where she starts her utterance with 'would you', the respondent incorporates the phrase 'I wouldn't' into his own turn.

In extract (9) the respondent displays an orientation to the salience of self-identification by describing himself by using a category which is applicable to anyone, thereby undermining the relevance of a specific subcultural category. But in addition to this, he produces a spate of talk which more explicitly displays his sensitivity to, and rejection of, the kinds of self-identification work the interviewer's turn was designed to elicit. Finally, in subsequent exchanges from extract (5) (reproduced below as extract 10), a respondent exhibits a further explicit orientation to the kinds of interactional tasks the interviewer's utterances were designed to accomplish.

(10) 2G:F:T1SB [KHS]

```
                ((Tape starts))
1       I:      °right° (.) SO as: a said I'm doing stuff
2               on style and appearance can you tell me
3               something about yourselves th- (.3) the way
4               you look
5               (1.6)
```

6	R1:	>w-wu-wh't d'you< mean li:ke,
7		(.3)
8	R1:	what do you mean (.) about ourselves
9		's a bit general huhh
10		(.4)
11	I:	well:. how would you describe (.) what
12		you're wearing
13	R1:	ehm (.) what I feel (.4) be(hh)st in hhuh
14		(.4) what I feel is sort'f (.3) myself
15		(1)
16	I:	what about you,
17	R2:	uhM::
18		(5) ((*alarm in background*))
19	R2:	I just find it really offensive when people
20		(.6)
21	I:	sorry,
22	R2:	I just find it really offensive when people
23		try to la::bel (.) what you look like and so
24		(.3)
25	I:	yeah=
26	R2:	=(then) go away and write a magazine article
27		and say oh they're gothic (.2) or they're
28		hippy or something.

In this case the first respondent seeks and obtains a clarification from the interviewer, and then provides an answer (which, noticeably, does not involve a categorical self-identification). But observe the behaviour of the second respondent when the interviewer addresses her for an answer to the same question: she forcibly protests about the kind of self-identification which the interviewer's first turn was designed to achieve.

To summarise, briefly: in this chapter we have been concerned to identify some communicative procedures through which our respondents undermined the criterial relevance of their subcultural identity. In particular we focused on insertion sequences directly after the interviewer's first question, but we also noted some other techniques by which respondents could mitigate the central relevance of their subcultural affiliation for their personal identity. These observations differ markedly from what would have been predicted by New Subcultural Theory. Remember that members were assumed to draw upon subcultural resources to alter their self-image and self-identity, and to mark their difference from other people. The implication is that subcultural identity should figure prominently in the replies to the question which invited the respondents to tell the interviewer something about themselves. In this sense, our analysis provides further criticism of the overcommitted image of sub-cultural identity prevalent in New Subcultural Theory (the image, that is, of persons whose primary if not sole identity is being a punk or whatever). But we have gone further, in that our analysis reveals how the ascription of subcultural identities may be resisted in favour of a non-categorical or ordinary identity; precisely the kind of identity that implies *non*-distinctiveness. Of course, it could be argued that our respondents must have been marginal members; hence they do not accept the label as readily as proper members would. But on what grounds could we distinguish marginal and proper members, especially when several respondents subsequently readily accepted the subcultural category label as a self-description? Indeed, it is both more fruitful and appropriate to consider what constitutes 'proper' membership as a complex members' concern (and in Chapter 7, we show how the issue of authentic and shallow membership is negotiated by respondents).

Perhaps the overriding conceptual point to be drawn from the analytic observations presented in this and the previous chapter is that the discursive negotiation and resistance of a social identity can be a delicate and sensitive business. By examining the subtle procedures through which identities are occasioned, resisted, and negotiated in interaction we begin to appreciate social identities as utterly fluid, variable and context-specific. This is partly because the very meaning, content and form of identities are made contextually relevant to address contingent interpersonal concerns. And attending to sequences of talk as forms of social action necessarily engenders a dynamic conception of self and social identity.

Our emphasis upon the dynamic quality of social identity is mirrored in the mainstream social psychological literature, and in postmodernist critiques of psychology generally. However, we think that detailed analysis of the organisation of talk as a vehicle for interaction permits a more sophisticated and elegant appreciation of the dynamism of social identities than either the traditional, or the critical positions.

Consider the way that the self has been conceived in postmodern accounts. Here, the fluidity of the self and identity is embodied in the vision of a fragmented subject. There is not one self waiting to be discovered, but a multitude of often contradictory and diverse selves occupying (sometimes fleeting) positions in discourse. It is claimed that the meaning of selves is not fixed but fluid: continually constructed and reconstructed (Henriques *et al.*, 1984; Hollway, 1989; Parker, 1992; Potter and Wetherell, 1987; see also Wetherell and Potter, 1992). With some exceptions (notably Davis and Harré, 1990), however, this perspective fails to realise the continually shifting nature of identity in practice. Instead, there is a tendency to select aspects of individuals' accounts in order to identify the discourse within which a person is embedded (see Parker, 1992). As a consequence, we are left with a rather static account of identity: it is as if the person merely hops from one discursive position to another. In other words, there is an absence of any empirical consideration of how people move, discursively or otherwise, from one position to another, and of the ways that social identities can be occasioned as resources to address specific interactional or inferential contingencies.

The idea of the 'fragmented self' again raises the issue of motivation and agency; in particular, it has been argued that without some notion of a core self we cannot produce an account of the 'mechanism' or motivation for positioning in discourses and hence identities (Henriques *et al.*, 1984; Hollway, 1989). In the absence of such an explanation the implication is that we are discursively determined. By contrast, we wish to argue that the problem lies not in the absence of an underlying core self, but because the level of analysis fails to provide a proper appreciation of *how* different identities are achieved and resisted in turn-by-turn sequences of talk, and the local functions that are served.

By contrast, the mainstream approaches make explicit assumptions about a core, agentic self. They are built around a distinction between 'I', the centre of experience and the agent who perceives the world and structures experiences and cognitions, and 'me', the content of those cognitions, including stored identities. (This distinction derived originally from James, 1890 and Mead, 1934.) Motivation is similarly built into traditional social scientific accounts as an internal or psychological construct (see, for example, Markus and Nurius, 1987). Mainstream social psychological and sociological perspectives are not therefore plagued with concerns about issues of agency and motivation.

However, a different problem arises, and this concerns a long debate regarding the nature of the self-concept (Gergen, 1971; Mischel, 1976). 'The controversy can be summarised as concerned with the question of whether the self-concept possesses unity, continuity and consistency across situations or whether it is multidimensional, transient, inconsistent and situation-specific' (Turner, 1982:18). The problem arises because on the one hand it is assumed that individuals *possess* identities which are stable enough to permit their measurement (for example, Breakwell, 1986; Markus, 1977; Mischel, 1976, Stryker, 1987; Turner, 1982; Turner *et al.*, 1987). On the other hand, Turner states that 'the self-concept as subjectively experienced at any given moment (which can be called the self-image) varies directly with the contemporary environment and immediate social context' (Turner, 1982:18–19).

The problem of identity and diversity of self is most commonly resolved by distinguishing between 'identity' (which is 'stored' or internalised) and the self-image or level of self-perception (which is situation-specific). Thus, Turner (1982), suggests that there has been

a failure to distinguish between the self-concept as a cognitive structure and the self-images which are produced by the actual functioning of that structure at any given moment. We shall hypothesise that the self-concept is a relatively enduring, multifaceted system which is carried about in the head from situation to

> situation. It has the overall coherence and organisation which produces a sense
> of unity and consistency and yet structurally and functionally its parts are highly
> differentiated. They are apparently able to operate relatively independently of
> each other. Thus in any given situation a different part or combination of parts
> of the self-concept could be at work with the subjective consequence that dif-
> ferent self-images are produced. By analogy with an orchestra we can think of its
> musical technology and basic instrumentation as the cognitive structure and the
> actual sounds it makes as the varying self-images. (Turner, 1982:19)

Having made the distinction between identity and self-image, the problem
then becomes one of translating identities into self-images; and it is in the
pursuit of the solution to this (theoretical) problem that Self-Categorisation
Theory describes how identities become activated or salient (Turner, 1985;
Turner *et al.*, 1987).

Thus, Self-Categorisation Theory (hereafter SCT) is primarily concerned
with the processes underlying a cognitive transformation: the change from an
individual's subjective sense of a unique self to the perception of themselves
as a member of a group. According to SCT, when this change has occurred –
when people perceive themselves as members of groups – they are said to
have become depersonalised. Depersonalisation occurs through the interaction between aspects of the person and of the situation.

The person dimensions that are important are as follows. First, in order to
become salient, a social category must already be available to the perceiver:

> An individual who defines him- or herself as an 'Australian', for example, may
> never think about nationality for days at a time, yet if that self-definition did not
> exist as a latent identity, it could hardly become salient in relevant settings.
> (Turner *et al.*, 1987:54)

The available category must also be *accessible* to the person at the time.
This refers to a state of category 'readiness' which is determined by learned
expectations and background knowledge of what tends to go with what in the
environment (people will be more ready to perceive someone as a punk if
they are at a punk rock gig); the person's current motives (the person is
looking for a punk); goals and values; and the degree to which that identity is
highly valued and central in self-definition.

In order for an accessible self-category to be made salient, it must fit the
situation or the perceptual frame of reference in two ways: comparatively and
normatively. The comparative aspect of fit depends upon the perceived differences in attributes and behaviour and so on between individuals belonging
to different (implicit) groups compared to the differences perceived between
individuals belonging to the same (implicit) groups (Oakes *et al.*, 1991).[3] The
perceived differences between potential categories of people must also match
our stereotypic preconceptions of the characteristics of those groups. That is,
there must be normative fit.[4]

Thus, particular social categories or social identities become salient when they are available to a person, accessible, and they fit the situation. When a social identity becomes salient, people are said to engage in a process of depersonalisation or self-stereotyping whereby they 'come to perceive themselves more as the interchangeable exemplars of a social category than as unique personalities defined by their individual differences from others' (Turner *et al.*, 1987:50). In order to make proper sense of this aspect of their theory, we have to think of the individual as a perceiver or observer of a situation, watching what is going on from the sidelines before categorising themselves (see Wetherell and Potter, 1992).

So the SCT approach conceptualises a mechanism or process through which identities come to function as self-images. Here, the focus is on the perceptual and intrapersonal processes which are said to constitute the underlying (internal) basis of identity salience or functioning self-images, and through which people become depersonalised. Internal motivation influences the accessibility of a particular identity. Finally, the situation is important in the determination of identity salience, or rather, the person's *perception* of the situation; they perceive similarities and differences within the frame of reference provided by the context. It is largely because of our perception of changing circumstances or relevant social relationships that the self is fluid, variable and context-specific.

This is the way that SCT accounts for the dynamism of social selves. It rests upon a (supposed) tension between a (hypothetical) stable internal entity and the external expression of fluid identities. In addition to its rather cumbersome theoretical complexity, SCT makes questionable assumptions about the nature of the individual. For example, the individual is portrayed as a discerning information processor, watching social situations to decide upon which kind of self-categorisation to adopt. This portrayal has been challenged from many quarters of the social sciences and philosophy, for it is a monadic view which reinforces individual/social dualism. For our present purposes, however, it is important to emphasise that at any moment, identities are treated as the products of psychological processes which precede social interaction (Oakes *et al.*, 1994). By contrast, the analytic approach adopted here emphasises the importance of participation in social interaction which is organised in turn-by-turn sequences. Identities are regarded as products of verbal interaction, and there is no need to invoke hypothetical psychological processes either as explanatory constructs, or as the starting point for analysis.

When we describe, for example, how the design of utterances addresses inferential or interactional tasks, we are not claiming that the speakers *intentionally* used specific strategies because they were motivated to achieve certain effects. When we talk of the respondents' use of insertion sequences to achieve some specific interactional end, we are not claiming that the individuals concerned were merely expressing through their utterances a pre-arranged plan, or executing their intentions through these turns. Our observations concerning the functional significance of these strategies were derived from our analysis of the sequential and social organisation of the interaction, and the way that specific social identities were produced with respect to that organisation.

Moreover, there is an empirically grounded observation to suggest that an attempt to correlate the use of this device with psychological predispositions would not be fruitful. If we continue extract (3) we will see that the respondent subsequently accepts without hesitation the category label offered by the interviewer.

(3) 1 P:F:T7SA [KR]

```
                 ((Tape starts))
 1      I:       RIght how would you describe your sty:le,
 2               (.6)
 3      R:       how would I describe ┌the style
 4      I:                            └yeah
 5               (.4)
 6      R:       well (.4) it's:: (.) different it's
 7               usually dirty and scruffy and ripped
 8               ˙hh loads of chains (.) leather
 9               (.3)
10      I:       mm hmm
11      R:       sometimes coloured but mainly
12               (.5)
13      R:       often black
14               (.5)
15      R:       er:: and belts and handcuffs
16               (.7)
17      R:       erR:r: and er spi:kes
18               (.3)
19      I:       mm hmm
20      R:       an(d)- (.) er coloured hair
21               (.4)                        |smiley voice|
22      R:       sticking up in all d ir ec ti o ns
23               (.3)
24      R:       (kk) ˙hhh
25      I:       would you call yourself a punk?
26      R:       yeah I would
```

If respondents were deliberately (that is, intentionally) using insertion sequences to avoid providing a subcultural self-identity, we would expect that in subsequent stretches of the interview they would likewise reject the interviewer's attempt to suggest or impose a category, but as we saw in subsequent turns in extract (3), that is not the case. (And there is a similar lack of consistency in those cases where the respondents did not produce insertion sequences: in some cases, they volunteer a self-identification, or accept one subsequently offered by the interviewer; and in some cases they do not.) However, we should not be disheartened by the absence of such consistencies; indeed, the very absence of a pattern in the data which would support the investigation of such individualistic concerns itself suggests the importance of explaining the social organisation of these events.

Conversation analytic research has focused on talk-in-interaction as a domain of social activity that is inherently ordered, and not as a representation of mental processes, or as a way of gaining insight to speakers' motivation or intentions. Yet Sacks was aware that his mode of analysis could be taken to imply that he was engaged in an attempt to model or describe the psychological processes which underpinned competence in language use. He was at pains to be clear about this, and said, at the end of his first lecture

> When people start to analyze social phenomena . . . then, if you have to make an elaborate analysis of it . . . you figure that they [speakers] couldn't have thought that fast.
>
> I want to suggest to you that you have to forget that completely. Don't worry about how fast they're thinking. First of all, don't worry about whether they're 'thinking'. Just come to terms with how it is that [the detail of talk] comes off. Because you'll find that they can do these things. . . . Look to see how it is that persons go about producing what they do produce. (Sacks lecture 1, Fall 1964: published as Sacks, 1992:11)

There is a further point we want to emphasise. Conversations comprise a series of acts which follow a trajectory in which each conversational act depends for its sense and relevance on both the prior turn and subsequent uptake. In Chapter 4 we argued that this feature of conversation made it imperative that we regard products of interaction such as identities as jointly accomplished. It also means that there is a functional coherence which is intrinsic to the progress of talk; the logic of utterances and what speakers thereby achieve derive not from imputing underlying intentions to a speaker, but from their embeddedness within a particular trajectory of talk.

In many respects these methodological concerns resonate in later social constructionist writing. Shotter (1993), for example, argues that the basis or possibility of identities is provided for within the ongoing, current contexts of social activity. He draws upon Vico's notion of *divine providence*: the idea that the resources required to shape and develop practical actions are intrinsic to those actions. (This echoes the conversation analytic claim that utterances are context-shaped and context-renewing.) Consequently, our past activities (including previous turns in verbal interaction) create an 'organised setting' for their continuation:

[R]ather than acting 'out of' an inner plan or schema, we can think of ourselves in our current activities as acting 'into' our own present situation, in terms of the opportunities and barriers, the enablements and constraints that it offers. (Shotter, 1993:69)

Continuity, agency and motivation, then, should be understood in the ongoing flow of human activity. We may have no explicit plan, purpose or intention to do certain things, but only certain kinds of consequences can at any one time ensue: those for which a provision exists in our current social context. In this way, intentionality is located in the interaction between people rather than within an individual; it is embedded within the ongoing flow of talk rather than a discrete cause of single acts or identities. Clearly, this is different from the theoretical account provided by Self-Categorisation Theory, which attempts to identify universal mechanisms which produce discrete identities at any one point in time, however momentary.

Social identities, and the motivation for them, are enmeshed in the fabric of social interaction, not ancillary to interpersonal encounters. Therefore, the problem is perhaps not so much in requiring a motivational explanation, but in also viewing motivations as within individuals rather than visible in the functional significance of the devices employed in the ongoing flow of activity and conversation. In this sense, an analytic approach which focuses on the dynamics of language use does not avoid the issue of intentionality, but instead provides an alternative way of understanding it.

Notes

1. It is indeterminate from the ensuing interaction whether the interviewer was referring to these characteristics as a single unit, or whether she mentioned them as discrete features. For the purpose of this chapter we will treat 'style and appearance' as a single unit of two components.
2. Remember that we are not claiming that the respondent actually interpreted the interviewer's question in this way; rather, we are simply pointing to the interactional and sequential consequences of a turn designed to exhibit that this was the kind of interpretation of the previous turn which informed the design of this particular utterance.
3. It is important to bear in mind here that in SCT categories are formed and exist in (meta)contrast to other categories. That is, for Turner *et al.*, identities are stored as self-categories. They claim that like all categories their existence, constitution and meaning depends on their contrast with other relevant categories. Social identities, or social self-categories which define individuals as members of 'ingroups' therefore depend on their contrast with relevant 'outgroups'. So, processes of comparison are important in determining the relevance of a particular category in a particular situation.
4. A hypothetical example may help to clarify what Turner *et al.* are proposing here. Imagine yourself observing a scene in a pub which is filled with men and women, who are also Scottish and English. Your (perceptual) task is to decide whether the

people you see are most appropriately defined as Scottish or English, or whether gender categories provide a better fit. On this basis, you decide who you are for the purposes of acting appropriately in this situation. Imagine that all the women are talking, and all the men are drinking, some Scots and some English people are drinking, others talking. The behaviour you observe therefore correlates with their division into the categories 'men' and 'women' (but not national categories). So, there is comparative fit with gender categories.

Nevertheless, the observed similarities and differences must be consistent with the normative and stereotypic content of the relevant categories. To continue the above example, let us assume that, stereotypically, women go to pubs to socialise and men go to pubs to drink; if the women are all talking, and the men are all drinking, their behaviour fits normatively with the categorical division. If, on the other hand, the men are talking and the women are drinking, this does not fit normatively, and the division into men and women is unlikely to become salient.

Chapter 6

LANGUAGE, ACTIONS AND IDENTITY
The use of self

In this chapter, we investigate further the ways that a specific social identity – again, that of an ordinary person – can be made relevant through the use of language. And we will emphasise the inferential consequences of these discursive procedures by focusing on the way in which the establishment of an ordinary identity can warrant the legitimacy of a specific social action: making a complaint.

But there are new, broader methodological points we wish to raise. It may appear strange that, in a detailed study of the language of youth subcultures, we here embark on a second substantive empirical chapter which focuses upon the ways in which our respondents warrant their identity not as punks, or gothics or rockers, but as ordinary people. But through our analysis we go on to show that even in talk by which respondents warrant their ordinary identity, they display an acute sensitivity to the fact that they are simultaneously visible as members of a specific subculture. With these observations in mind, we extend our discussion of the relationship between identity and action. This allows us to raise the issue of the status and explanatory utility of underlying cognitive and motivational processes.

Our analysis focuses principally on two extracts from two separate interviews, one with a female punk, one with a male punk (although occasionally we will be drawing on other data extracts to indicate the generality of the phenomena we discuss). In the first extract, the speaker expresses a negative assessment: a complaint in which membership is described as entailing significant disadvantages. We will argue that the way the speaker designs these utterances addresses a very sensitive issue. She is formulating a complaint to illustrate a feature of her life as a member of a subcultural group: in this instance, punk. The character of the complaint is crucially dependent upon this identity: she couldn't complain about aspects of life as a member of a specific group if she wasn't actually a member herself. Therefore, by making such a complaint she is explicitly orienting to, and occasioning as a relevant feature of her talk, her social identity as a punk.

It is possible, however, that negative common knowledge about this group may be invoked to account for the behaviour of those people about whom the speaker is complaining. That is, what is known generally about the group is always potentially available as a set of resources by which to interpret the activities of any specific member. For example, the conspicuous mode of dress, the grubby, unwashed appearance and the reputation for violence – some of the stereotypical features of the subculture – may be invoked to rationalise the reactions that the speaker has encountered, and thereby to undermine the legitimacy of the complaint. Thus, she is faced with a problem: to justify her complaints, and design her descriptions so that the basis for her complaints is seen as warranted, while at the same time deflecting the type of response we may characterise as 'Well what do you expect looking like that?'. The object of this analysis is to furnish a technical appreciation of the way in which the speaker orients to and negotiates this problem. That is, we want to identify and explain the tacit reasoning practices which inform the speaker's use of specific phrases, words and illustrative examples to build this sequence, and through which she provides for its character as a recognisable complaint.

In the second extract, the speaker is describing violent incidents which occurred after a concert by a punk rock band. In this descriptive sequence the speaker reports the actions of the police at the concert. Our interest in this descriptive work is the way the speaker asymmetrically characterises the behaviour of the two relevant groups, punks and police, so as to warrant the inference that the subsequent violence was due to the actions of the police, rather than stemming from the violent inclinations of the punks. There are, however, many other interesting features of the speaker's description which contribute to the depiction of the punks as the passive recipients of unwarranted and unwanted police actions. And, in this sense, this speaker is also making a complaint; however, he is not complaining about the way that he as an individual has been treated, but the way that the punks who were at the concert that night were treated. But we will see that his descriptions are also guarded and designed with respect to the kinds of negative common knowledge about punks which could be used to account for the incidents which followed the concert.

Making a complaint

Consider the following extract.

(1) 1P:F:T1SA [KHS]

```
1    I:    can you tell me anything ↑else
2          about (.3) punk=what's it like to be a °punk°,
3          (1.2)
4    R:    it can be quite difficul(t)
5          'cos like when you wanna go into a pub
6          or somethin: you get (.2) sor(t)'ve (.4)
```

7   in some pubs they say "get out"
8   ('cos) of the way you look.
9   (.8)
10   I: yea:h.

The speaker's complaint is that, broadly, she is refused service in pubs, and this is produced as one negative consequence of her subcultural membership.[1] The speaker begins to illustrate the basis for her negative assessment with the utterance ''cos like when you wanna go into a pub or somethin:'. In this she describes an activity, which she then goes on to claim she was prevented from doing. As we noted in the previous chapter, activities can be described so as to make relevant a specific category or classification of the people who do them (Sacks, 1972; see also Schegloff, 1972). For example, the activity of going to a psychology lecture makes relevant the identity of psychology student for the particulars of the talk in which such a formulation may be introduced. In contrast to this example, the activity of going to a pub does not furnish such a strong set of inferences about the category of people engaged in it. Apart from certain specific inferences, for example, that the people actually going into the pub are (or look) above the legal drinking age, there is otherwise little that can be gleaned about the identity of the people so described. Therefore, it may be termed an 'anybody's activity': the sort of thing any ordinary person might do.

There is a related issue. This activity could be described in a number of different ways, for example, having a few beers, going drinking or going out on the town. These formulations furnish a different set of inferences from going to the pub, because they hint more towards revelry – a night out. By contrast, the formulation presented by the speaker is a particularly routine description, it orients instead to the conventional or institutional character of going to the pub as something that a large number of people do regularly.

One final point is that going to a pub is one of the archetypal social activities in the United Kingdom, and one which often entails a variety of other social activities. People usually go to pubs with friends, or to meet friends, play various games, talk to other people and so on. In the speaker's description of this activity the nature and existence of these related social activities are implicit because she does not provide reasons for going to the pub. Thus there is no explicit reference to the *social* character of going to pubs. It is worth considering the kinds of inferences that we might have drawn from her description if it had included explicit reference to the social character of going to pubs. Had she said that she went to pubs to meet friends, or with friends, it is possible that recipients may infer, quite reasonably, that it is likely that her friends share her interests, taste in clothes and music and values, etc.: in short, that they too may be punks. If this inference is made, it may be argued that a group of punks going into or drinking in pubs could be viewed as threatening or alarming, and such inferences may be used to defend the reasonableness of the reactions ('get out') that she later describes. In other words, a slightly amended formulation of the same activity – one which suggested the activity of a number of individuals – could furnish very different sets of inferences about events; and these could in turn be cited as the (legitimate) basis for the reactions about which the speaker is complaining. It therefore seems that the way her description is formulated displays an awareness of and excludes these possibilities.

Our point is this: that the description of the activity is designed to furnish certain inferences about the speaker. In representing her activity as an 'any-body's activity', she occasions the relevance of her own character as an ordinary person; that is, in attending to the pragmatic business of making a complaint she is doing 'being ordinary' (Sacks, 1984) as an interactional resource.

In the following data there are further examples of the way in which activities are described by members of subcultures so as to provide for their routine and ordinary properties.

(2) 1P:F:T1SA [KHS] (The speaker is describing some of the disadvantages of being a punk.)

```
1      R:     well it's the police
2             an' some pubs you go into
3             yuh think "(oh'll)
4             all I wanna do is go
5             for a quiet drink"
6             then you ge⌐t thrown out
7      I:              ⌊yeah,
```

(3) 1P:M:T9SA [KHS]

```
1      R:     you can be standing at a bus stop
2             or something and it sort of,
3             you can sit on one of the seats
4             at a bus stop and all the seats will be packed
5             but people won't sit next to you
```

(4) 2P:M/F:T8SA [CM]

```
1      MR:    >↑YEa-< All these people=you're
2             >walk'n ng down the stree(t)<
3             'nd yuh get so m-
4             the majori(t)y o' them go,
5             "look at the state of them=
6             they're bla:ck they're dirty.
7             they're ↓smelly, (.2) they're agg↓ressive"
8             (.3)
9      MR:    >know (ut) ah mean,<
```

In each of these cases, the speakers employ the same resources. They describe only the most routine and everyday features of their activities: in extract (2) 'wanting to have a quiet drink', in (3) 'standing at a bus stop', and in (4) 'walking down the street'. These formulations occasion the relevance of the speakers' ordinary identity.

There are some further, related points about the target utterance ''cos like when you wanna go into a pub or somethin:'. In routine conversation, actions and events can be prefaced by formulations of intention or expectation. For example 'I wanted to arrive on time'. When such prefaces as these are used it is noticeable that the intended action usually does not occur, as in 'I wanted to arrive on time but the train was delayed'. People do not routinely construct utterances such as 'I wanted to arrive on time, and I did' unless they are specifically emphasising the virtues of effort, or some particular feature of the circumstances relevant to the conversation. Thus, the speaker formulates her description to portray her exclusion from a general class of activities.

Second, this utterance does not refer to a specific incident. In illustrating her assessment she constructs an utterance which has the character of a hypothetical example. The use of hypothetical examples, instead of, say, reference to an actual event, has a number of interactional consequences. It allows the speaker to distil recurrent features from a number of events and bring them together in a form which may not strictly represent their occurrences in real life. Furthermore, hypothetical examples have a defensive property in the following sense. Making a claim about one specific incident raises the possibility that we may be asked to justify our version of that event, or expand upon specific particulars of the circumstances: when did this happen, who else was there, what were you doing? With a hypothetical example, however, no specific incidents are proffered, and thus there is no recourse to a direct interrogation of the details of the events.

Third, the addition of 'or somethin:' at the end of the utterance registers that she is making a statement about a general class of activities, rather than one specific kind of event. It suggests that it is not just going to the pub which can be problematic, but also other activities. In so doing, she also heads off the potential argument that, given the essentially mundane character of 'going to pubs', being prevented from doing so is hardly the basis for a serious complaint about the way she is treated. Instead, she suggests that it is the pervasiveness of this kind of reaction that is problematic.

By using these resources the speaker is able to provide for a set of inferences about the activities she is describing. For example, that she is not making a claim about a specific event, but about recurrent events. Furthermore, she is not making a claim about a specific activity, but a general set of ordinary activities of which the one cited is an example. Finally, she has described these general activities to indicate that she is recurrently precluded from engaging in them.

Let us now consider lines 6 and 7 of extract (1) in which the speaker describes the reactions of other people: 'you g<u>e</u>t (.2) sor(t)'ve (.4) in some pubs they say "<u>g</u>et out" '. The first observation about this sequence is that the speaker does not mention an 'I' or a 'we' to whom these reactions occurred. Thus, the description may be heard as one that happens generally. In addition, in order to understand why this omission may have functional significance, it is worthwhile considering the inferences that might be drawn from her utterances had she made reference to herself or a group of people. It seems likely that the use of 'I' or 'we' would focus the description of others' reactions on a specific person or a particular group. This in turn could increase the likelihood that the recipient may resort to 'common knowledge' about the group in order to locate a possible warrant for the others' reactions. So, the way that the utterance is formulated has the effect of reducing the possibility of this kind of interpretative work by the recipient.

Similarly, the speaker does not say explicitly who she claims has said 'get out'. Given the context, it seems reasonable to presume that she is referring to publicans. Yet she does not name them directly as publicans. In one of his early lectures (published as Sacks, 1984), Sacks made some interesting observations about authority figures, in particular, police officers, and people's reasoning practices about such authority figures. He noted that when we see police officers attending to an incident, or talking to someone, it is common that our first reaction will be to wonder what has happened, or what that person has done wrong. Similarly, many people will be familiar with the phenomenon of thinking 'have I done anything wrong?' when they see a police officer approaching them. What Sacks was pointing to is a powerful inclination in some people to try to see how it is that the police are going about their business legitimately and not, for example, causing trouble or behaving without justification.

Building on this observation, we suggest that a similar range of considerations applies to other authority figures, such as publicans. So that, had the speaker said 'the landlords say "get out" ', or 'the owners tell us to get out' the recipient may be inclined to wonder what the speaker had done to justify such a reaction. That is, an official or occupational identity such as publican may be used as an interpretative resource with which the recipient could find a warrant for the reaction of the people so described. By not furnishing this description of the people who ejected them from pubs, or prevented them going into pubs, the speaker ensures that this interpretative resource is not made explicitly available to the recipient.

A further point is that in this utterance the speaker actually formulates a version of the words used on those occasions when she has been excluded from pubs. Moreover, her utterance is designed so that these words may be heard as reported speech. The basis for this claim is that these data were initially transcribed by someone who had no knowledge of the analytic issues we wished to explore in the data, nor of conversation analytic transcription conventions.[2] That she heard these utterances as reported speech, and marked them accordingly in her transcription, we take to be strong evidence that this reading is one that is conventionally available, and that this is how the speaker designed them to be heard. Thus, she creates the impression of reporting the words which were actually said to her. 'Get out' is an imperative order. It formulates in the harshest possible terms what could otherwise be described as a request to leave. In this way the speaker provides for the severity of the others' reactions: it is not merely that she was ejected, but that the manner in which this happened was positively vehement.

Similarly, in extract (4) above, the speaker used reported speech to provide for the extreme and uncompromising reactions of other people. In the following extracts there are further examples of the way the people we interviewed used reported speech when describing others' reactions to them. It is interesting to note that in extract (6) the speaker's description of other people's thoughts is said in such a way that they may be heard as reported speech.

(5) 2G:F:T1SB [KHS]

```
1      R:    and the police are (.) v:ery prejudiced
2            against us
             some lines omitted
3      R:    (ev'n) my boyfriend's got a bi:ke,
4            (.3)
5      I:    ⌈°mm°
6      R:    ⌊and >abou(t)<=he's been stopped.
7            he got stopped three times in one week
8            just walking along with it
9            (.)
10     R:    just tuh=you know they said
11           (.)
12     R:    "WHere >dj'a get that bike from,
13           y' nicked it< didn't you, >y'nu(w)<"
```

(6) 1R:M:T5SB [RRF]

```
1      R:    it's 'coz've of what you wear,
2            people think
3            "o:h God they're violent"
```

We propose that the target speaker is building a contrast between her activity and the response it receives. We observed earlier that the speaker has designed her description of her activity to provide for its routine and mundane character, and that by virtue of this pragmatic work she has occasioned the relevance of her own ordinary identity. Yet in describing the reactions of other people she uses such resources as reported speech to formulate a general and extreme response. Her descriptions therefore display an asymmetry between the response of other people, and the activity which prompted that response.

In recent years the analysis of naturally occurring language has yielded considerable information about the character and use of contrast structures in a variety of discursive circumstances: in political discourse (Atkinson, 1984a and b; Heritage and Greatbatch, 1986), in selling techniques (Pinch and Clark, 1986) and in an account of a young woman's decline into mental illness (Smith, 1978). In these forms of language use, inferences about the preferability of one item are exposed and easily available from the contrast. In this case, however, there is no direct comparison of one item with another: the contrast is embedded. These utterances are designed to invite the recipient to inspect the two components – the action and the reaction – and find that the latter is unwarranted given the character of the former.

Formulating embedded contrasts between occasioned ordinary identities and their associated activities, and reactions to those activities, is a common resource in the interviews we collected. We provide just one example here.

(7) 2P:F:T1SB [KHS]

```
1    R:    this way* y'know you walk* down the street
2          and you look like this='nd people y'know
3          like "O:h"
4          (.6)
5    R:    y'know "she's a punk",
6          "she's this" y'know=I mean, I walk down
7          the street people s:pit at me, you know
```

In extract (7) the speaker reports her activity as 'walking down the street', and describes people spitting at her by virtue of [looking] 'this way*'. In this case, and in the case of the target extract we are examining, the extreme responses of others are implicitly contrasted with the ordinary activities which stimulated them. Moreover, in both cases, the speakers occasion the relevance of their own ordinary identity as a resource to provide for this contrast.

Finally, we turn to the utterance in line 8 of our focal extract (extract 1), '('cos) of the way you look.', with which the speaker formulates a reason for the reactions of other people. Her utterance attributes to these other people the reasoning procedures which inform their actions. By doing this the speaker implicitly ascribes a theory of social behaviour to these other people: namely, that they assume that people who dress in a certain way, be it punk, gothic, or heavy rock, are likely to cause trouble, warrant suspicion and deserve contempt. We propose that the way in which the speaker addresses this issue is a further resource to heighten the contrastive effects of the prior two utterances.

First, we may note that the speaker portrays the others' extreme and negative reactions as being based not on firm evidence, such as, for example, personal experience, or common and accepted knowledge, but on a very superficial feature: the way in which she dresses. Second, the way in which she describes her appearance renders its more startling features as unimportant; instead she portrays it as just another appearance, as just another look. By implying that her appearance is not in any way radically different from other modes of dress, she undermines the possibility that her appearance may be legitimately used as the basis for negative and damaging inferences about her. A further example of this is illustrated in the following extract.

(8) 1P:F:T1SA [KHS]

```
1      I:      ↑Are there ti:mes when you sort've (.) see
2              yourself or think of yourself as a punk and
3              other ti:mes when you just see yourself as
4              (.4)
5              as Mary Smith or whatever you⌐r name is
6      R:                                   └°nah° ah'mean I
7              (1)
8      R:      ah mean I know ah'm a punk know
9              but I jus:(t) (.) I just feel as thou:gh,
10             I'm the same as everyone else=I mean I dress
11             diff'rently ('h) >bu(d)air< again everyone
12             dresses different to everyone ↓else.
13             (.5)
14             so li⌐ke
15     I:          └yeah,
16             (.3)
17     R:      when people look at me
18             as if I'm an alien, it sometimes=it gets
19             me really annoyed because (.3) you know
20             I'm just the same as everybody else
```

Finally, by constructing her appearance as a routine matter – just another way of dressing amongst many others – and by formulating others' reactions as being based upon superficial features, the speaker in the target data makes available the inference that such theories of action are inherently weak and unreliable. One implication of this is that others' behaviour is seen as motivated not by reason, but by less worthy factors, such as blind prejudice. A particularly striking example of this is illustrated in extract (9).

(9) 2P:M/F:T8SA [CM] (The speaker claims to have observed police attacks on women and children who were members of the Stonehenge 'hippy convoy'.)

```
1      FR:     they done that at Stone↑henge
2              thou⌐gh didn't they, or: somewhere=
3      MR:        └(yeah?)
```

```
4    FR:    =they come (.5) there was like a coach
5           with (.3) women and that
6           (.7)
7    MR:    they ┌don't care
8    FR:         └'nd she came out holdin' a ba:by
9           or som'in'. and they said
10          "naw(h) don't hi(t)- (.) don't come in here
11          there's loads of kids and that"
12          (.3)
13   FR:    and they just paused for a couple of seconds
14          and thought "what the fuck,"
15          'nd they just (.) laid in.
16          (s) it's not human
```

So far, the analysis has begun to reveal the pragmatic resources which the speaker used to design her utterance, and to explicate the tacit reasoning procedures which informed her use of these resources. We have argued that, through the way in which her activities are described, she has occasioned the relevance of a specific social identity – that of an ordinary person. Additionally, her account of the others' reactions to her is designed to provide for their extreme and unwarranted character, given the identity she had occasioned in the immediately prior utterance. Furthermore, in describing why the others reacted in this manner, we argued that she provided for the inference that the others' reasoning procedures are premised on superficial characteristics, and are thereby unwarranted. This in turn heightens the contrastive effect, accomplished through the prior utterances, between the ordinariness of the speaker and the extraordinary behaviour of other people. Thus, we have revealed the ways in which the speaker occasions the relevance of an ordinary identity as a resource to address a specific interactional task.

Many of these analytic themes will emerge also when we consider the following extract. This comes from an interview with a male punk, during which he describes in general terms the police's hostile attitude to the concerts of punk rock bands. We are examining this extract for the following reasons. Whereas in extract (1) the speaker is making a complaint about the way *she as a punk* is treated, in the following account the speaker is complaining about the way that *a group* of punks was treated. Second, in extract (1) the speaker is describing the way that she is treated by others, but these others are not named explicitly. So, although we can reasonably assume that she is referring to publicans and landlords when she reports that 'they say get out', the referent of 'they' is not actually explicit. But in the following case the speaker is explicit about the other group with whom the punks are in conflict.

(10) 2P:M/F:T8SA [CM] (The male respondent in this extract spoke with a strong Scottish accent.)

1	MR:	and the po̲lice were all outside there,
2		(.) (ehr) at the co̲:ncert̲,
3		there wasnae a bit of trouble 'part fro(m)'nside
4		one or two wee scra̲:ps, you know?
5		(.2)
6	MR:	But that ha̲ppens=ev'ry one- every gig
7		⌈there's a scrap?
8	FR:	⌊°mm°
9	MR:	>(th)'s all's< so̲mebody doesnae like somebody else.
10	FR:	Mm:
11	MR:	dunna mattah w̲:ha̲:t it is (.4) i's always ha̲ppenin',
12		'hh y' know you cannae sto̲:p that?
13		(.6)
14	MR:	an' (.) we go outside. and there they are.
15		(.8)
16	MR:	fucking ei̲ght hu̲ndred old b'll,³
17		(.2)
18	MR:	just wai̲:tin' for the cha̲:nce,
19		(.3)
20	MR:	riot shields truncheons (.2) and you're ↑not
21		doin' nothin' you're only trying to get doon
22		to the tube and gae hame 'hh
23		so what do they do?=you're walk(n) by 'en
24		they're pu̲shing you wi'tha' (.) truncheons
25		an' ·h they star(t) hattin' the odd punk
26		here and there,
27		(.3)
28	MR:	and what happens?=the punks rebe-rebel, they
29		don' wanna get hit in the face with a truncheon
30		↑nobody does 'hhh so what do you do,=you push
31		yer copper back and (>then<) wha' happens?
32		ten or twelve of 'em are beatin'
33		the ⌈pure he̲ll out of some poor bastard
34	FR:	⌊mm
35	MR:	who's only tried to keep somebody off his back,
36		(.7)
37	MR:	Now:* that started a ↑ri̲ot.

To develop our understanding of this sequence, it is necessary to consider again the range of culturally available stereotypes about the category punks. As punks and punk rock emerged in the mid-1970s, tabloid press coverage focused on and glorified the more extreme characteristics of their lifestyle and the music: rejection of societal convention, self-mutilation as personal decoration, violence, uncleanliness, rebellion and so on. The sometimes violent exploits of bands like the Sex Pistols and some of their followers ensured that the punk subculture was ideally suited to be the subject of a media-initiated moral panic (cf. S. Cohen, 1972). These stereotypical representations of the punk lifestyle permeate our culture, and constitute a powerful set of lay assumptions and common-sense knowledge. It is always possible that the behaviour of someone who seems to fit the category punk rocker can be explained and interpreted by reference to this largely negative stock of knowledge.

In this sequence, the speaker has to contend with this background set of assumptions and knowledge. But more important, perhaps, is the fact that he is describing an incident at which violence did take place, and he has to formulate his descriptions accordingly, thereby minimising the likelihood that a recipient might reason that the punks were somehow responsible for the disturbances. We will examine first some of the ways that the speaker describes the actions of punks at the concert so as to emphasise their character as routine, *everybody's* activities, rather than group-related activities.

In lines 2 to 7 there is a short sequence in which the speaker describes some violent incidents which happened at the concert. (This part of the account is examined in a later section.) Then the speaker begins a series of descriptions of the actions of the punks, and the actions of the police. So in lines 14 to 22 the speaker says 'an' (.) we go outside. and there they are. (.8) fucking eight hundred old b'll, (.2) just wai:tin' for the cha:nce, (.3) riot shields truncheons (.2) and you're ↑not doin' nothin' you're only trying to get doon to the tube and gae hame'.

Note that the first reference to the punks' behaviour is a very minimal description of what they did after the concert: 'And we go outside'. The second reference provides a further characterisation of the unexceptional nature of their behaviour: 'doing nothing' and simply 'going home'. It is interesting to note that the speaker's reference to the punks changes in the course of the segment. He says first that 'we go outside' but then he reports their subsequent behaviour as 'you're only trying to [go home]'. There is a sense in which 'we' clearly marks the speaker as a member of a specific group or collectivity. But the characterisation of their attempt to go home as 'you're only trying . . .' does not invoke such a clear affiliation. Indeed, it appeals to what everybody does or what anybody would do. Initially, we might assume that this is simply an idiosyncratic and 'one-off' way of engendering a recipient's sympathy for the events that befell the punks on the night of the concert. As we progress through the rest of this account, however, we shall see that the character of this specific segment is tied to the broader organisation of the whole account of the incidents.

There is a contrast between the way that the behaviour of the punks is described, and the way in which the speaker reports the presence of the police. The speaker provides a numerical evaluation of the police officers in attendance after the concert which, regardless of its accuracy, portrays the police presence as excessive. Furthermore, he reports that the officers came equipped for violent confrontation. So, he builds a contrast between the actions of the punks and the subsequent response by the police: the behaviour of the punks is portrayed as quite unexceptional and routine, whereas the response of the police is portrayed as extreme.

In lines 23 to 26 the speaker reports 'you're walk(n) by 'en they're pushing you wi'tha' (.) truncheons an' 'h they star(t) hattin' the odd punk here and there'. As in the previous extract, there is first a description of the punks' behaviour and then a description of the actions of the police. And, like the previous segment, the behaviour of the punks is reported in minimal everyday terms: they are simply 'walking by'. By contrast, the police are portrayed as initiating violence in that they start 'hattin' [hitting] the odd punk'. Note also that the violence is portrayed as being indiscriminately inflicted, rather than directed at specific individuals, or as part of the police response to a particular contingency. This serves to undermine the warrant for such police behaviour. Furthermore, it portrays the police's actions as being propelled not by any rational motives or plan of action. It suggests that at best they are pursuing a callous policy, at worst that their response is prejudiced if not irrational. Thus, the speaker's description in this segment further emphasises the contrast between the behaviour of the punks and the police.

In lines 28 to 35 the speaker then recounts the events which culminated in what he describes as 'a riot', and provides a characterisation of the punks' contribution to the escalating violence. Note, first, that this issue is raised via his posing the rhetorical question 'And what happens?' as a consequence of the police indiscriminately hitting the punks. Note also that the use of the verb 'rebel' portrays the punks' first active involvement in the violence as being responsive to, and a consequence of, police provocation, oppression, etc. Furthermore, this response is warranted by an appeal to 'how any one would respond in these circumstances': punks 'don' wanna get hit in the face with a truncheon ↑nobody does'.

Finally, the speaker provides the first reference to violent actions actually perpetrated by the punks after the concert: 'you push yer copper back'. It is clear that he is not describing one specific event, or any number of specific incidents; rather, he describes a general response, which is again warranted by an appeal to what 'anyone would do in this situation'. There are two interesting features of the description of the punks as 'pushing back'. 'Pushing' is not a particularly aggressive act, and its use here portrays the punks' behaviour as being defensive, rather than offensive. Also, the characterisation of the punks as pushing back demonstrates that their actions are a form of resistance to an ongoing physical assault, rather than any attempt to initiate conflict.

Some interesting differences are emerging. So, for example, the behaviour of the punks is described as entirely mundane; they are characterised as simply doing what any ordinary person might do. They are also portrayed as passive recipients of violence, rather than aggressive perpetrators; even when they are actively involved in violence the punks are portrayed as using physical force to effect the most minimal form of self-defence. The description of the behaviour of the police, however, is couched in terms of their orientation to, and pursuit of, aggressive confrontation: their presence is excessive and they engage in random physical assaults. Thus, the speaker portrays the ordinary and mundane activities of the punks, but formulates the behaviour of the police through a series of descriptions which emphasise the aggressive and extraordinary behaviour of the police. The speaker uses a contrastive organisation to emphasise the extreme nature of the police response. Indeed, the inference that the presence of the police and their subsequent behaviour were unwarranted in part rests upon the juxtaposition of police action with the seemingly inconsequential and ordinary behaviour of the punks.

It is important to remember that we are not assessing this account to try to discover whether the speaker's description is accurate, or whether he is distorting 'what really happened'. Rather, we are interested in the descriptive resources which are used to construct this version, and to sketch what dynamic and functional properties it has. (Of course, it is quite possible that the same linguistic resources could be used to achieve the opposite ends: it is not hard to imagine how the punks could be described to portray their extraordinary and potentially aggressive demeanour, thereby warranting the appropriateness of the police response.)

Let's take a more detailed consideration of a much smaller data segment: 'one or two wee scra:ps,' (line 4). We will start with the word 'scrap'. Of all the ways which could be used to describe two people hitting each other – 'fighting', 'violence', 'a punch up' – the word 'scrap' clearly minimises the seriousness of the incident. Indeed, 'scrap' evokes images of schoolboy tussles in playgrounds rather than incidents in which people may incur severe physical damage. The characterisation of the incidents as 'wee scraps' further portrays the relative insignificance of the incidents.

Consider also the numerical evaluation '*one or two* [wee] scraps'. A first point is that 'one or two' clearly registers the 'occurring more than once' character of the incident being described. Referring to a number of violent incidents could easily be used by a sceptic to undermine the general thrust of the speaker's claim that the police presence after the concert was unwarranted. However, 'one or two' provides the most minimal characterisation of more than one. Second, note that the speaker does not say one, or two, but 'one or two'. In one sense, this marks the speaker as not knowing the precise number of incidents. More important, however, is that the display of not knowing marks the precise number as not requiring clarification, and therefore as being relatively unimportant. Third, in this sequence the speaker concedes that violent disturbances occurred at the gig. Thus the speaker makes an admission which could be damaging to his overriding claim that the punks were not to blame for the subsequent riot. However, conceding such a potentially delicate point is one method by which the speaker can minimise the likelihood that his account will be seen as a biased version of events. This in turn augments his implicit claim to be an accurate reporter of what really happened. So, although the speaker does reveal that indeed there were some violent incidents at the concert, he does so in such a way as to portray the 'more than one' number of incidents as minimally as possible, while at the same time registering the relative insignificance of these events, and portraying himself as an honest observer.

Finally in this section we consider lines 6 to 11, 'But that happens=ev'ry one- every gig there's a scrap? >(th)'s all's< somebody doesnae like somebody else. dunna mattah w:ha:t it is (.4) i's always happenin'. A first preliminary observation: note the instances on which the speaker uses the words 'always' and 'every'. Pomerantz (1986) has studied the use of words like 'always' and 'never' in ordinary conversation. She provides a technical identification of this, referring to such words as extreme case formulations. Other examples are never, brand new, nobody, everybody, completely innocent and forever. Such formulations serve to portray the maximum (or minimum) character of the object, quality or state of affairs to which they refer.

In lines 6 to 11 the use of words like always and every might appear to be a case of simple exaggeration, with little indication that there is something systematic about their use. But let us return to Pomerantz's (1986) analysis of extreme case formulations in everyday conversation. She found that speakers use extreme case formulations to influence the judgement or conclusions of co-interactants, *especially in circumstances in which the speaker may anticipate that the account, story or claim being made will receive an unsympathetic hearing.*

We can now return to the instances of extreme case formulations in the punk extract. Recall that the speaker has just revealed that there was spate of violent activity at the concert he had attended. He then says: 'But that happens . . . every gig there's a scrap? >(th)'s all's< somebody doesnae like somebody else. dunna mattah w:ha:t it is (.4) i's always happenin','.

Observe the work that the use of extreme case formulations does here. Specifically, the phrase 'every gig there's a scrap?' portrays violence as being related to a general kind of social occasion, namely, rock concerts. Note that he does not say that these violent incidents occur at every punk rock gig. Rather it is the *gigs* that are associated with the disturbance, and not the gigs of bands whose following comes from a specific youth subculture. The second extreme case formulation '>(th)'s all's< [there's always] somebody doesnae like somebody else' characterises violence as arising inevitably from interpersonal conflict. Such conflicts are portrayed as having their roots in idiosyncratic clashes of personality, irrespective of the social groups to which individuals may belong. Finally, 'i's always happenin'' marks such conflicts as a recurrent and consistent feature of human existence, and not peculiar to specific sections of the community.

In reporting the violence which occurred at the concert, the speaker makes no reference to the fact that the combatants were punks. Indeed, he has done considerable work to portray the incident as something which occurs routinely at rock gigs generally, or which arises from two people's dislike for each other, and which is endemic in human society. In so doing, he minimises the relevance of the social identity of the combatants as punk rockers, and thus implies that their subcultural membership is merely incidental to this violence and not the reason for it.

Throughout the passage, the speaker is making the claim that the 'riot' which followed the concert was a consequence of the unwarranted presence of the police, and their subsequently provocative behaviour. However, the occurrence of a spate of violence at the concert could easily be interpreted in the light of negative stereotypical knowledge about punks: namely that their lifestyle and attitudes lead them to seek rebellion, confrontation with authority and violence. The mere fact that there was some disturbance could warrant the inference that the violence was another instance of typical punk behaviour. Clearly, such a conclusion would severely undermine the validity of the speaker's (implied) claim that the problems after the concert were a consequence of the police presence. The design of the speaker's descriptions in lines 6 to 11 displays his sensitivity to precisely these kinds of alternative interpretations. He uses extreme case formulations as a rhetorical device to minimise the likelihood that his account of the violence following a punk rock concert may be called into question by reference to 'what everyone knows about punks'.

To summarise: we view identities as *achieved;* not fixed but negotiated products of the ongoing flow of interaction. By this, we mean that identities are features which people can occasion as relevant in their day-to-day dealings with each other. Our detailed inspection of two instances has revealed ways in which a specific identity is made relevant and used by an individual to attend to broadly interpersonal issues. Throughout, our concern was with the details of how identities are negotiated, and with the functional significance of that achievement.[4] That is, we focus on the action orientation of identity accounts, as well as how identities are drawn upon as a resource in accounts of violent or unjustified action. So, we begin to see a close link between identity and action. It is useful to consider how this relationship has been addressed elsewhere, and the implications for the issues of agency which we raised in the last chapter.

In many areas of sociology and social psychology it is assumed that there is a link between identity and action. For example, McCall (1987) notes that role theories have been informed by the symbolic interactionist axiom '[p]ersons must first make self-identifications before they can organise and direct their own activity' (Spitzer *et al.*, 1970:9). From a role theory perspective, self-identifications are internalised roles, whose external manifestation relates to particular kinds of behaviour. Thus, it is assumed that the more central or salient a role-identity for an individual, the more intensely or consistently should their behaviour reflect that identity (R. H. Turner, 1987). Conversely, the more we perform a particular role, the more likely we are to come to see ourselves as the kind of person embodied in that role.

In Self-Categorisation Theory, the level of self-perception, or the ways that individuals conceive of themselves at any particular moment, has a causal influence on the kinds of behaviour in which they engage. In particular, Self-Categorisation theorists have been concerned with group action and its apparent uniformity. It is argued that depersonalisation is the basic process which underlies and enables group behaviour. This is the process where individuals conceive of self in terms of a social identity and stereotype themselves accordingly. Depersonalisation makes group behaviour possible because it 'provides group members with a shared psychological field, shared cognitive representations of themselves, their own identity, and the objective world in the form of shared social norms of fact and value' (Turner and Oakes, 1986:250). According to SCT, under these conditions, we all perceive ourselves as the same, and we attribute the same behavioural norms to ourselves. Hence we behave collectively: in the same category-appropriate manner. Therefore, like role theorists, Self-Categorisation theorists regard identity as the precursor of and causal influence in group behaviour.

Nevertheless, despite the apparently firm assumption that there is a causal relationship between identity and behaviour, empirical studies have not always warranted this faith. R. H. Turner (1987) notes a discrepancy in empirical studies between verbalised self-identities and behaviour; and Markus and Nurius (1987) state that there are throughout the literature accounts of unsuccessful attempts to link the self-concept to behaviour (see Wylie, 1979, for a review). Such discrepancies have not, apparently, shaken the belief that there is a connection.

To address these discrepancies, and to establish a more indirect relationship between identity and action, there has been an attempt to incorporate the concept of motivation into theoretical explanations. So, instead of being described in terms of the direct translation of identities into identity-relevant behaviour, identities are said to *motivate* action in the service of fulfilling goals, hopes and fears which are related to self-conception. For example, Markus and Nurius (1987) suggest that it is the vision of what we could be, or what we do not want to become, that motivates action: our *possible* rather than actual selves are linked to action. They do not deny the behavioural effects of unconscious desires and so on, nor the influence of socio-structural factors, but they suggest that

in those situations that can be construed as self-relevant or self-revealing, an individual will be invested in his or her behaviour and attempt to regulate it, and it is then that behaviour . . . will be importantly controlled and regulated by possible selves. Whenever the situation is of a type that allows for flexibility in individual construction and interpretation (i.e. one that is not so highly constrained as to override all individuality) people will use their possible selves as blueprints for action. (Markus and Nurius, 1987:160)

They argue that the concept of possible selves helps us to understand better how the self regulates behaviour. Nonetheless, there remains the question of the relationship between identity and motivation. In social cognitive terms, the important issues are how motives, goals and values are cognitively represented within the self-system, what structures carry them, and how they function (Markus and Nurius, 1987:161). Whereas traditionally, motivation has been analysed as if it were impersonal, instinctual or unconscious (see Nuttin, 1984), they argue that the concept of possible selves renders motivation more personalised and concrete. This is because, in their view, motivations are 'carried in specific cognitive representations of the self in future states' and one's actions may be shaped by attempts to realise or avoid these states. For example, it is not the abstract goal of 'earning a degree' that is the significant determinant of behaviour, but the possible self, 'me having a degree'.[5]

Abrams (1990) provides a more cognitive resolution to the problem of the relationship between identity and action. He criticises the social identity approach for assuming that the link between identity, or self-perception as a group member, and behaviour such as discrimination, is automatic. He argues that what is missing is an account of the processes that relate self-perception to social behaviour. Integrating Self-awareness and Social Identity approaches, he identifies different conditions under which a salient personal or social identity will lead to different kinds of behaviour, depending on the amount (low or high) of self-focus and the domain (public or private) of self-attention.

By contrast, the empirical approach to identities and language use collapses the theoretically achieved distinction between social identity and social action in three ways. First, our analysis focused on an instance of social (inter)action in which a particular social identity was inextricably implicated. So, our interest has been in the pragmatic use of social identities (of self and the group) as linguistic resources in interaction. Second, we focused on the ways in which the nature, content and relevance of particular identities were achieved. For example, our analysis showed that the activity of going to public houses was characterised to portray it as an essentially mundane and routine experience, the sort of activity an ordinary person would do. Moreover, this characterisation was defensively designed for it displayed a sensitivity to the possibly damaging and negative inferences about groups of punks in pubs. The point is that the actual characteristics of the activities associated with a category may be formulated to circumscribe the range of inferences that may legitimately be drawn about the speaker. Therefore, identity is not seen as a thing that *we are*, a property of individuals, but as something *we do*. It is a practical accomplishment, achieved and maintained through the detail of language use. Third, identity accomplishment is regarded as functional insofar as the details of identities are designed with a view to achieving some task or in pursuit of everyday concerns. In our analysis of the first extract, the category ordinary person was negotiated with a view to the type of action the speaker was engaged in: making a complaint. Other analyses have shown how categories may be used in ascribing motives (Watson, 1983); teasing (Drew, 1987); mitigating actions (Wetherell and Potter, 1989; Wowk, 1984); or claiming authentic identity (Widdicombe and Wooffitt, 1990).

In many areas of the social sciences, then, it has been assumed that there is a separation between identity and action: they are regarded as different orders of phenomena. As a consequence, the theoretical focus is on the (causal) links between identity and action. Since, empirically, there is apparently little evidence of a direct link, the concepts of motivation, goals, ideals and self-awareness amongst others are invoked to sustain the theoretical assumption that there is a relationship.[6] In contrast, however, we have tried to avoid this dualism; we have sought to reveal the inseparability of identity and action. Moreover, we do not conceptualise motivation as a separate mediating construct; instead motivation is enmeshed in the action orientation of the achievement of particular identities. By dissolving the relationship between identity and action, and by focusing on the pragmatics of identity *as* action, we are able to produce analytic conclusions without relying on underlying internal mechanisms or motivations. In common with other discursive approaches to selves, identities and other 'cognitive constructs', we have pursued a deliberately non-cognitive analysis.[7]

There is a final point we want to address. Within some readings of Self-Categorisation Theory, increasing emphasis is given to the idea that the primary underlying basis for action is our *representation* of the social context and our place within it in terms of relevant categorisations. Action and identity are deemed, then, to spring from our construal and representations of the world; representations enable us to act in the world. But the view that action depends upon our first representing the world and our place in it fails to appreciate our embeddedness in the world and constitutes an obstacle to the achievement of a fully integrative understanding of social selves. Representations function theoretically as a 'bridge' between the world and the agent which reinforces the dualism which both traditional and postmodern psychologists work to overcome. By contrast, our concern is not with our *representation* of social relations but our *participation* in social relations and activity. The dynamics of interaction rest not on the continual representation of 'the social context' but on the flow of interaction; the sequential, turn-by-turn flow in which different characterisations of the situation may be made relevant according to the interactional business at hand.

In this part of the book we have outlined our analytic approach to identities, and we have tried to relate this approach to some shared concerns with both the postmodern and more mainstream social psychological and sociological literatures. We have further developed points made in the introduction to this book about the nature of identity and its relation to motivation and action, and we have shown that identity and action are implicated in debates about human agency and motivation.

So far our substantive observations have focused on the organisation of verbal interaction, and in particular, the way that subcultural identities can be negotiated and resisted. But this is a counter intuitive finding. When we began this research, our questions were based on the theoretically informed assumption that our respondents would happily proclaim their membership of subcultures. But as we have seen, there were occasions when the expected affiliations were resisted. In the next part of this book, we shall begin to explore this resistance; and indeed, examine some of the ways in which subcultural affiliation itself is produced in talk.

In contrast to previous chapters, we shall not be focusing so exclusively on the sequential and interactional foundation of identity management. While retaining our interest in the underlying descriptive devices through which our respondents address issues of self and identity in their talk, we shall also try to broaden our analytic perspective to examine some of the substantive topics they raise in their talk about their lives as members of specific subcultural categories. Thus, our focus shifts from identity and action to an empirical study of individuals and social groups.

Notes

1. In this analysis we will not begin to investigate why the speaker elected to discuss a negative consequence of her subcultural membership at this point in the interview. Although this merits attention, we shall focus here exclusively on the design of this specific sequence.
2. In this chapter we highlight those stretches of talk which are produced as reported speech by using speech marks conventionally employed in fictional writing.
3. '[O]ld b'll' is a version of 'Old Bill', a British slang expression for the police.
4. The accounts in this chapter detail incidents in which the speakers complain of unfair treatment by other people. However, we have not addressed explicitly issues concerning discrimination against punks, or wider societal discrimination against specific social categories. This is because our analysis is concerned with the organisation of language use in the production of discursive identities. Consequently, it is beyond the scope of this book to address issues of prejudice and discrimination but it is important to be clear that we do not deny the experience or the existence of prejudice and discrimination. Wetherell and Potter (1992:62) make a similar point in relation to racism.

> [W]e are not suggesting that there is a kind of 'unreality' to racism or that racism is simply accounts and words. If we think for a moment of how racism is made manifest. Words are central to that process but racism is made manifest, too, through physical violence, through material disadvantage, and through differences in opportunities and power. However, to

understand that pattern, we have to develop some account, whether as social scientists, as politicians, as subjects of racism or as the initiators and beneficiaries. The crucial aspect, as always, is whose story will be accepted and become part of the general currency of explanation, whose version of events, whose account of the way things are? (Wetherell and Potter, 1992:62)

5. Markus and Nurius (1987) are not alone in linking identity and motivation. For example, Foote (1951) believed that all motivation was a consequence of one's set of identities; we are motivated to express our identities so that action is an expression of those identities. Erikson (1956) too viewed all important behaviour as motivated by our need to meet and resolve identity tasks. More recently, Stryker (1987) talked of how identity salience motivates relevant role performances, because performing roles *validates* those identities. Thus, motivation is seen as a reflection of what individuals hope to accomplish in their lives and what they would like to become, or to avoid becoming.

6. There is an interesting parallel here with social psychological approaches to the question of the relationship between attitudes and behaviour. First, it is assumed that attitudes like identities are internal constructs, and that they have a causal influence over behaviour. The lack of empirical success in demonstrating a direct relationship between the two has led, not to the abandonment of the idea that there is a link, but to theoretical efforts to show that the relationship is indirect. In Fishbein and Ajzen's (1975) influential Theory of Reasoned Action, attitudes and subjective norms together determine *intentions* to act; they do not directly affect action. More complex models have not always yielded clearer statistical relationships, however. Thus the concept of motivation or intention is no guarantee of success in linking internal constructs and behaviour. Moreover, intentions to do something are, as we all know, no guarantee that we will actually behave in accordance with our intentions. Eiser (1986; Eiser and van der Pligt, 1988) suggest that a more useful solution is to examine attitudes (or identities) and behaviour separately, rather than assuming a causal link between them.

7. It is this non-cognitive stance which has been the focus of criticism of discursive approaches. Given the centrality of cognitivism to current ways of thinking about selves as agents, this is perhaps no surprise. An issue of such importance needs to be discussed in some detail and so we will address this criticism in the concluding chapter.

Chapter 7

AUTHENTICITY IN AUTOBIOGRAPHY

The question of how, and why, individuals become affiliated with subcultural groups is the subject of academic theorising and lay speculation. Rarely, if ever, have researchers considered autobiographical accounts of how individuals first became interested in, or a part of, a recognisable subcultural group. In this chapter we investigate the descriptive strategies and communicative skills which inform the ways in which our respondents construct such accounts. In particular, we want to argue that their accounts are produced against a background of academic and lay assumptions about the reasons for, and processes of, affiliation. Consequently, we begin by examining some themes which permeate the sociological and social psychological literature on adolescence, and we then show how similar themes have filtered into common sense and media accounts.

In Chapter 1, we noted Brake's (1985) efforts to explain subcultural group membership in terms of the functions it serves for individuals. For example, it may be regarded as a solution to socio-structural problems for those with little investment in the system. In addition, it provides a pool of resources and a collective identity which young people may draw upon in their attempt to make sense of their situation, construct a viable self-identity, and resolve existential dilemmas thought to characterise adolescence.

A similar functional emphasis can be found in the literature on adolescent groups, a literature which is highly pertinent to subcultural groups, not least because it is commonly assumed that individuals affiliate with subcultures during late adolescence and for some of the same reasons. For example, it is assumed that peer groups[1] are very important in the lives of young people; in particular they are regarded as playing three complementary roles. First, the peer group plays a *supportive* role in helping individuals cope with the developmental and maturational changes which all young people face. Second, the peer group plays a role in *identity formation and change*; this is presumed necessary because adolescents need to differentiate themselves from adults, locate themselves in social terms, and overcome feelings of insecurity and fears of loneliness. Finally, the peer group plays an *influential* role in framing the values, attitudes and activities of members as they become interested in social and political issues, and they have access to increased leisure time and spending power.

How does the peer group accomplish these roles? This question has been answered in a variety of ways. For example, Coleman and Hendry (1990) argue that peer pressure is a primary mechanism for transmitting group norms and maintaining loyalties among group members. C. Sherif (1984), by contrast, emphasises interaction as the vehicle through which group norms are developed and come to regulate members' behaviour. She argues that natural groups are formed when adolescents facing problem situations realise that they can be dealt with most effectively through coordinated actions. Therefore, young people interact and over time stabilise into a social unit referred to as 'we' which constructs roles and social norms.[2] These norms regulate the behaviour of individuals both when alone and together. Change in self-conception is achieved through adopting these norms. Similarly, Brake (1985) argues that style is learned in social interaction with significant subcultural others and is used for a variety of meanings.

Social identity theorists have adopted a different approach: they have been concerned to reconceptualise the notion of peer pressure by making social identity the driving force towards uniformity. The model of Referent Informational Influence (see Turner, 1982) regards 'group pressure' as self-stereotyping according to one's *beliefs* about what constitute group norms.[3] This model thus gives the individual a more agentic role in adopting norms and so on than the more usual assumption that pressure comes from powerful or influential members. Specifically, it assumes that the individual first defines him or herself as a member of a social category, say, punk or gothic. He or she then forms or learns the stereotypic norms and criterial attributes of that category (for example, style characteristics). Finally, he or she adopts these features him or herself and 'conforms to those attributes which define the category' (Reicher, 1987:181). So, the idea is that adolescents will adopt what they regard as criterial features because these are ways that social identity as group members is realised.

There are several important features of these theories that are worth noting. First, whatever the mechanism of group influence, the result is conformity. Coleman and Hendry (1990), for example, argue that because all peer groups are oriented towards fostering identity development, they encourage conformity. Second, two key areas in which young people conform are style and music. So that

> individual adolescents may behave differently from their parents' – and sometimes their own – values because of peer group pressure, and may appear to rebel against adults' values though in a totally conformist way – by wearing almost exactly the same style of clothes and hair fashion as their friends. (Coleman and Hendry, 1990:106)

Similarly, the norms to which Sherif (1984) refers include nicknames, jargon, distinctive styles of dress and rules for acceptable treatment of one another and outsiders. A third feature concerns the impression that young people are almost *predisposed* to conform; Coleman and Hendry (1990:126) talk of 'compulsive subcultural conformities' which relate in particular to adolescents' fear of isolation and need to experiment with roles. Finally, it is assumed that the price of group membership is a transitory loss of self or individuality.

These are academic accounts of why young people are attracted to subcultural groups. But these forms of explanation also permeate everyday common-sense or lay assumptions about group membership. Lay conceptions, like those produced in academic papers and journals, are *outsiders'* accounts; they are culturally available resources for individuals who are not committed to a specific subcultural lifestyle to talk and reason about individuals who are. More important, these lay conceptions undermine the personal significance of commitment to a specific subculture. To illustrate this we need only consider the following extract, taken from a British newspaper article on youth subcultures, which neatly encapsulates outsiders' understanding of, and accounts for, young people's affiliation to subcultures. '[A] teenager's desire to identify with a tribe – and to follow religiously its dress code – is entirely normal' (*Today* 7/7/90). The article goes on to say that teenagers today are making a statement by 'banding together and adopting their own fashions, fads and language'. We have already noted several key features of academic theorising which have some resonance here: the need for identity and predispositions to conformity. But it is worth examining this statement to reveal how it subtly articulates a set of largely negative assumptions about membership of youth subcultures.[4]

Note that membership of a subculture is characterised in terms of tribal affiliation. This description trades on (largely outdated and discredited) anthropological accounts of the organisation of 'primitive' societies (that is, societies which simply display customs and forms of social organisation which are markedly different to those found in Western societies). The unfortunate implication to be drawn from this (implicitly racist) characterisation is that membership of a subculture is not, for example, the rational choice of an enlightened individual, but constitutes instead a primitive response more usually associated with the uncivilised behaviour of 'savages'. Similarly, the claim that young people 'religiously follow' subcultures characterises individuals without independent or critical thoughts on their actions.

Consider also the implications of the use of the term 'teenager' to refer to the people who join these 'tribes'. As Sacks pointed out in many of his early lectures (Sacks, 1992), the term teenager emerged as an adults' term through which to categorise young people and their activities. Certainly in the United States at the time Sacks was lecturing, but also to an extent today, the term makes available a number of unfavourable inferences about the people that it is used to describe (they are rebellious, truculent and so on). This in turn portrays young people's membership of subcultural groups in an unsympathetic light; for example, that it was an act of rebellion against parental strictures. Similarly, because the term teenager usually refers only to people between the ages of thirteen and nineteen, its application facilitates the conclusion that the actions of people so designated are 'just a phase they're going through', and will therefore be abandoned at some later (presumably more mature) stage in their development.

Finally, the extract fosters the impression that youth subcultures can be equated with (and, by implication, amount to nothing more than) styles of dress. This in turn diminishes the political, moral or personal significance which may be derived from membership of a subculture.

So, lay assumptions about the reasons why young people join subcultures are largely negative. Moreover, they provide a set of culturally available interpretative resources with which to portray the actions of individuals who become punks, gothics, or whatever, as shallow, a condition of youthful immaturity, and merely a transient phase in their maturation towards adult-hood. Thus, when young people provide accounts of their interest and in-volvement in subcultural groups, they do so against a background of precisely these kinds of lay assumptions about, and explanations for, subcultural be-haviour. In this chapter we will investigate some of the kinds of discursive resources used by respondents to minimise the relevance of these kinds of lay assumptions for their involvement in subcultural groups. We are interested, then, in the ways they construct their own *authenticity* as members of sub-cultures. We begin with a discussion of some ways that respondents charac-terise their initial interest in the music and style associated with a specific subculture.

Accounting for change

In our interviews, respondents consistently reported that it was their liking for a specific musical style that precipitated their interest in, and eventual involve-ment with, the subculture with which that music was associated. In the follow-ing two extracts the respondents describe how friends at the time were influential in introducing them to a particular sort of music.

(1) 1R:M:T5SB [RRF]

1	I:	When and how did you get inta
2		being a rocker?
3	R:	it must have been when I was about
4		fourteen or fifteen (.) some friends
5		at school were (.)
6	I:	mmhm
7	R:	an' they- an' I said oh heavy metal's
8		rubbish', they said nah it's not
9		an' they gave me some tapes to listen

```
10                to an' I did enjoy it, did ┌like it
11      I:                                   └mmhm
12      R:    and that's when I s-sort of started
13            getting into it (.) before I sort of liked things
14            like Duran Duran and Spandau Ballet
15            (.) huh ˙hh
16      I:    mmhm and then I ┌mean how-
17      R:                    └but that's 'cos
18            I hadn't heard heavy metal you see
```

(2) 4M:R:T15SA [H]

```
1      I:     C'n you tell me something about why you ↑changed?
2             (.2)
3      R2:    erm (.) yeah it was: really very simple
4             u:m (.)
5      ?      ('cos he's ┌creep)
6      R2:               └on the bus on the way to college
7             I always used to sit with them
8             a:nd I used to, take the mickey out their
9             music never really knowing anything about it
10     I:     ┌ahha
11     R2:    └and one day they played me it
12            an I was s'prised to find I actually liked it
```

These accounts are formulated to portray a series of circumstances in which speakers developed an enthusiasm for heavy metal music. But even in these passages the respondents' talk displays their sensitivity to potential claims that their progression towards the relevant subculture was motivated by shallow or flimsy concerns. So, if it is known that an individual adopts a liking for novel musical style on the basis that his or her friends like it, then we may question the sincerity of that person's claims. We may also question the extent to which this positive evaluation would be sustained; if a previous musical style was abandoned due to peer influence, we might expect current tastes to be similarly subject to whim, and therefore equally disposable.

The respondents' accounts in extracts (1) and (2) display their orientation to the kinds of inferences which may be drawn from an admission of the importance of the influence of friends. This concern is evident in the way that the respondents' conversion to heavy metal is characterised in a series of discrete circumstances. They portray, first, their initial impressions about heavy metal in a mildly derogatory fashion. So, the respondent in extract (1) reports that he would say to his friends that 'heavy metal's rubbish' (lines 7 and 8); and the respondent in extract (2) claims that he would ridicule his friends for liking that kind of music. Second, they produce an account of the circumstances through which their friends subsequently exposed them to the music: in extract (1) 'they gave me some tapes to listen to' (lines 9 and 10) and in extract (2) 'one day they played me it' (line 11). Finally, they emphasise their subsequent positive reactions: in extract (1) 'an' I did enjoy it did like it' (line 10); and in extract (2) 'I was s'prised to find I actually liked it' (line 12).

Built into these descriptive sequences, then, is an implicit contrast between the basis for the earlier negative evaluations, and the basis for subsequent positive assessments of the music. So, in extract (1) the respondent reports his initially negative evaluation of heavy metal as having been formed prior to his friends providing him with tapes. Similarly, in extract (2), the respondent states that he derogated his friends' music taste while 'never really knowing anything about it', thereby characterising his initial evaluation as at best, formed in the absence of any exposure to the music, and at worst, simply prejudice. By characterising their first impressions of heavy metal as having been formed in the absence of any direct experience of it, the respondents can warrant their claim that their subsequent conversion was due to a genuinely positive assessment of that kind of music, thereby warranting the sincerity of the change in their musical allegiances.

In extracts (1) and (2) the respondents do not provide a direct account of their affiliation with the relevant subcultural group, and neither do they refer to other aspects of subcultural affiliation, such as style. In the following extracts, however, respondents describe how, having developed a preference for the music, they began changing aspects of their appearance.

(3) 1M:H:T5SA [RRF]

1	I:	wh-when and how did you sort of
2		get inta (.8) being a hippy
3		(1)
4	R:	err dunno someone lent me an Iron Maiden
5		tape yeah? (.) and I really liked it so (.)
6		an' then I got into Rush an' stuff,
7		then I started going to concerts (.1)
8		an' sort of sa:w everyone around you
9		and you didn't really fit in at the concerts
10		an' that (.4) an' it (.) jus felt li-
11		I've always felt like growing my hair long
12		since I was little (.)
13	I:	>mmhm<
14	R:	so I jus decided to grow it long
15		much against my dad's will n everything

(4) 2G:F:T1SB [KHS]

| 1 | I: | well what made you choose (.) the way |
| 2 | | you two look |

3	R2:	em (.) it's just a sort of progression for-
4		you like <u>cer</u>tain types of mu<u>sic</u> (.)
5	I:	yeah
6	R2:	and it's just how I <u>fe</u>lt,
7		this is how I <u>wan</u>ted to dress

An intriguing feature of these extracts is the ways that speakers initially begin to build descriptions which seem to support the assertion that their commitment to a subculture was due simply to a desire to look and act the same as those who were members of the group. However, the respondents then do pragmatic work to formulate this change as a reflection of deeper personal inclinations and commitments. For example, in extract (3) the speaker characterises the nature of the change in his appearance (letting his hair grow long) as an expression of a deep-rooted and persistent inclination: 'I've <u>al</u>ways felt like growing my hair long since I was little' (lines 11 and 12). Second, he observes that this occurred against the wishes of his father (line 15). This characterisation stands as a practical demonstration of a deeply held commitment to a style of appearance common to the subculture.

In these two extracts, the respondents refer to feelings and desires when characterising their developing commitment to features of subcultural style: 'it (.) jus felt li- I've <u>al</u>ways felt like growing my hair long since I was little' (extract 3, lines 10 to 12); and 'it's just how I <u>fe</u>lt, this is how I <u>wan</u>ted to dress' (extract 4, lines 6 and 7). In Western society, social scientists and lay people alike draw distinctions between cognition (such as thoughts, beliefs, attitudes, intentions) and emotions (such as feelings, desires, impulses). Conventionally, cognition and cognitive processes are within conscious control and associated with rational thought and decision-making; emotions, on the other hand, are regarded as potentially beyond rationality and conscious control. The implications of each as the basis for, say, changing appearance are thus very different. Change which has its basis in cognition is regarded as intentional, deliberate and planned. By contrast, change that is seen to be a result of feelings is not under conscious control, and by implication, it is more sincere because it is an expression of the real self.

There is a further point: in extract (3) the speaker characterises his underlying feelings as long-standing and consistent: 'I've <u>al</u>ways felt like growing my hair long'. Similar formulations are used in the following extracts to characterise feelings, interests and preferences as the basis for respondents' choice of clothing.

(5) 1M:R:T5SA [RRF]

1	I:	can you tell me abou- (.) <u>more</u> about
2		<u>how</u> you got into it
3		(.)

4	R:	err (.4) well (fr) start I I've always
5		felt comfortable in <u>j</u>eans, so I always
6		wear <u>j</u>eans, if I can (.) I don't like
7		wearing baggy trousers
8		or anything like that 'tsalways
9		gotta be <u>tight</u> (.) and it just
10		worked up from ↑there (.2) s-sort of
11		you I mean you see rock bands on the telly

(6) 3G:2M/1F:T17SA [KHS]

1	MR1:	it's like I was <u>a</u>lways int'rested-
2		I <u>know</u> it sounds a
3		cliché looking like this- but
4		I was always interested in the:: (.) things like
5		<u>horr</u>or (.) horror stories and horror.
6		and I was always writing
7		horror stories at sch<u>ool</u> <u>ev</u>er since
8		I can re<u>member</u> (.)
9	I:	ahha
10	MR1:	and it's like (.) it was just a(.) an
11		es<u>cape</u> from everything else and I was
12		<u>interested</u> in things
13		like the super<u>nat</u>'ral (.) and I I jus
		((*few lines omitted re. the supernatural*))
14		and that's <u>why</u>: it started to <u>show</u>
15		with clothes, and hair, and make up
16		n everything as ↓well

In each of these extracts, speakers refer to category-bound attributes of particular subcultures. In doing so they employ extreme case formulations (Pomerantz, 1986; see Chapter 6) to portray their deep-rooted commitment to those activities, clothes or conventions. So, in extract (5) the respondent reports that he 'always' felt most comfortable wearing jeans, the traditional attire of rockers and heavy metal fans. In extract (6) the respondent claims that he was 'always' interested in horror stories; a concern with all things macabre and gothic is a characteristic associated with gothics. Moreover, by characterising their preferences and so on as 'always' existing, they suggest that these preceded subcultural affiliation. This is reinforced by specifying a period in their lives in which they were manifest and during which individuals are not expected to be interested in subcultural groups: for example, 'I was always writing horror stories at sch<u>ool</u> <u>ev</u>er since I can re<u>member</u>' (extract 6, lines 6 to 8). Therefore, by constructing the enduring nature of their interests, speakers imply that their status as members of subcultures is a simple expression of an intrinsic self-identity, and thereby indicate their authenticity. Prototypical aspects of appearance are thus construed as vehicles through which to exhibit the 'true' self (see also Widdicombe, 1993).

The nature of change

In their autobiographical accounts, speakers construct the nature of change as a gradual or sequential process.

(7) 1R:M:T4SB [RRF]

```
1    R:    and ma-ma mates like (.8) it was
2          through their big brothers (.) they- they
3          go gradually into it you know listening to:,
4          big brothers' albums and that
5    I:    mmhm
6    R:    an' then err (.) tch hangin around wi'em
7          (.6)
8    R:    playin all these tapes an' everything
9          you jus sorta gradually like gi'us a lend
10         a that (.) s-sort a (.) s-slip (.)
11         s:tick it into the: °cassette deck
12         or whatever an' err°
13         (1)
14   R:    gradually just buying albums an' (.)
15         all of a sudden it happen ( ) tss (.)
16         you grew the hair a wee bit (.) °you know°
```

In extract (7) change is constituted through a description of a sequence of circumstances in which the respondent is portrayed as playing an increasingly active role. The respondent's involvement in the music was initially through 'hanging around' with his friends, then requesting albums from them and finally buying albums himself. In this way, he indicates that his commitment to features of the subculture evolved over time. In this and the following extract, the respondents emphasise that their affiliation with the subculture, or aspects of the subculture, was *gradual*.

(8) 2G:F:T1SB [KHS]

```
1    R1:   yeah it's sort of like drifting into it.
2          gra:dually it's not um (.) you suddenly
3          wake up one mo:rning go out and
4          buy all the clothes dye your hair
5          put on the ma:ke-up
```

6		(.2)
7	I:	ahha
8		(.2)
9	R1:	like I've been s:ort of getting gradually
10		more extreme for about (.) ↑four years?
11	R2:	yeah
12	R1:	I dyed my hair about four years ago:
13		but (.4) it didn't look like thi:s
14	I:	mmhm (.) CAN YOU
15		(.)
16	R1:	changing and experimenting an' things

The speakers provide an explicit contrast between two characterisations of the process of change: 'drifting into it. gra:dually' (lines 1 and 2) and 'you suddenly wake up one mo:rning go out and buy all the clothes dye your hair put on the ma:ke-up' (lines 2 to 5). In the latter, change is accomplished abruptly and completely. Moreover, the speaker's use of the definite article, *the* clothes and *the* make-up imply a pre-defined image which is intentionally adopted. 'Drifting into it' does not have the same implications since it suggests that change was accomplished over time and in the absence of intended consequences. The first respondent explicitly denies the relevance to their own cases of the abrupt version and her denial is reinforced subsequently by the second respondent. She illustrates the process of 'getting gradually more extreme' (lines 9 and 10) with reference to dying her hair; this process is constructed as one of 'changing and experimenting an' things' (line 16).

The following extracts exhibit a further resource upon which speakers draw in constructing the process of changing their appearance: the absence of their own personal agency in the process of becoming a member of a group.

(9) 1M:R:T4SA [RRF]

14	R:	gradually just buying albums an' (.)
15		all of a sudden it happen ( ) tss (.)
16		you grew the hair a wee bit (.) °you know°

(10) 1P:F:T7SA [KR]

1	I:	↑how: (.) and when did you get into.
2		being a hippy punk (.) ˙hhh
3		(.2)
4	R:	dunno (t) just came gradually-sort of
5		after I left school
6		(.)
7	I:	mmhm=
8	R:	=sort of changed slowly I s'ppose

Wooffitt (1992) observed that accounts of paranormal experiences can be described as an 'it' that 'happened'. He notes that the kinds of events that are characterised as things that happen *to* people are past events whose occurrence was not contingent upon human agency and involvement. He argues that, in describing their experiences in this way, speakers are trading on conventions which inform the way we refer to events which exist independently of the speaker's agency, actions and intentions. By doing so, speakers establish the 'out-thereness' of the paranormal phenomenon and minimise their own active involvement in its occurrence. Similarly, in the extracts above, speakers portray the absence of their own agency and involvement in the changes that occurred: instead they characterise the emergence of their own subcultural affiliation as, for example, an 'it' that happened. Thereby they portray their personal development as the expression of a deep-rooted and genuine commitment, rather than the result of a conscious decision to adopt a particular style.

Negotiating the potential influence of others

In this and the following section we examine ways in which respondents may address one prevalent common-sense understanding of why someone might change: the influence of a peer group. Such an influence is potentially problematic in that the imputation of the salience of a peer group could be taken to imply that affiliation to a subculture was not a true expression of self, nor the consequence of a deep personal commitment, but was due simply to the influence of others. We describe some procedures through which these implications can be addressed by looking in detail at one sequence taken from an interview with three gothics, one female, two male.[5] We identify two types of resources used to manage the delicate issue of the existence and potential influence of relevant others.

In the following extract the respondents discuss the origins of their change to unconventional clothing.

(11) 3G:2M/1F:T17SA [KHS]

```
                     ((tape starts))
1       I:           conventional clothing (.) or
2                    high street fashions
3                    (1)
4       MR1:         yeah when I was younger
5       I:           ahha (.) ┌what kind of age
6       MR1:                  └(when I was er)
7                    e:rm up till about the age of fifteen
8                    (.2) (an' I) I just wore conventional clothes (.)
```

9	I:	mmhm
10	MR1:	but I didn't listen to conventional <u>music</u>
11		(.6)
12	FR:	mm I wore
13	MR1:	( )
14	FR:	yeah I wore I wore my- I sort of started (wearing)
15		s-sort of like (.) <u>unconven</u>tional clothes
16		when I was about thir<u>tee:</u>n an' like it took
17		me a whole <u>hour</u> to s-sort of put this
18		long black s<u>kir</u>t on to actually walk
19		down the <u>str</u>eet (.)
20	I:	ahha?
21	FR:	see what I mean it took me a
22		long <u>ti</u>me that's when I s<u>tar</u>ted
23		'hh but I didn't know anybody, else
24		dressed in black or <u>any</u>thing (.)
25		I just did it purely for my<u>self</u>

((*some lines omitted*))

26	FR:	yeah I-I <u>di</u>dn't know anybody, at <u>a:</u>ll ·hh
27		I came from a really tiny. s-sort of really
28		<u>sma:</u>ll. little <u>vi</u>llage ⌐an' like
29	I:	└ahha
30	FR:	everything I did was under close s<u>cru</u>tiny
31		(.2) (but) it wasn't until <u>fi</u>fteen
32		that I <u>re</u>alised there was like
33		<u>l</u>oads of other <u>pe</u>ople
34	I:	mmhm
35	FR:	(who) s-sort of dressed the same way as <u>I</u> did
36		or: <u>sor</u>t of the same way, things like that
37		(.2)
38	MR1:	yeah 'cos I started wearing <u>ma</u>ke up, and
39		I didn't even know about <u>o</u>ther people
40		<u>wea</u>ring it I st- I star- I just started
41		<u>wea</u>ring it and putting on these <u>b</u>lack
42		clothes and things like that an' then
43		⌐I went
44	I:	└ahha
45	MR1:	I went into <u>town</u> one <u>week</u>
46		because like I was considered <u>re</u>ally
47		<u>free</u>ky by <u>ev</u>erybody (.) because 'hh all these
48		people who lived on this estate hadn't
49		ever seen <u>any</u>body like <u>me</u> before (.)
50		I went into <u>town</u> one <u>eve</u>ning an'
51		walked by this <u>pub</u> an' saw <u>l</u>oads of people with

52	hair, spiked up an' things like that an' er
53	a lot more way out than me even though I was
54	considered the biggest freak of the area- they
55	were a lot more way out than me- I was-
56	I was jus- overawed by the fact th-
57	that there was more people, who
58	actually dressed differently to wh- what everybody
59	else (wears) round the a:rea

In this account, the what and when of change are formulated in the context of speakers' denials of their knowledge of others who dressed in similar ways. So, the second respondent (FR) states that she 'sort of started (wearing) s-sort of like (.) unconventional clothes when I was about thirtee:n' (lines 14 to 16) but 'I didn't know anybody, else dressed in black or anything' (lines 23 and 24). Similarly, the first respondent (MR1) says that 'I started wearing make up, and I didn't even know about other people wearing it' (lines 38 to 40). As we said earlier, when speakers describe change to an unconventional appearance, hearers may draw negative inferences regarding the reasons for that change; they may infer that speakers were copying or influenced by others, or conforming to a particular image. In order for such inferences to constitute a legitimate reason for change, however, one needs to have some knowledge of the existence of unconventional others, and of the attributes that render them unconventional. Formulating change in the context of denying knowledge of potentially relevant others has the following inferential consequences: it directly denies the likely assumption that these respondents changed their appearance to conform to a particular image; it acknowledges the existence of potentially relevant others; and finally, it implicitly acknowledges that their existence could, in other circumstances, provide a reasonable explanation for change.

Their denial of knowledge of potentially relevant models is reinforced in two ways. First, both respondents provide an account of an occasion on which they became aware of the existence of potentially relevant others. These accounts clearly establish the temporal order of events: the origins of change occurred prior to the discovery of similarly alternative others, even though these others did exist at the time. The first respondent states that he started changing his appearance and then he 'went into town one evening an' walked by this pub an' saw loads of people with hair, spiked up . . .' (lines 50 to 52). His reaction to this discovery further confirms the temporal order insofar as he was 'overawed by the fact th- that there was more people, who actually dressed differently . . .' (lines 56 to 58). The second respondent states that she began changing her appearance at about the age of thirteen although 'it wasn't until fifteen that I realised there was like loads of other people (who) s-sort of dressed the same way as I did' (lines 31 to 35). Additionally, these descriptions allow respondents to exhibit their awareness of similarly alternative others, while at the same time establishing that the presence of these others could not be cited as an explanation for their own change to an unconventional appearance.

Second, both respondents refer to the locale in which they grew up and in which change took place. These descriptions demonstrate that the speaker's decision to begin dressing differently was not influenced by people who lived in their respective communities. Indeed, in the account produced by the second respondent she portrays her anxieties about beginning to wear alternative clothes in her home town. She says: 'it took me a whole h<u>ou</u>r to s-sort of put this long black sk<u>ir</u>t on to actually walk down the <u>str</u>eet [   ] it took me a long <u>ti</u>me' (lines 16 to 21). She then claims that 'I came from a really tiny. s-sort of really sm<u>a:</u>ll. little <u>vi</u>llage an' like everything I did was under close sc<u>ru</u>tiny' (lines 27 to 30). This description invokes the conservatism of the speaker's home community, and hence establishes that there were unlikely to be potential role models for the emergence of her own subcultural style.

The nature of relevant others

The first respondent in extract (11) makes three references to 'unconventional', and hence potentially relevant, others. Each reference to these unconventional others avoids focusing upon, or emphasising, similarities between their appearance and his own. For example, he draws an implicit contrast between those features of his own and of others' appearance that indicates nonconformity. So, their nonconformity is indicated by 'hair, <u>sp</u>iked up an' things like that' (line 52), his by wearing make up and black clothes. In his second reference he makes a direct comparison between his own appearance and theirs: they were 'a <u>lot</u> more way out than <u>me</u>' (line 53). Finally, he says that he was 'over<u>aw</u>ed by the <u>fa</u>ct th- that there <u>was</u> more <u>pe</u>ople, who actually <u>dr</u>essed differently to wh- what everybody else (wears) round the <u>a:</u>rea' (lines 56 to 59). Thus the speaker establishes not only that both he and these other people are different, and deviate from conventional forms of dress, but that he and they deviate *in different ways*. This in turn permits the speaker to substantiate his implicit claim that his own progression from 'normality' to an alternative style is not a consequence of the influence of relevant others.[6]

In denying knowledge of similarly dressed others, speakers refer to collections of others or 'loads of people' whose appearance is characterised by black clothes, spiked up hair and so on. The features that the speakers describe make available, in this context, particular category labels or terms: namely, goths or punks. Building upon this observation, it would seem intuitively plausible that the respondents' attempt to undermine the implication that they were conforming to a particular image would be better served simply by denying explicitly that they were aware of the existence of punk or gothic subcultures. It is interesting, therefore, that they do not employ such labels.

Wooffitt (1992:104ff.), however, suggests that being able to name some state of affairs or objects implies having knowledge about them, such that one can recognise what *counts* as that object or state of affairs. Moreover, naming suggests a commitment to the in-principle existence of the object so named, and can be taken as an indication of interest in the phenomenon. Drawing upon these observations, had either of the respondents in extract (11) named the relevant others as gothics or punks, it might inferred that they were able at the time to recognise these others as members and thus that they had the appropriate criterial knowledge of what counts as gothic or punk. This in turn could be cited as the warrant to claim that the speakers had some interest in those subcultures. The availability of such inferences would, however, undermine their implicit claim that they were not motivated by a desire to conform to a particular image at the time.

Comparative devices and authenticity

One of the primary resources for establishing one's own claims for authenticity is to undermine the authenticity of other people's motivations for joining a subculture. In an earlier study (Widdicombe and Wooffitt, 1990) we observed that speakers use three primary resources to accomplish their negative assessments of other members.

The use of labels

In the following extracts, the speakers apply labels to some members of the subculture: 'mini goths', 'plastic goths', 'pseudo goths' and 'Eighties punks'.

(12) 2G:F:T1SB [KHS] (*Referring to the gothic subculture.*)

1	I:	have you noticed. <u>cha:</u>nges (.) in this time?
2		(1.8)
3	R1:	well there's been The Mission that's just started
4		an' so it's become a lot more <u>pop</u>ular (.)
5	R2:	yeah=
6	R1:	=specially with yo<u>un</u>ger people
7		there's (a) <u>mini</u>-goths now
8		(.2)
9	R2:	'hh heh heh

(13) 3G:2M/1F:T17SA [KHS]

1	MR1:	'cos like. with <u>some</u> people with <u>some</u> people
2		it's <u>im</u>age (.)
3	I:	ahha
4	MR1:	and like <u>they:</u>re (.) what <u>I'd</u> call <u>pla</u>stic goths

(14) 3ex-G:1M/2F:T11SA [RRF]

```
1        MR:     =there's quite a few people who'll just
2                do it when they go ou:t, on the weekend
3                (.)
4        FR:     yea:h
5                (.)
6        MR:     hh pseudo goths
```

These labels draw attention to the difference between factions and permit the speakers to say something specifically about the labelled members. In extract (12), 'mini' with its connotations of smallness, works as a derogatory label. In extracts (13) and (14) the terms 'plastic' and 'pseudo' imply artificial affiliation with gothic and hence also denigrate the members so labelled.

Emphasising the shallowness of new members

In the following extracts, speakers describe the involvement of some members.

(15) 2G:F:T1SB [KHS]

```
1        R2:     ye:ah it's:, going downhill re:ally an'-er
2                a lot of sort of really naff people are
3                latching onto it 'cos they ┌like
4        R1:                                 └ye:ah
5        R2:     the style and dressing up like that
6        R1:     it's become really tr:endy
7                ┌now (.) to be gothic ┌'hh
8        R2:     └yeah                  └yeah
9        R1:     yeah
```

(16) 2G:F:T1SB [KHS]

```
1        R1:     (         ) a:nd so, the mini-goths
2                tend to be the people who've only
3                just recently cottoned on to
4                The Mi ┌ssion >'cos they're only about<
5        R2:            └°yeah°
6        R1:     a ye:ar ┌old now
7        R2:             └they're very sh- (.)
8                they're shallow (.) s-sort of they've
9                just got into the- you know they're jus
10               dabbling in the (.) the outskirts of the music
11               (so) y' ┌know huh huh
12       R1:             └you kno:w
```

In these extracts descriptions are constructed to indicate the kinds of motives which lead these individuals to affiliate. For example, in extract (16), R2 makes an overt reference to the shallowness of the new members which is then reinforced by the charge that they are only 'dabbling in the (.) the outskirts of the music'. By implication, their motives are insincere insofar as they are not adopting the overarching lifestyle of the subculture.

Ascription of prototypical features

In extract (17) the speaker makes several references to prototypical features of the punk style. However, he establishes that these characteristics in themselves are no guarantee of 'a true punk'. Indeed, it is by the ascription of these prototypical features that the speaker is able to characterise the inauthenticity of those to whom he is referring.

(17) 1P:M:T6SA [KR] (*The respondent in this extract spoke with a strong Scottish accent.*)

```
1    R:    NOO it's like a uniform like hhh=
2          =if you've no' got a mohican and
3          tartan trousers you're no' a punk ·hh hh=
4    I:    =what d'you mean by a uni↑form
5          (.)
6    R:    (t)s like. (as) everybody thinks a punk's
7          got a leather jacket an' a pair of
8          tartan trousers an' a mohican (.) hh but
9          all punks are no like that ken wha'
10         I mean ⌜hh
11   I:            ⌞mmhm
12   R:    when I used to have an' (.) eighteen
13         inch mohican: (.) hh bu' it dinnae prove nothin-
14         it dinnae make me a better punk
15         (.2)
16   R:    becaus:e (.2)
17   ?:    anybody got a pound ((voice in background))
18   R:    it doesnae prove nothing to have a
19         big mohican>YOU can be a punk if you wear
20         ordinary cla:es:
21         (.)
22   I:    mmhm
23   R:    (i)ts what you think that cou:nts
```

In extract (18) the speaker employs a particularly artful categorisation to delineate the insincerity of new members.

(18) 2G:F:T1SB [KHS] (*Referring to new gothics.*)

```
1     R2:     (so) y'┌know huh huh
2     R1:          └you kno:w they
3             throw away the white stilettoes
4             and buy buckle boots a:nd (.3) I dunno
5             it's jus quite funny
```

The speaker establishes the shallowness of other members in the way that she characterises the process through which females reject their previous lifestyle and adopt that of the gothic subculture. She claims they 'throw away the white stilettoes and buy buckle boots'. White stilettoes are conventionally associated with trendies, or those who follow conventional, High Street fashions and who frequent nightclubs at weekends. Buckle boots, on the other hand, are a prototypical feature of the gothic subculture. By equating them with white stilettoes, she provides for their character as equally trivial. Moreover, the process of transition is described as throwing away items associated with one lifestyle and buying those associated with another; but genuine membership cannot be bought.

In the following extract, the insincerity of members is reinforced by characterising the process of transition as one in which previous trendies go out and buy the 'image package' on the basis of a sudden decision.

(19) 2G:F:T1SB [KHS]

```
1     R1:     =and ONE day
2     R2:     >a bit wicked<
3     R1:     you could be:
4     R2:     uh heh heh hhh
5     R1:     wandering around w- you know with blond hair
6             and white jacket and (.) y- it's
7             really aMA:zing that some people y'see
8             the very next DAy they'll all come in with
9             dyed black hair- great big group of them-
10            they'll be sitting in a gra:ve-yard
11            and ┌hh
12    R2:         └nhuh huh huh
13    R1:     talking about
14            The Mission an' things it's jus
15            (.4)
16    R2:     mm
17            (.4)
18    R1:     I s'ppose it's quite a:rrogant
19            to say o:h you know well they're shallow
20            and we're not (.) bu:t (.)
21            people tend to do it
```

In summary, we have observed a number of resources used by speakers to portray the inauthenticity of other members. Thus, speakers labelled some members, and the label itself provided a negative assessment of the faction so labelled. They also made explicit reference to the shallowness of some members. Less explicitly, others' shallowness was made available through the characterisation of their motives (for example, to be fashionable), the lack of interest in the values and overarching lifestyle of the subculture and in their transitory involvement and hence lack of commitment to the subculture. Finally, other members' shallowness was established through the ways that speakers characterised their adoption of prototypical features of the subculture: for example, 'buying into' the subculture overnight. In these accounts, speakers draw implicit and explicit contrasts with genuine members. Genuine members have a personal moral investment in the subculture and their commitment is characterised as deep and protracted, and based in intrinsic feelings, desires or other aspects of their selves.

Similar observations are reported by Fox (1987) in a rare ethnographic study of punks who frequented a bar in the United States. She investigated how the punks she studied distinguished different strata in the punk subculture in terms of their commitment to the punk style and lifestyle, and the category labels used to refer to members. For example, *hardcore* punks embodied punk fashion and lifestyle codes to the highest degree and were committed to punk ideology. The *softcore* punks were visually indistinguishable and they were committed to the lifestyle, but not to punk as an ideology or an intrinsically valuable good. *Preppie* punks were concerned with the novelty and the fashion, they bought into the image and turned it on and off at will (for example, by having their hair cut such that it could be made to look either punk or conventional). They did not lead the lifestyle of the core members and were frequently derogated by the core members which 'served to separate, for the committed punks, "us" from "them" ' (Fox, 1987:363). She too notes that preppies' commitment was described as transitory: 'they do it just on weekends'.[7]

There is, however, a discrepancy between Fox's ethnographic interpretation of the punks' accounts and our analysis of the language through which respondents' constructed their autobiographies. In particular, she uses the accounts she collected to illustrate the punks' deep commitment to ideological features of the subculture, to punk identity and to punk as an external reality. Fox's interpretation is therefore an illustration of the tendency to interpret the behaviour and identity of individuals who *could* be categorised as punks *solely* in terms of that identity.

This raises an important point. Fox's analysis of subcultural membership is like many other lay and social scientific explanations in that it is insensitive to the issue of individuality. That is, these explanations assume that commitment to the subculture or a peer group is an important feature of adolescence; therefore it is assumed, implicitly or explicitly, that one consequence of a social identity derived from group membership is a commensurate *loss* of individuality.

In Fox's account, and in other social scientific accounts, this loss is not regarded as problematic. However, this is somewhat paradoxical, given that society places great value on individuality, uniqueness and autonomy. Yet theoretical formulations of adolescents' search for collective identity in subcultural forms fail to acknowledge this. However, the analysis of members' own autobiographical accounts indicates that they are designed to address precisely the kinds of assumptions about social identity and conformity which would jeopardise claims of individuality. That is, the tension between social identity and individuality, ignored in theoretical explanations, permeates the accounts produced by individuals for whom a subcultural identity is actually, or even potentially, relevant.[8]

The analysis of the extracts we have presented in this chapter suggests that motivation is a recurrent basis for differentiating genuine from non-genuine members. It is important to note, however, that in claiming this, we are not referring to motivation as a cognitive entity, but as a linguistic or pragmatic construct which respondents draw upon in their accounting. Some members were portrayed as having shallow grounds for joining the subculture: they adopted prototypical features of the subculture in order to be fashionable, or because the image is appealing. By contrast, in their autobiographies, or in making distinctions between genuine and non-genuine members, authenticity was warranted through the description of more genuine motivations, for example, the emergence and realisation of deeply held personal feelings and desires.

We have suggested elsewhere (Widdicombe and Wooffitt, 1990) that these motivational and conceptual asymmetries relate to a distinction made by Watson and Weinberg (1982) between *being* a member and merely *doing* membership. In their study, Watson and Weinberg (1982) found that speakers distinguished between being homosexual and performing activities which could be classified as homosexual. They cite many other studies which have found a similar distinction in people's accounts. It seems, therefore, that the being/doing distinction is general and pervasive; that it is part of our common-sense knowledge or competencies through which we reason about our social worlds. Being a member, or being a punk, can only be achieved by having the right *grounds* for possessing category-related attributes; shallow members are merely 'doing' punk, gothic and so on – they do not have the correct grounds or reasons for their performance.

In our earlier paper (Widdicombe and Wooffitt, 1990), we said that the right grounds for joining were implied rather than articulated explicitly. Our analysis in this chapter allows us to specify more clearly the common-sense competencies which inform the nature of these genuine or proper grounds. Specifically, we can now suggest that the 'right' or genuine grounds for membership are tied to individualistic notions such as feelings, personal desires, intrinsic difference, and to personal motivation for realising or expressing these feelings and so on.

This is unsurprising given conventional assumptions about authenticity, genuineness and sincerity (Silver and Sabini, 1985; Trilling, 1972). These notions refer to the mode of acting, or to what is inferred to lie beneath the act, rather than the content of that act. It is not what a person does that makes her a genuine person, but what informs or motivates her actions. In this sense, authenticity relates to what we conventionally understand to be a person's inner, private life, such as thoughts, feelings and motives: dimensions that make us unique individuals. Heidegger (1927) and Sartre (1958), in fact, equated authenticity with the necessity for each person to realise their own uniqueness or individuality. The authentic life was seen to consist in a realisation of one's isolation and freedom.

If we take issues of authenticity seriously, then, we are faced with an interesting paradox regarding group membership and its so-called criterial attributes. For conventional social scientific accounts, a particular style is taken to indicate membership of a particular category or group. The authenticity of, and the motivation for, group membership are deemed to be tied to the presumed need or desire of the individual to acquire the collective identity on offer by the category. But the analysis of our respondents' accounts, and the tacit reasoning which informs their accounts, suggest a different picture. Here, authenticity is established by reference to the emergence and maintenance of a true or inner self which just happens to reflect, or mesh with, the underlying values of the group. Indeed, in their accounts the speakers characterise the inauthenticity of some members by portraying their need or desire to acquire the collective identity of the group. Inauthenticity could be established precisely by the ascription of the kinds of criterial features of a category which, in the social scientific literature, are treated as motivating genuine affiliation.

In this chapter we have explored a tension between individual and collective identity in the accounts of our respondents. In particular we have considered the way in which issues of authenticity are made relevant in accounting for one's emergent identity as a member of a subculture. Many of these themes will be explored further in the next chapter, in which we begin to examine the ways in which young people characterise the benefits of group membership.

Notes

1. The term 'peer group' is sometimes used to encompass different kinds of groups; for example, 'crowds' or larger, reputation-based collections of adolescents, and smaller 'cliques' which are based in frequent interpersonal interactions and shared activities (for example, Coleman and Hendry, 1990; Steinberg, 1993). However, researchers are not always explicit about the kind of group to which they are referring.

2. Sherif notes that adolescent peer groups are not isolated from the wider socio-cultural context in which they exist. The collectively endorsed values or social norms are simultaneously reflections of the adult world (and hence the larger socio-cultural context), reactions to it, and the creation of individuals participating with others in activities with considerable significance to them. In this way, membership of peer groups may help individuals realise their assigned position within larger society.

3. An important feature of this model is that individuals don't conform to the observable behaviour or image of others, but to their own beliefs about appropriate behaviour for category members.

4. We are not claiming that this extract reveals the author's own personal beliefs, nor that it reflects a specific editorial policy on 'youth issues' or 'young people's affairs'. Indeed, it is irrelevant whether or not these attitudes are held by institutions or individuals. We are merely indicating their salience as interpretative resources which pervade our culture, and cite this extract as an instance of their mobilisation in popular culture.

5. The arguments in this and the subsequent section are made in more detail in Widdicombe (1993).

6. The second respondent similarly appears to display such sensitivity when she corrects her initial statement that she realised there were 'other people (who) s-sort of dressed the same way as I did' (lines 33 to 35) to one that is less resonant of coincidence and similarity: 'sort of the same way' (line 36).

7. Moreover, Fox reports similar comments made by the hardcore punks in her study to those made by our respondents. For example: 'Punk didn't influence me to be the way I am much. I was always this way inside. When I came into punk, it was what I needed all my life. I could finally be myself' (Fox, 1987:353). Here the speaker characterises her subcultural identity as the expression of her 'true' or 'inner' self.

8. Similarly, we can find in the literature at least two other empirical studies which indicate young people's sensitivity to problems of group membership. Brown et al. (1986), for example, asked 1,300 US adolescents to explain why belonging to a peer group was (or was not) important to them. They derived six categories of reasons from their content analysis of responses. Each category (with the exception of 'identity') included reference to both positive and negative aspects of group membership. For example, crowd affiliation was described as both a source of activities, and as imposing restrictions on activities; and the crowd was regarded as providing and restricting opportunities for meeting people and making friends and so on (and similarly for the categories 'reputation' and 'support'). One of their categories, which they labelled 'conformity versus individuality' encompassed statements that being similar and fitting in is desirable; and that the peer group impedes individuality, autonomy and independence. Brown et al.'s (1986) findings thus suggest that young people are sensitive to the double-edged common-sense wisdom about the consequences of collective identity and group affiliation (although the salience of these different aspects changed with age).

Kitwood (1980) observed that the need to develop and maintain a distinct character, or a sense of being a person distinct from others, was a primary concern amongst the British adolescents that he interviewed. He suggested that this need arises from several sources. It is partly engendered through problems encountered by being a member of a peer group with shared values, and of spending much of their time in the company of others of similar age and background. In addition, Kitwood proposes that a person's sense of uniqueness is threatened as social horizons are widened because they become less self-centred and begin to appreciate their insignificance as they become increasingly aware of others in a similar social position. We may add that distinctiveness and individuality become important issues because of the prevalent assumptions that young people are in search of a social identity through conformity in a society in which such notions are incompatible with individuality.

Chapter 8

THE BASES OF AFFILIATION

What is the basis of continued affiliation to a subcultural group? Although a range of answers is offered by the social psychological literature, these tend to reflect a concern with the factors that make a group cohesive.[1]

One dominant theme is that our sense of who we are, and our self-worth, are intimately bound up with our group membership. One of the consequences of joining a group is a change in the way we define ourselves (Brown, 1988). To leave the group therefore would entail a *loss* of identity and precipitate a need to change our understanding of self. Consequently, our investment of self in the group through identity is likely to ensure continued commitment to that membership. Indeed, for Social Identity theorists, identification of self as a group member is the central feature which defines a collection of people as a group, and ensures the cohesion of the group (Hogg, 1987; Turner, 1982, 1984).

But joining a group is not just a question of a change in identity, it also involves some kind of initiation rite through which potential members are accepted as novices into the group and subsequently become fully fledged members (for example, Moreland and Levine, 1982). Brown (1988) argues that initiation rites serve at least three functions. First, they mark the boundaries, symbolically if not actually, between insiders and outsiders. Second, they constitute an apprenticeship into the normative standards and skills required of members. Finally, they elicit loyalty from the new member. In the case of subcultural groups, initiation is said to involve learning and adopting the style, music preferences, lifestyle and ideological beliefs of the subculture; it also involves learning the skills of performance, that is, playing the role with sincerity (Brake, 1985). Because of the role played by such attributes in initiation and in defining the group as distinct, identification with the group should also involve commitment to style, lifestyle and ideology; this commitment should in turn ensure continued affiliation.

Moreover, when people join groups, their experiences, activities and outcomes are linked in some way to those of the other members: they become interdependent. Lewin (1948) proposed that one way that members become interdependent is through a sense of shared or *common fate*. So it may be the shared perception of similarly grim future prospects that provides the impetus for affiliation with subcultures. Affiliation is also said to be derived from the way that members come to depend on each other for the satisfaction of personal and social needs (Lewin, 1948), and the attainment of goals (Deutsch, 1949, 1973). Similarly, Bass (1960) defined a group as a collection of individuals whose existence as a social unit is rewarding to the individuals. So, group membership serves functions for members, and as long as the group mediates rewards, members are likely to remain in the group. There is resonance between these sociopsychological conceptualisations of group affiliation and Brake's (1985) argument that subcultural groups provide solutions to socio-structural problems and existential dilemmas. Therefore, individuals will continue to affiliate as long as they experience such problems and find relief in group membership.

A third feature of group affiliation concerns the development of social structure in the form of group norms, roles and expectations. We saw in the last chapter that the Sherifs believed that norms were central in the formation and functioning of adolescent groups (for example Sherif and Sherif, 1969; see also C. Sherif, 1984). From this perspective, adherence to group norms and expectations is the basis for continued affiliation and group cohesiveness. Moreover, Brown (1988) discusses a number of individual and social functions of norms. For the individual, norms constitute frames of reference through which the world is interpreted; they thereby enable the member to structure and predict his or her environment. Similarly, Brake (1985) noted that one of the functions of the subculture was to provide a perspective for making sense of the world and members' experiences. In addition, norms function to regulate the behaviour of individuals both alone and in the group. Norms also fulfil social functions. For example, they facilitate the achievement of group goals by helping to coordinate group members' activities. They also serve to express, enhance and maintain aspects of the group's identity. According to Brown (1988) this latter is especially true of norms concerning particular styles of dress; these norms help demarcate members of the group from non-members and thus define that group's identity more clearly. Norms and the social structure of the group therefore serve important functions as well as providing the means through which members continue to affiliate and hence they ensure that the group is cohesive.

Finally, members may continue to affiliate because they like the other members, either as individuals (for example, Lott and Lott, 1961, 1965) or as group members (Hogg, 1987, 1992). Interpersonal attraction has been regarded as central in the cohesiveness of the group because 'without at least a minimal attraction of members to each other a group cannot exist at all' (Bonner, 1959:66). Similarly, Heider (1958) argued that positive sentiment relations (liking for others) and positive unit relations (a sense of oneness or togetherness) are inextricably linked. The basis of attraction is, however, the source of some dispute. For example, Lott and Lott (1965) argued that interpersonal attraction, or cohesiveness, arises through rewarding interaction.

Festinger (1950, 1954), by contrast, argued that people are attracted to and affiliate with others in order to validate their opinions, attitudes and beliefs. So that, according to Festinger, mutual interpersonal attraction reflecting shared attitudes is the basis of group affiliation.

On the basis of the social psychological literature it is possible to predict that members have an investment in the group for one or more of the following reasons. It constitutes part of their identity, and the costs and effort of initiation generate a commitment to features of the group. Also, membership may continue because members derive certain benefits, such as the satisfaction of needs, the attainment of goals, or simply rewarding interaction. Alternatively, individuals may be committed to group norms and performing the requisite roles. Finally, they may simply like the other members.

These considerations of the bases for members' affiliation, and the group's cohesiveness, informed two of the questions in the original interviews. First, we asked if membership of the group or being a punk (or whatever) was important to the respondent (this question was used successfully by Gaskell and Smith, 1986 for the same purposes). Second, we invited respondents to talk about the benefits or advantages of their membership of the subculture.

We begin our analysis by considering the following account.

(1) 2G:F:T1SB [KHS]

```
1        I:      mmhm is being gothic very impo:rtant ta ya?
2                (.)
3        R2:     yes
4        R1:     yes
5                (.)
6        R2:     I ⌈wouldn't definitely⌉ =
7        I:       ⌊c'n you tell me     ⌋ =
8        R2:     =⌈wouldn't change it
9        I:      =⌊mo:re about it
10       R1:     I wouldn't change.
11               I love being eh being like this
12               I don't like s-sort of being stared at
13               by all the grannies an' stuff
14               but I like ⌈to stand out
15       I:                 ⌊mhm
16       R1:     I like being different
17               and I don' think I'd I I-I won't change
18               for a long time I don't think=
19       R2:     =also it's really
20       R1:     I really enjoy being
21       R2:     ⌈it's jus
22       R1:     ⌊it's jus
```

23		(.)
24	R1:	it's nice being=
25	R2:	it's jus
26	R2:	=yeah=
27	R1:	=part of an identity
28		th-there's some se<u>curi</u>ty
29		in it 'cos er (.5) it's (.) I don't know=
30	R2:	=you find people that're
31	I:	mhm
32	R2:	the same as you
33		because they dress the same as you
34		and you find they have a similar mentality
35		so it's a very easy way of finding friends
36		who're similar to you (.)

In this account, the first respondent invokes several of the conceptual under-standings of why one might affiliate with a subcultural group. For example, she mentions the desirability of a distinct yet shared identity. She also ad-dresses personal and social benefits: security and finding friends with a similar outlook and set of interests.

There are, moreover, other features of this account which are interesting. Note that *initially* both respondents provide minimal, positive, one-word an-swers to the question, and that these responses are followed by a next ques-tion from the interviewer which seeks further elaboration. But when this elaboration is provided, the speakers do not refer immediately to positive aspects of their lives as gothics. Instead the second respondent says 'I wouldn't definitely wouldn't change it', a sentiment which is partially echoed by her friend. So, although the first respondent does indeed talk about the kinds of anticipated benefits of being a member of a group, she mentions these only after saying that she would not change. For the second respondent, the claim that she would not change is produced as the complete answer to the request for further elaboration. So, even though the respondents refer to identification and to the benefits derived from involvement in a subcultural category, these are not produced in an unmitigated way.

These preliminary remarks are not only relevant to the features of extract (1). Indeed, out of nineteen interviews in which these two questions were asked, there are only five cases in which the respondent(s) formulated an-swers which portrayed unhesitatingly the significance of identification or any other personal and social benefits. This means that in thirty-three cases in which respondents could have elaborated the predicted bases of involvement in a subcultural group, they declined to do so. However, as we shall see, it is certainly not the case that our respondents unanimously claimed that mem-bership was insignificant, nor did they claim that there were no benefits to be derived from their membership of a subcultural group. Indeed, it would have been bizarre for such a claim to be made, for it would have invited the response that if membership is not important, and if there are no benefits, why persist in affiliation?

The focus of our analysis, then, will be on the discursive devices and strategies through which our respondents accounted for their (continued) commitment to the subculture. First, we examine responses to the question concerning the importance of identity or membership. We will then analyse the ways they addressed the question of the benefits of group membership.

Importance of membership

In this section we will look at three discursive strategies which underpin respondents' replies to the question 'Is being an X important to you?'. We begin by examining a strategy through which respondents formulate in minimal terms the importance of their subcultural membership.

(2) 1 Hippy/Punk:F:T7SB [KR]

```
1       I:      huhha. is it very important to you,
2               being punk hippy?
3       R:      ah dunno I jus sort of (.) happy
4               as I am I jus (it's)
5               the way I want to be so (.)
6               that's that 'hhh
```

(3) 1H:M:T5SA [RRF]

```
1       I:      ↑is it very impo:rtant to you (.)
2               being a hippy?
3               (.)
4       R:      er
5               (1.2)
6       R:      I dunno y'know I- well
7               I wouldn't like to be anything else
8               °put it that way°
```

Extracts (2) and (3) share three properties. Both respondents employ the particle 'ah (I) dunno' at the beginning of their answers (extract 2, line 3; extract 3, line 6). Note also that the answer they subsequently go on to provide is produced immediately after the 'ah dunno' particle. There is no gap or delay which would suggest that the respondents are using the phrase here to mark a genuine lack of knowledge about the state of affairs on which they are being asked to comment. So, the use of 'ah dunno' may be motivated by more interactional contingencies. Indeed, it appears that the 'ah dunno' particle marks the beginning of a turn which is in some way disjunctive to the prior turn.[2] That is, in both cases the respondents have been asked a question which makes relevant some type of affirmative or negative answer. Neither respondent, however, provides a simple or extended yes/no answer. Therefore, their answers are misaligned with respect to the type of question they are addressing.

Instead, the respondents characterise their subcultural membership in terms of personal preferences: in extract (2) the respondent announces that 'I jus sort of (.) happy as I am I jus (it's) the way I want to be' (lines 3 to 5); and in (3) the respondent says he 'wouldn't like to be anything else' (line 7). Since each assessment is formulated in terms of one specific point (personal happiness and rejection of alternatives), we may characterise these as *minimal evaluative responses*. Finally, both responses are followed by closing particles: in extract (2), lines 5 to 6, 'so (.) that's that 'hhh,' and in extract (3), line 8 "°put it that way°'.[3]

Some analytic remarks can be drawn from our observations regarding the nature and properties of these answers. Specifically, we suggest that through these design features respondents characterise the question they have just been asked as *irrelevant to them*. The inappropriateness of the question is manufactured in the detail of their responses. So, the use of the 'ah dunno' particle displays the respondents' orientation to the sequential misalignment between the type of turn made relevant by the prior question and the type of turn they go on to provide. The basis of this misalignment is generated primarily through the provision of minimal evaluative responses. That is, their evaluations of their membership are produced as a 'just is' statement, which in turn renders irrelevant questions which address the *importance* of subcultural involvement. The 'just is' character of these responses is further displayed in the 'final comment' phrases. Here the respondents orient to the 'nothing else to say' character of their assessments, while at the same time terminating their utterances.

These responses are, in many senses, curious; what might account for the respondents' disinclination to furnish the type of yes/no answer projected by the interviewer's prior question? One consideration is that a simple 'no' answer would then invite questions as to why the respondent continued to dress in a manner associated with a specific subculture. It is important to note also that both respondents had either volunteered their subcultural identity, or had accepted such an identity when proffered by the interviewer. Having established the relevance of a subcultural identity, it would be an accountable matter for the respondents subsequently to claim that their involvement in that subculture was of no significance to them.

An answer which affirmed the personal importance of subcultural membership could entail equally problematic implications. In the previous chapter, we argued that young people's accounts of their involvement in subcultural groups are conducted against a background of largely sceptical and unsympathetic lay assumptions about, and explanations for, subcultural group membership. For example, that subcultural identity is accomplished through conformity and peer pressure. We noted, too, the common assumption that the price of group membership is the loss of individuality. Such lay assumptions may be relevant to the design of the respondents' answers in extracts (2) and (3). An admission of the importance of involvement in a subculture might invite the charge that the individual concerned is simply 'following the crowd' or, more importantly, that their self-identity is defined through that group membership rather than through idiosyncratic characteristics. This in turn may implicate the shallowness of their affiliation and their lack of self-authenticity.

In the light of these considerations, the respondents' answers in extracts (2) and (3) display a delicate sensitivity. They do not provide either a negative or affirmative answer to the interviewer's question. More significantly, however, they formulate their involvement in a subculture as something that 'just is' a feature of themselves for which measures of importance are simply irrelevant. Their answers therefore have an evasive, or even defensive character.

In contrast, in extracts (4) and (5), we see instances of more affirmative responses. Through an analysis of these extracts, we will identify a second strategy used by our respondents to answer the question 'is being an X important to you?'.

(4) 1P:M:T9SA [KHS]

1	I:	is being punk very important to you?
2	R:	yep
3		(.)
4	I:	why?
5	R:	well I won't change the way I look
6		(.) to get a job or (.) th- anything
7		like that I think (.) that (.)
8		they can accept me as I am or (.) ((staccato))
9		they don't accept me

(5) 2P:F:T2SB [CAM]

1	I:	yeah is it very important to you, being punks?
2		(.4)
3	R1:	yeah
4		(.)
5	R1:	yeah
6	R2:	fairly
7	R1:	yeah
8	I:	can you (.) tell me
9	R2:	fairly
10	I:	something about why?

11	R2:	um (.3) it's like at work
12		like I've (.) had hassle at work
13		about the way I look an' everything like that
14		a:nd I'm not prepared to totally
15		change myself a-er-and everything
16		that I sort of believe jus jus
17		to get a job really

In extract (4) the respondent answers 'yep', while in extract (5) the first respondent says 'yeah', and the other says 'fairly', which is less emphatic but still positive. Both sets of answers are produced as complete turns. In neither extract is there any indication that after the 'yep' or the cycle of 'yeahs' and 'fairlys' the respondents intended to go on. For example, there are no 'ums' and 'er's' which would indicate that there is 'more to come' in the turn. Furthermore, the interviewer's production of a supplementary question displays her recognition that the respondents were not going to continue and elaborate upon their minimal answers.

The responses to the follow-up question 'why (is being an X important)?' have some interesting properties. The most noticeable feature is that neither subsequent turn actually answers the question. Instead of saying why it is important, the speakers provide a *measure* of the importance of subcultural involvement. So, in extract (4) the respondent's subsequent turn is prefaced with 'well', thereby marking what follows as an explanation for some point, rather than an attempt to address explicitly the interviewer's follow-up question. He then goes on to characterise the personal significance of his subcultural involvement by describing how he would not alter his appearance to obtain something which might be desirable; in this case, a job. Similarly in extract (5), the second respondent explains that, despite experiencing difficulties at work because of her appearance as a punk, she would not change. In both cases the repondents' refusal to change to attain something desirable (a job, a 'hassle-free' environment) is cited to index the importance of their subcultural involvement.

Respondents claim that they would not change in any way to achieve something as significant as employment. In general, this is a typical way in which an individual can illustrate a commitment to an aspect of his or her life or behaviour. These accounts, however, have a formulaic or idiomatic character to them. The respondent in extract (4) closes his account with the bravado statement 'they can accept me as I am or (.) they don't accept me'. The staccato production of this statement emphasises its idiomatic character. In extract (5) the second respondent initially acknowledges that she *has* a job by beginning to report difficulties she has experienced at work. By the end of the account, however, she is establishing her commitment to her lifestyle by saying that she would not discard it *in order* to get a job. So although her account begins by referencing actual events, she eventually changes to the production of a more formulaic account to illustrate her commitment.

Extracts (2) to (5) share some common properties. Both sets of answers are misaligned with respect to the kind of next action projected by the interviewer's prior turn, and they do not directly address the immediately prior question. But unlike the respondents in extracts (2) and (3), respondents in extracts (4) and (5) do affirm the importance of their subcultural involvement. Yet when they are pressed to elaborate why such involvement is significant, they do not cite, for example, the significance of group identification, nor the social benefits which accrue from membership, nor do they invoke any of the other kinds of lay assumptions we have so far discussed. Indeed, they decline to mention *any* benefits. Instead, they index the importance of their subcultural involvement by citing a formulaic example of the extent to which they could not change deeply held personal beliefs or change something as fundamental as their self-identity.

It is now clear that our respondents address subcultural involvement in such a way that they can be seen to be affirming its importance without explicitly orienting to any benefits of that involvement nor to the positive consequences of shared identification. This feature of our respondents' accounts is particularly clear in the final strategy used to address the question 'is being an X important to you?'.

To identify this phenomenon we will consider the following four extracts. The strategy we wish to identify has several discrete components: an answer/assessment; a rejection of alternatives; a nomination of rejected alternatives; a list of attributes of the rejected alternative; and a summary/upshot. Although not all components are represented in each of the extracts, there are sufficient commonalities to warrant examination of these four extracts together.

(6) 1P:F:T7SA [KG]

1	I:	is being a punk very ((*smiley voice*))
2		important to you?
3	R:	yeah very indeed
4		I couldn't imagine myself being
5		straight at all
6		(.) like dressing neatly in tidy
7		nice clothes an' having my hair
8		down and all that 'hh
9		na I can't imagine=probably
10		in a couple of years' times
11		I'll be like that but I-I-
12		at the moment I can't imagine it at all
13	I:	mmhm=
14	R:	=I mean it's that. way I wanna be
15		an' I wanna stay an' really
16		that's it (huh huh)

(7) 1P:M:T6SB [KGR]

1	I:	is being a punk very ((*smiley voice*))
2		impo:rtant to you?
3	R	˙hhh I couldna see mysel'
4		any other way (.) you know
5		(.) I mean I couldna see myself
6		walking doon the s- doon the street
7		wi' a suit or anything like that
8		(ugh) no way
9		˙hhh that'd take too long
10	I:	so is that important?
11		(.)
12	R:	ye:↑ah

(8) 1H:M:T5SA [RRF]

1	I:	↑is it very impo:rtant to you (.)
2		being a hippy?
3		(.)
4	R:	er
5		(1.2)
6	R:	I dunno y'know I- well
7		I wouldn't like to be anything else
8		°put it that way°
9		I wouldn't like to be 'orrible trendy
10		smelly yellow shirts
11		an' things like that (.) so
12		I s'ppose it is in a way
13		yeah (.) it's jus
14		it's the only thing that I like
15		(I think that) everything else
16		is pretty bent really
17		°it's quite annoying°

(9) 1R:M:T4SB [RRF]

1	I:	is being a rocker very impo:rtant to you?
2		(1)
3	R:	er
4		(1.3)
5	R:	ahha aye (.)
6		it's jus the way I am er
7		(.4)
8	R:	couldn't imagine life (.) of er

```
9                 (1.3)
10      R:        of say I lived wi'
11                (1.8)
12      R:        °I dunno (.3) bu'°
13                (.2)
14      R:        I remember the Royal Family you know
15                (having) a go at these people
16                (as er) you know an' er
17                going about wearing suits an' everything
18                going to all these functions and
19                do's an' that er
20                driving about in a Ferrari
21                I jus couldn't see it (.)
22                I mean (.3)
23      I:        °mmhm°
24      R:        it's easier being being the way I am
25                it's jus (.)
26                jus' comes na┌tural ken?
27      I:                     └mm
28      R:        after a while
```

Following the interviewer's question the respondents produce an *answer* or *assessment* component.

(From extract 6)

```
1       I:        is being a punk very         ((smiley voice))
2                 important to you?
3       R:        yeah very indeed
```

(From extract 9)

```
1       I:        is being a rocker very impo:rtant to you?
2                 (1)
3       R:        er
4                 (1.3)
5       R:        ahha aye (.)
6                 it's jus the way I am er
```

In extracts (7) and (8) the assessment component is absent. However, in all cases the respondents go on to produce, or at least begin to produce, a *rejection of alternatives* component, in which the respondents claim that they could not be anything other than a member of their respective subcultures. For example, from extracts (7) and (8):

(From extract 7)

```
1    I:    is being a punk very          ((smiley voice))
2          impo:rtant to you?
3    R:    ˙hhh I couldna see mysel'
4          any other way (.) you know
```

(From extract 8)

```
1    I:    ↑is it very impo:rtant to you (.)
2          being a hippy?
3          (.)
4    R:    er
5          (1.2)
6    R:    I dunno y'know I- well
7          I wouldn't like to be anything else
```

Respondents then go on to illustrate what exactly they could not be by *designating rejected alternatives;* sometimes through a reference to a specific alternative category. For example, in extract (6) the respondent claims that he could not be 'straight', a term used to denote young people who have no subcultural affiliation; and in extract (8) the respondent nominates the category 'trendy'.

(From extract 6)

```
1    I:    is being a punk very          ((smiley voice))
2          important to you?
3    R:    yeah very indeed
4          I couldn't imagine myself being
5          straight at all
```

(From extract 8)[4]

```
7    R:    I wouldn't like to be anything else
8          °put it that way°
9          I wouldn't like to be 'orrible trendy
```

In extracts (7) and (arguably) in (9), however, the respondents invoke the categories 'business person/yuppie' and 'upper class jet set' by describing and rejecting patterns of dress and behaviour which are conventionally associated with those groups.

(From extract 7)

```
5    R:    (.) I mean I couldna see myself
6          walking doon the s- doon the street
```

7   wi' a suit or anything like that
8   (ugh) no way

(From extract 9)

14   R: I remember the Royal Family you know
15   (having) a go at these people
16   (as er) you know an' er
17   going about wearing suits an' everything
18   going to all these functions and
19   do's an' that er
20   driving about in a Ferrari

Having explicitly or implicitly invoked a category, respondents then list attributes of that category. As is common in conversational discourse, these lists have a three-part structure (Jefferson, 1991).

(From extract 6)

(.) like dressing neatly in	
tidy nice clothes	**1**
an' having my hair down	**2**
and all that	**3**

(From extract 7)[5]

going about wearing	
suits an' everything	**1**
going to all these	
functions and do's an' that er	**2**
driving about in a Ferrari	**3**

(From extract 8)

I wouldn't like to be	
'orrible trendy[6]	**1**
smelly yellow shirts	**2**
an' things like that	**3**

Finally in this sequence, the respondents produce a *summary assessment component*, in which they either describe the gist of their prior talk, or instead formulate the upshot or consequences of what they have just been saying. For example:

(From extract 9)

21   R: I jus couldn't see it (.)
22   I mean (.3)

```
23      I:      °mmhm°
24      R:      it's easier being being the way I am
25              it's jus (.)
26              jus comes natural ken?
```

The summarising character of the final component is particularly evident in extract (8), in which the respondent uses the word 'so' to mark the beginning of an upshot of his prior talk.

(From extract 8)

```
11      R:      an' things like that (.) so
12              I s'ppose it is in a way
13              yeah (.) it's jus
14              it's the only thing that I like
15              (I think that) everything else
16              is pretty bent really
17              °it's quite annoying°
```

The descriptive device or summary assessment in extracts (8) and (9) displays a sequential organisation; the structural components appear in the same order. In the light of this observation, consider the interviewer's question in line 10 of extract (7).

(Extract 7)

```
1       I:      is being a punk very          ((smiley voice))
2               impo:rtant to you?
3       R:      'hhh I couldna see mysel'
4               any other way (.) you know
5               (.) I mean I couldna see myself
6               walking doon the s- doon the street
7               wi' a suit or anything like that
8               (ugh) no way
9               'hhh that'd take too long
10      I:      so is that important?
11              (.)
12      R:      ye:↑ah
```

The question 'so is that important?' is produced immediately after the respondent describes a nominated alternative category. In the other extracts, this component is followed by a summary assessment of the respondent's prior talk. Notice, then, that the interviewer's next question is produced right at the point where a summary assessment would have been relevant. And the type of question produced by the interviewer is one designed to exhibit her upshot of the prior talk (Heritage and Watson, 1979). This suggests that both respondent and interviewer have a shared orientation to the sequential organ-isation of this strategy (which may in turn indicate its character as a culturally available resource).

To summarise some of the features of this third descriptive device: respond-ents address the importance of their subcultural involvement by naming and describing the attributes of social categories with which they would not like to be involved. These alternative categories range from the simple term, straight, designating someone without any subcultural affiliation, to trendy, yuppies and the upper-class jet set. There is also an asymmetry, in that respondents decline to discuss characteristics of the lifestyle of their own subculture, but seem happy to list the kinds of activities and conventions associated with the category they have designated as being the kind of person they could not be. Furthermore, the descriptions of these alternative categories are negative or depreciatory. But perhaps most significant is that again we see respondents address and affirm the importance of membership of a subcultural group without actually referring, say, to the lifestyle, beliefs or activities associated with that subculture.

Therefore, the three discursive strategies we have identified so far in this chapter seem to be resources through which respondents can avoid, or suggest the irrelevance of, importance as a dimension appropriate to evaluating membership.

Of course there are exceptions: in some cases respondents do refer to the attributes of their own subcultural group. However, it is noticeable that in these cases the respondents mitigate or deny the importance of their sub-cultural involvement. For example, in the next extract, the respondent de-scribes features of rockers' lifestyle and tastes. Specifically, she mentions a certain type of clothing and names a popular rock band, but this description is produced in the context of her claim that being a rocker is *no longer important* to her.

(10) 1R:F:T4SA [RRF]

1	I:	is is being rocker very im-important to you?
2		(1.2)
3	R:	n:no it's just that I like it
4		it used to be when like I was
5		thirteen and that 'cos like
6		you're influenced a lot
7	I:	mmhm
8	R:	by the bands 'hh an' I remember (ah)
9		always wanted to dress like
10		Jon Bon Jovi or 'hh you know
11		goin about in fringed jackets an'
12		(.2) 'hh spandex

13		but now I don' bother
14		it it doesn't matter what you dress like
15		jus as long as you like the music
16		an' that's all I do
17	I:	°mhm°
18	R:	so I jus dress the way I want

And in extract (11), the respondent describes several features of the lifestyle associated with the hippy subculture. Moreover, she does accept that these are important to her, but she does so only after spending time denying her affiliation with that category (whilst acknowledging that others could see her as a hippy).

(11) 2H:F:T3SB [FP]

1	I:	is being hippy very impo:rtant t' ya?
2	R1:	I don' really look on myself as a hippy
3		like ah said I jus' do what I wanna do
4		an' if people call me a hippy 'hhh
5		then I'm a hippy to em an' it (.)
6		don't insult me, coming from
7		someone like you (.)
8		but er I-I dunno (I'd) my way of life
9		is very very important to me so I s'ppose
10		yeah it is it is it's er 'hhh my mates (.)
11		an' me bike an' drugs are the main things
12		to me really an' I'm not ashamed to say it
13		'cos they don' fuck me up d'ya know
14		wha' I mean 'cos I know (.4)
15		well I don' ⌐know
16	R2:	└we know
17	R1:	we know=
18	R2:	=⌐we know the main things=⌐
19	R1:	└the main things about ┘
20	R2:	=about drugs an' everything
21		an' our mates an' everything that (is).
22		I feel we're all the same really
23		it is very important to how we are

So, even when respondents produce a summary assessment of the importance of being a member, they do so in such a way as to undermine or limit the significance of their own affiliation.

On the basis of the analysis so far, we suggest that the respondents were addressing a particularly delicate issue in their answers. They were not merely answering a substantive question about the importance of their membership of a subculture: they were also displaying a sensitivity as to the kinds of inferences which could be warranted by a simple positive assessment of their identity or lifestyle as punks or whatever. That is, they seem to be orienting to the way a characterisation of affiliation in terms of identity or identity relevant features, or the social benefits of affiliation, could make available certain unfavourable inferences about the basis of and motivation for their involvement. For example, to affirm the importance of subcultural identity may invoke implications of conformity and the loss of individuality. On the other hand, characterising affiliation in terms of the benefits thereby accrued may be taken to imply that the motivation for affiliating is simply based on what they get out of it; that is, membership is merely instrumental rather than a matter of commitment.

There is an intriguing upshot of some of the remarks we have presented so far. There is a considerable body of research which suggests that assessment of an ingroup can be achieved by derogating an outgroup (see Brown, 1988; Hogg and Abrams, 1988). And we have reported on some of the ways in which respondents described the kind of category to which they *could not* belong as a way of indexing the importance of the group to which they *did* belong. But these formulations were not simple expressions of social psychological or cognitive strategies to affirm self or group membership. Rather, the design of these utterances was motivated more by interactional contingencies relevant to occasions in which affirmation of one's membership of a group could entail largely unsympathetic responses. What social psychologists may have identified, then, is a feature of the way talk is organised to address inferential concerns, rather than the verbalised operation of a psychological mechanism for affirming self in group membership.

Advantages of membership

Similar concerns seem to inform some of the strategies employed when answering the question, 'what do you get out of it, what advantages are there?'. Obviously, the design of these questions takes for granted that there are advantages. So, instead of inviting speakers to assess whether there are, in fact, advantages of being a member, the question invites them to characterise the nature of the assumed advantages.[7] As we shall see, their responses did not conform to the kinds of answers we had anticipated for good (theoretical) reasons. Consider the following two extracts.

(12) 1 Hippy/Punk:F:T7SB [KR]

2   I: 'hh what d'you get out of it

3   (.4)

```
4       I:      what advantages are there
5               (.)
6       R:      dunno there aren't any
7               I don't think 'hh
8               just that people take the
9               mickey out of you all the time
10      I:      'hh huh
11      R:      huh so: huh
12              I can't really think of
13              any advantages
```

(13) 1P:M:T9SA [KHS]

```
2       I:      what d'you get out of it,
3               what advantages are there
4               (4.2)
5       R:      I don't know if there's
6               any advantages really
7               (.5)
8       R:      I think
9               (3)
10      R:      advantages? phhh
11              (4)
12      R:      °no°
```

In both cases the respondents deny that there are advantages to be derived from their membership. However, these are not flat denials. Instead, respondents' statements that there are no advantages are formulated so as to indicate the basis for their assessment; that is, these answers are produced to be heard as being contingent on the respondents' mental processes. For example, in extracts (12) and (13) the claim that there aren't any advantages is accompanied by the phrase 'I don't think'. The point is that respondents' claims are apparently designed to be heard as a statement derived from a process of thinking and self-reflection.

Edwards and Potter (1992) have observed a similar phenomenon in their study of the rhetorical organisation of public political disputes. Citing Latour and Woolgar (1986), they suggest that formulations of a state of affairs can be conceptualised as lying on a continuum of modalisation. At one end of this continuum are statements which are taken to be so commonplace and taken-for-granted that their basis does not need to be formulated; the basis of the statement can be assumed simply as an objective fact about the world. At the other end of the continuum are statements which are prefaced by such phrases as 'I think that . . .', 'I believe that . . .' and 'I know that . . .' and so on; such statements about the world are made highly contingent on the mental processes, knowledge and desires of the speaker.

Returning to extracts (12) and (13), respondents produce answers which can be heard as reports or observations of their own personal experiences. There are inferential advantages to this strategy. A flat denial that there are no advantages would be contradictory to something which is commonplace, and which seems intuitively obvious. This denial itself would then be an accountable matter. But by portraying their denial as a reflection based on personal experience the respondents can more effectively rebut these taken-for-granted assumptions; that is, they counter lay assumptions not with denials, but by 'hinting' or alluding to their own experiences.

A similar strategy is used by respondents in the following two extracts.

(14) 1R:F:T4SA [RRF]

1	I:	what good things do you
2		get out of it- what sort of
3		advantages of (.) being a rocker
4		(.4)
5	R:	hhh em
6		(1)
7	R:	there isn't all that much
8		really

(15) 1P:M:T9SA [KHS]

1	I:	what d'you get out of it,
2		what advantages are there
3		(4.2)
4	R:	I don't know if there's
5		any advantages really

The respondents' use of the word 'really' to characterise their version orients to a distinction between what is *apparently* the case and what is *really* the case. It simultaneously acknowledges that while it is conventionally or generally known that membership entails personal benefits for the individual, the reality is different. As with extracts (12) and (13), designing their responses so that their statements are contingent on reflection on personal experience, provides a more credible basis for counter intuitive claims than, say, a simple denial or flat assertion.

In extracts (16) and (17) below we see a rather different formulation.

(16) 1R:M:T5SB [RRF]

1	I:	what- what good things
2		d'you get out of being a rocker
3		(2)

4	R:	ah-don't actually get good things
5		I jus sort of enjoy the music

(17) 2P:F:T2SB [CAM]

1	I:	what do you get out of-
2		I mean what advantages are there
3		tuh being punk
4	R1:	u::m
5		(.2)
6	R2:	huh huh huh.hh
7	R1:	none
8		°I don't think°
9	R2:	˙hhh none huh ha huh ˙hh
10		I shouldn't think
11	R1:	hh ˙hhh
12	R2:	huh huh huh
13		˙hhh I jus enjoy it
14		huhH huh huh
15		˙hh I s'ppose
16	I:	mhmm

In formulating their assessments, speakers refer to enjoying the subculture, or some aspect of it: 'I jus enjoy it' (extract 17), and 'I jus sort of enjoy the music' (extract 16); that is, having denied that there are any advantages or 'good things' derived from membership, speakers produce a positive aspect of affiliation. However, they characterise this positive aspect – enjoyment – through the use of the term 'just'. Their use of 'just' minimises the significance of enjoying the music, or the subculture, and thereby exhibits a depreciatory meaning (Lee, 1987). Moreover, focusing on enjoyment implies a pleasurable but not important or significant experience. So, although speakers do produce a positive assessment of affiliation, its significance is very much played down.

The effect is emphasised through the explicit contrast with the prior utterance in which speakers refer to 'getting good things' or advantages; that is, speakers draw a distinction between advantages and their (mere) enjoyment, and they deny that there are any advantages. In this way, enjoyment is not characterised as a positive benefit of group membership.

In this chapter we have examined some of the features of responses to two questions in our interviews. One question invited respondents to assess the importance of their membership; and the other invited them to describe the benefits derived from their involvement. These questions were informed by prevalent theoretical assumptions about the bases of commitment and continued affiliation to the subcultural group. These theoretical explanations initially led us to believe that the respondents would discuss matters of identity, and the significance to them of attributes like style, lifestyle and ideology. We also expected some account of the personal needs that are fulfilled or the social benefits that are derived from their involvement: for instance, rewarding interaction, shared activities, solutions to problems. In short, we expected to receive the kinds of reasons that are enshrined in both formal social psychological theories *and* lay interpretations of group membership and adolescent behaviour.

The question about the importance of being a punk (or whatever) was designed to elicit discussion about the way that membership of the subculture, and the characteristic features of style, lifestyle and so on, enabled a positive social identity. Respondents acknowledged the question's intent insofar as their responses did address issues of identity but they also indicated the inappropriateness of assessing the *importance* of their identity. Sometimes, even when they affirmed the importance of the lifestyle, or of being punk (etc.), they did so, for example by stating that they would not change aspects of their identity, despite the personal and social difficulties they experienced as a consequence. Other respondents affirmed the importance of their subcultural involvement by reporting and denigrating the kind of social category to which they would not wish to belong. In a sense, then, respondents assessed their social identity through invoking 'who I am not'.

We are not alone in this observation. For example, Kitwood (1983:143) noted in relation to South Asian Muslim adolescents that 'through an understanding of what they are not, they have a more assured understanding of who they are'; and Said (1978) argues that identity is often acquired negatively through a sense of what 'we' are not.[8] However, these earlier studies assume a clear demarcation between the 'real me' and 'not me' which respondents simply articulate. By contrast, our respondents' invocation of 'who I am not' seems to be strategically designed to address more inferential concerns.

Consider some of the points we have made about social identity. For example, in Chapter 7 we began to consider self and identity in relation to group affiliation. We described lay and academic assumptions that some young people, in need of a collective identity, conform to criterial attributes of the group, and use them to bring about a change in their self-conception. The analysis has shown, however, that these kinds of assumptions are used as resources to characterise the *inauthenticity and shallowness* of some members. And in their autobiographical accounts, respondents displayed a sensitivity to these kinds of theoretical and lay assumptions; in various ways their accounts were designed precisely to avoid the implication that they were simply conforming to group norms. We noted that accounts of the process of changing self were acutely sensitive to issues of authenticity, and that in our culture self-authenticity was tied to notions conventionally regarded as aspects of individuality. In short, our argument was that the problem with making group membership relevant is that it raises delicate issues concerning the loss of individuality, and hence the inauthenticity of self.

Similarly, in this chapter, we examined the bases of continued affiliation with the group: drawing from the theoretical literature, it seemed reasonable to assume that a central factor would be the positive social identity that was thereby achieved and which becomes an intrinsic aspect of the self. But our respondents employed a number of devices which enabled them to avoid affirming or disconfirming the importance of group membership; indeed, in some cases, responses were constructed to exhibit the *irrelevance* of membership.

The examination of the tacit practical reasoning processes which inform the accounts reveals the kinds of common-sense or inferential issues relevant to our respondents when they are reporting on their lives as members of youth subcultures. One such inferential concern seems to have been that defining the self through group affiliation (and hence conformity) implicates the inauthenticity or shallowness of self-identity. Instead, our respondents' accounts exhibit their tacit understanding that authenticity is achieved when a social identity is a realisation of deeply held personal beliefs, desires or idiosyncratic characteristics.

The conventional social psychological explanations emphasise the positive importance of the social identity that can be attained from affiliation to, and continued membership of, subcultural groups. For example, Turner *et al.* (1987) conceptualise a change in self-perception such that the self comes to embody characteristics of the group. And in a sociological vein, Brake (1985:13) implies that authenticity is accomplished through 'good' performance of the subcultural role, or by accomplishing a change in self-image through resources provided by the subculture. But these explanations neglect common-sense notions about what is required in order to be an authentic person. Indeed, in the design of their talk, young people do discursive work to exhibit that these forms of explanation are not relevant to them. Thereby they display their tacit understanding of the potentially negative inferential consequences of having their own affiliation and membership described in this way.

Our analysis of the ways the participants responded to the question of the advantages of group membership demonstrated a similar concern with issues of authenticity and the motivation for affiliation. Questions about the advantages of group membership assumed that people derived benefits from their involvement. But we also noted that assertions about the benefits of membership could warrant the inference that their involvement is based on the rewards they expect to derive from their membership. And if it is asserted that one's involvement was motivated solely by instrumental concerns, such claims would undermine the authenticity of that affiliation. These kinds of implications are resisted through denying the assumption that there are advantages (and the invitation to list them). Where positive aspects are mentioned, this is done in a way that trivialises them, and the way they are formulated indicates that such aspects are not characterised as advantages of membership.

Respondents design their talk to resist attempts to assess affiliation in terms of what is thereby gained.[9]

Theoretical assumptions about group membership, then, seem strangely removed from the kinds of concerns which actually inform the various ways in which young people talk about their involvement in subcultural groups. The majority of the answers did not address the kinds of benefits and advantages we would have expected from social psychological explanations and lay assumptions about group affiliation.

So far we have considered two main aspects of members' biographies. In Chapters 4, 5 and 6 we examined the subcultural category in relation to issues of self-definition and characterisation of the self, and we described some ways in which respondents made relevant their non-categorical or ordinary identities. In this and the previous chapter, we have been concerned with accounts of involvement with subcultural groups. In these accounts, respondents displayed a sensitivity to issues of individuality and self-authenticity: their utterances were designed to avoid unsympathetic or damaging inferences about themselves which could be warranted by their subcultural affiliation.

In the final analytic chapter we examine how repondents address a final crucial feature of biographical accounts: the *meaning* of the subculture.

Notes

1. The topic of group cohesiveness is long-standing and controversial in the history of social psychology, not least because it is part of the debate about the very existence of social groups as social and psychological realities (see Chapter 2 for further discussion of why the establishment of the group's existence is theoretically important).
2. We owe this observation to Paul Drew.
3. Whereas it is clear that 'that's that' has the character of 'final comment' to a stretch of talk, it is not so obvious from the transcript that the same is true of 'put it that way'. However, two points are relevant. The phrase 'put it that way' was said quite softly, much quieter than the surrounding talk (as indicated by the degree signs) and this feature of its production augments the likelihood that it will be heard as a closing remark. But more significant is that it appears in extract (3) in the equivalent structural position occupied by the phrase 'that's that' in extract (2).
4. Parts of extract (8) were examined earlier in the chapter. In that analysis, we focused only on the first few lines, arguing that the phrase 'put it that way' constituted a 'final comment' on the respondent's turn. Clearly, it did not in fact mark the end of the respondent's answer because he continues. In the light of this it is necessary to warrant our analytic claims about the use of 'put it that way'. There are three points. First, as we mentioned earlier, there are features of the way in which this phrase is produced which make it hearable as final comment. Second, we also noted that it appears in this extract in the equivalent structural position occupied by the phrase 'that's that' in extract (2). Third, observe that after 'put it that way' the respondent goes on to say 'I wouldn't like to be ''orrible trendy'.

1H:M:T5SA [RRF]

```
 1     I:     ↑is it very impo:rtant to you (.)
 2            being a hippy?
 3            (.)
 4     R:     er
 5            (1.2)
 6     R:     I dunno y'know I- well
 7            I wouldn't like to be anything else
 8            °put it that way°
 9            I wouldn't like to be 'orrible trendy
10            smelly yellow shirts
```

Embarking on this description, the respondent recycles the words 'I wouldn't like to be . . .', which were initially produced prior to the phrase 'put it that way'. What seems to be happening, then, is that the respondent does indeed finish his turn with 'put it that way', but then restarts his account, and to establish the continuation of his turn he recycles parts of an utterance produced prior to (what had been initially produced as) the closing comment. (See also Wooffitt and Fraser, 1993.)

5. Due to the transcription difficulties, and the unorthodox syntax, it is not clear what kind of utterance the respondent in extract (7) is making at this point. However, it seems possible if not likely, that he is using the category 'Royal Family' to introduce the kind of behaviour and activities in which he would not like to be involved. By recalling an incident in which the Royal Family were talking about these people, the speaker is able to demonstrate knowledge of the category of 'upper-class jet set' while indicating the absence of any personal experience of these sorts of people. Moreover, although the speaker does not refer to three separate items, he does refer to three distinct attributes conventionally associated with wealthy people in general: a formal style of dress, official events and what is for most people a prohibitively expensive type of car.

6. As we have already indicated, we are treating 'trendy' as a category designation, and not as an adjective used to elaborate the description of the shirts; and as such this term, and the use of a generalised list completer (Jefferson, 1991:676), establish the three-partness of this sequence.

7. It may be thought that the production of such a leading question is simply bad interviewing technique. In our defence, we would point to the substantial theoretical and empirical literature available at the time, both social psychological and sociological, which embodies the assumption that people join subcultural groups so as to derive some kind of personal or social benefits. At the time that these interviews were conducted, then, it seemed hardly contentious to ask a more direct type of question. And of course, at the time that these interviews were conducted, we had no interest in or concern for the interactional or discursive contingencies which inform the design of answers in interviews, and which we eventually came to focus upon in subsequent analyses.

8. See also, R. H. Turner, 1987; and Turner and Gordon, 1981.

9. However, we are not claiming that our respondents never talked of a collective, shared identity. Remember, in extract (1) the second speaker talked of identity, security and similarity to others. Consider also the following extracts in which respondents discuss relationships with other people, notably strangers.

2P:M/F:T8SA [CAM]

```
 1    I:     ˙hh ↑would you say that no:w, y-you felt
 2           some sorta bond with other punks
 3           that you Don't kno:w but you see around
 4           like at gigs or whatever=
 5    FR:    =yeah it's good that like if you GO: to a place
 6           which you DOn't kno:w ˙hh and you see punks
 7           th-that they'll accept you ┌don't they┐=
 8    MR:                               └aie aie  ┘
 9    FR:    they accept you 'cos they know
10           that (.) that you're alright because of your hair
11           or whatever- they know that you're not (.2)
12    I:     is th┌at- is that (.) ┐
13    FR:         └(          )    ┘
14    I:     important to you
15    FR:    i(t)s good that there's sort of like
16           it's good for the community
17           I think that everyone ought to be like that
18           it's just (.) ˙hh it's getting throught though ↓in↑nit
```

1R:M:T5SA [RRF]

```
 1    I:     ˙hh d'you feel tie:s or some sort of bo:nd
 2           with:- with other rockers that you DOn't know
 3           but you see at gigs: or: in the street=
 4    R:     =yeah ┌'cos
 5    I:           └or something
 6    R:     'cos you can sort of go up to them
 7           and say, ˙hh you got a fag mate an'
 8           they say ↑yeah sure have one sortve thing
 8           you know (.) ┌i-i- (.)   ┐
 9    I:                  └°mmhm°     ┘
10    R:     whereas- where you're all the same
11           you're all sort of like one big family
12           sort of thing ˙hhh (.)
13    I:     mmhm
14    R:     °it's really ┌good°
15    I:                  └is that,
16           feeling very important to you
17    R:     yeah 'cos I think it's sort of
18           it jus shows the amount of friendship
19           still ↑left in the world sort of thing ˙hh
20    I:     °mmhm°
21    R:     sort of within our circle
```

In these extracts, notions of kinship, community and sameness are drawn upon, and respondents produce positive assessments of this aspect of social or collective identification. They invoked the kinds of attributes that we expected in relation to their accounts of the importance of being a punk and the benefits that accrue. However, a crucial difference between the extracts above and those we analysed earlier in this chapter is that in the accounts above issues of self-identity and motivation for affiliation are not at stake. Instead, the focus is on characterising relationships with other people. These observations add weight to the argument that in circumstances in which issues of the self, identity and authenticity are at stake, the significance of social identity and group membership is minimised or trivialised.

Chapter 9

RESISTANCE THROUGH RITUAL?
Individualistic and oppositional narratives in formulating the meaning of punk

In Chapter 1, we examined sociological interpretations of the meaning and existence of subcultures and we noted that these neglected the biographical level of what the subculture means to its members. In this chapter, therefore, we present and analyse accounts of the meanings of the subculture provided by the participants in our study who identified themselves as punks at some point in the interview.[1]

Since we focus on the punk subculture, it is useful to recap briefly the main features of the sociological interpretation of the meaning of punk. Punk, like all working-class subcultures, was said to be a form of social and political resistance to dominant cultural hegemony which was achieved through the 'ritual' adoption of subcultural style. Thus, aspects of style symbolised alternative values and conveyed an oppositional message; for example, ripped clothing and the image of clothes that had been thrown together incoherently were seen as a celebration of chaos. Chains, bondage trousers, and similar accessories made public 'the perverse elements of sexuality such as bondage or fetishism . . . emphasising yet mocking it' (Brake, 1985:78). Moreover: 'The safety pins and bin liners signified a relative material poverty which was either directly experienced and exaggerated or sympathetically assumed, and which in turn was made to stand for the spiritual paucity of everyday life' (Hebdige, 1979:115). The punks' image and their claim to be nihilistic, anti-social and anarchic were regarded as a reflection of the recession and rising unemployment in Britain in the late 1970s (Brake, 1985:78). Finally, '[p]unk offered a parody, a taunting portrayal of popular culture, an attack on uncritical consumption of mass-produced artefacts and style' (Brake, 1985:79).

There are good reasons to assume that members' accounts will not reflect these sociological interpretations. An obvious point is that the sociological interpretation is too narrow: style is understood *only* in terms of opposition and resistance (S. Cohen, 1980). Yet even at the time, it was argued that for many members the punk lifestyle represented a hedonistic escape from, rather than a critique of, unfavourable material economic circumstances (Frith, 1978). Moreover, our interviews were conducted in 1987 and 1989, more than ten years after the first appearance of the subculture. In addition, we noted that when providing autobiographical accounts of their lives, members of subcultures could point to style or appearance as constituting an expression of underlying individual difference, intrinsic desires or feelings that *preceded* their public expression. So already we have seen some discrepancies between sociological explanations and members' accounts of the meaning of the subculture and style.

However, we do not wish to propose an alternative version of the meaning of the punk subculture. Indeed, we wish to challenge the assumption that there is *a unitary meaning* to be discovered. Any state of affairs can be described in a variety of different ways (Potter and Wetherell, 1987; Schegloff, 1972), and several researchers have noted that social categories do not have fixed meanings (see, for example, Condor, 1989; Potter and Wetherell, 1987). If we accept the possibility of multiple versions of the meaning of punk, we are liberated from having to view members' accounts as either verifying or disconfirming sociological theories and symbolic interpretations. Instead, we can begin to address new research questions. For example, we can explore some of the culturally available interpretative resources which permeate descriptions of the meanings of punk; and in so doing we begin to see how the subculture, its style and what it means to be a member are discursively fashioned.

In our interviews, we employed a range of questions to elicit accounts of meaning. For example, we asked respondents directly 'what is punk all about, what does it mean?'; we also asked whether, and if so how, punk had changed; and we asked respondents for their opinions on the popular conception of punk as rebellious and anti-establishment. Given our interest in the range of meanings of punk, and in contrast to the analyses presented in previous chapters, we have not restricted our analysis to responses to a specific question. Instead, we have drawn upon a range of circumstances in which accounts of meaning are produced.

In the first part of the analysis, we identify several descriptive strategies employed by speakers. We show how they function to avoid the production of a set of consensual attributes of the subculture, elevating instead the significance of individualistic notions. By contrast, in the second part of the analysis, we examine accounts in which the subculture is formulated as rebellious and anti-establishment, and we point to some interesting features of respondents' oppositional narratives.

Individualistic narratives and the evasion of consensual attributes

Defining punk with reference to the past

Consider the following responses to the question of what the subculture is all about.

(1) 2P:F:T2SB [CM]

1   I: WHAt's, w-<u>wh</u>at's punk all about 'hh

```
 2                (.2)
 3    R1:    hmm: good question hhh huh huh huh ˙hhh hh
 4                (.)
 5    R2:    well it was about (.) it was just a meaning a-
 6                it was a meaning (.) at first
 7                I don't think it is: (.) so much now it was=
 8    I:     =what d'you mean meaning
 9    R2:    well against (.) the system and agai:nst (.)
10                well basically the system (.)
11                the police an' all this sort of thing
12    R1:    I think ba- some of it- it still is a bit no:w
13    I:     ahha
14    R1:    but I think it started off more like that hh
15                (.2)
16    R2:    yea:h that's all it is against ┌everything
17    R1:                                       └°yeah°
18    R2:    °really°
```

(2) 1P:M:T9SA [KHS]

```
 1    I:     what's punk all abou:t?
 2                (2)
 3    R:     e:rm
 4                (2)
 5    R:     I dunno:
 6                (2)
 7    R:     I think (.) when it started
 8                it was (.8) about (.8) changing the system (.)
 9    I:     mmhm
10    R:     but now I don't think there's (.)
11                it's got- I don't think it's got the real,
12                ↑message now
```

In extracts (1) and (2) the speakers first define the punk subculture with
reference to its past meaning or character. So, in extract (1) the second
speaker says 'it was just a meaning a- it was a meaning (.) at first'; and in
extract (2) the speaker formulates a past goal of the subculture: 'I think (.)
when it started it was (.8) about (.8) changing the system'. The respondents
then formulate a comparison which reveals the present to be inferior in some
respect to the past. For example, 'it was a meaning (.) at first I don't think it is:
(.) so much now' (extract 1); and 'I don't think it's got the real ↑message now'
(extract 2). In formulating these contrasts, speakers orient to an ideological or
political dimension of the subculture's past; that is, the meaning was 'against
the system' and the message was about changing the system. In the following

extract, the speaker draws upon another ideological dimension, anarchy, as a
feature of the past.

(3) 1P:F:T7SA [KR]

```
1     I:    well ↑punk's bin around, f-for some ti:me now:
2           do you think it's the sa:m:e or different
3           being a punk ↓now: to what it was:, ten years ago
4     R:    it's definitely different yeah 'cos in the
5           beginning (.) 'hh (.) like, like I said w-
7           had more freedom
8           we could do what we want 'hh well I wasn't
9           here then so I didn:'t, really kno:w:
10          about the beginning you ↑know ┌'hhh
11    I:                                  └°mmhm°
12    R:    but it was definitely different
13          'cos we could, really (1.6) live anarchy 'hhh but
14          now we can't really        ((laughing voice))
15          anymore 'hh
16    I:    mmhm
```

There are two further features of the way speakers formulate the comparison between the past and present subculture. First, their formulations
indicate that the ideological or political dimension of the subculture's past is
diminished but not absent in the contemporary form. For example, in extract
(1), the respondent says 'it was a meaning (.) at first I don't think it is: (.) *so
much now*'; in extract (3) the respondent states that in the beginning 'we had
more freedom' and 'we can't really [live anarchy] anymore' (emphasis added).
By indicating that the specified qualities of the original subculture are not
absent in the contemporary form, the respondents portray the continuity of
the underlying meaning of the subculture.

Second, respondents state their characterisations of the past with certainty;
but they indicate that the meaning of the contemporary subculture is less easily
specified. That is, their references to the characteristics of the punk subculture
in the past are formulated as factual statements: for example, 'when it started it
was (.8) about (.8) changing the system' (extract 2). By contrast, references to
the contemporary meaning are made contingent on the respondents' own
thoughts or cognitions; that is, in extracts (1) and (2) remarks about the contemporary ideological force of punk are prefaced with the phrase 'I don't think'.
There is, then, an asymmetry in the ways that the past and contemporary
meaning of the subculture are described. Verdicts on the past are produced as
factual statements whereas verdicts on the contemporary scene are conditional:
these latter utterances are designed to portray specific views as the speaker's
opinion. But this is counter intuitive: presumably personal experience would

warrant more concrete and certain assessments of the contemporary meaning of the subculture. We may tentatively suggest, however, that one effect of portraying the contemporary meaning of punk as a matter of personal opinion is that speakers thereby avoid producing a set of consensual or criterial features through which to define the contemporary subculture.

Consider also the kinds of inferential work being addressed in extract (3). First, the speaker displays certainty that punks in the past did have more freedom and could follow an anarchic lifestyle. But notice that in lines 8 to 10 she says 'well I wasn't <u>here</u> the<u>n</u> so I didn:'t, really <u>kno:</u>w: about the beginning'. This admission works to portray the irrelevance of direct experience for making claims about the original features of the subculture. Second, throughout her description, she uses the pronoun 'we'. She thereby identifies herself with the subculture in the past and, by implication, with its earlier ideological content. Finally, by suggesting that this dimension is diminished but not lost, she provides an account of her present membership in a subculture now more than ten years old, the contemporary form of which she portrays as inferior.

Distinguishing the subculture and its members

The speaker in extract (2), however, continues his description of the meaning of the subculture.

(4) 1P:M:T9SA [KHS]

1	I:	what's punk all abou:t?
2		(2)
3	R:	e:rm
4		(2)
5	R:	I dunno:
6		(2)
7	R:	I thi<u>nk</u> (.) when it <u>started</u>
8		it was (.8) about (.8) <u>ch</u>anging the syste<u>m</u> (.)
9	I:	mmhm
10	R:	but <u>now</u> I don't think there's (.)
11		it's got- I don't think it's got the <u>real</u>,
12		↑<u>mess</u>age now more like- it's more, the <u>people</u>,
13		who like the music now rather than ⌐'hh
14	I:	└°mmhm°
15	R:	trying, to cha:<u>nge</u>, things
16		it's jus (.) the <u>people</u> who- who like the music
17		an' like (.) dressing the way they do

In lines 12 to 15, the speaker contrasts explicitly the concerns of the contemporary members with those of the earlier members. He states that 'it's more, the <u>pe</u>ople, who like the music now rather than trying, to cha:<u>n</u>ge, things'. Through this contrast between the basis of different members' affiliation, he makes relevant different dimensions of the original and contemporary subculture. That is, he implies that the original subculture was primarily based on an ideological dimension whereas the contemporary subculture is based on appearance and music tastes.

There is a further interesting feature of this extract. In the previous section, we noted that he defined the original subculture in terms of its ideological goal which he says is diminished in the contemporary form (line 4). But the contrast he produces in lines 7 to 9 above refers to *members* of the subculture. Similarly, when he produces his assessment of the contemporary meaning of the subculture in lines 16 and 17, it is the members to which he refers: 'it's jus (.) the *people* who- who like the music an' like (.) dressing the way they do' (emphasis added). The implication is that whereas the original subculture had a common ideological meaning and goal, the contemporary subculture is constituted through individuals with particular but personal preferences.

A similar though more subtle distinction is made relevant in the following extract. In this extract, however, the interviewer offers an ideological or oppositional dimension as potentially relevant in defining the subculture.

(5) 1Hippy/Punk:F:T7SB [KG]

1	I:	↑well <u>b</u>oth <u>pu</u>nks and <u>hi</u>ppies are of:ten
2		sort of por<u>tra</u>yed in the <u>me</u>dia as being re<u>be</u>llious
3		an: (.) anti es<u>tab</u>lishment and so on ˙hhh
4		d'you think that's ↑a<u>cc</u>urate
5	R:	<u>n</u>:ot re:ally I mean, you <u>ju</u>s:: sort of,
6		<u>do</u>ing what you want to <u>do</u>
7		it's just (.) it's: (.) just the way
8		you wanna <u>be</u> innit (w-) it's <u>no</u>: reason
9		why you gotta <u>dr</u>ess the <u>sa</u>:me
10		as <u>e</u>veryone <u>e</u>lse
11	I:	mm ⌐hm
12	R:	⌊it's just, you as a <u>per</u>son (.) <u>re</u>ally,
13		sort of not <u>fo</u>llowing the <u>sheep</u> and
14		<u>dr</u>essing e<u>xa</u>ctly how <u>e</u>veryone ↑<u>e</u>lse is (.)
15	I:	mmhm
16		(.)
17	R:	°really°

The interviewer asks about the accuracy of the media portrayal of punks and hippies as rebellious and anti-establishment. The respondent does not deny the relevance of these attributes outright: she claims instead that they are 'not really [accurate]'. She then produces an alternative account of subcultural membership. Her account is formulated as a three-part list in which she invokes the following features of a punk or hippy lifestyle.

1. you jus:: sort of, doing what you want to do
2. it's: (.) just the way you wanna be
3. it's no: reason why you gotta dress the sa:me
   as everyone else

We noted in previous chapters that listing may be used to indicate to the recipient that there is a general or common quality which connects the items in the list (Atkinson, 1984a and b; Jefferson, 1991). In the extract above, the three components make relevant the qualities of independence or autonomy in activities, appearance and lifestyle. The significance of individual autonomy is reinforced through the way she produces, undermines, and rejects an alternative basis of appearance. She says that 'it's just, you as a person (.) really, sort of not following the sheep and dressing exactly how everyone ↑else is' (lines 12 to 14) and 'it's no: reason why you gotta dress the sa:me' (lines 8 and 9). Her description thus portrays a picture of blind conformity in which it is implied that their sameness is due to a herd instinct.

The implication is that punks are individuals; consequently punk cannot be defined solely through ideological dimensions. Returning to the interactional circumstances within which this account is produced, we can suggest that the respondent interprets the question as focusing on the idea that the subcultures can be defined in terms of a relatively limited set of attributes. She resists this idea by undermining the definitional status of rebellion and anti-establishment views, and by emphasising individual rather than criterial reasons for adopting a particular lifestyle and style.

Although extracts (4) and (5) are clearly different in many respects, respondents in both make two significant distinctions. First, they minimise the relevance of ideological dimensions in defining the subculture, elevating instead the significance of appearance as one feature of the contemporary membership. Hence, built into their accounts is a contrast between ideology and appearance. Second, the respondents draw a further distinction between dimensions of the subculture and the basis of members' involvement.

The distinction between the subculture and individual members reflects a conceptual ambiguity in the sociological literature. In Chapter 1 we noted that the term 'punk', for example, was sometimes used to refer to the constellation of cultural elements such as style, music and values which exist independently of members. The term was also used to refer to a group of people who share values, experiences and lifestyle. In the accounts above, by drawing a distinction between them, it is implied that these two ways of portraying punk are not necessarily equivalent; that is, the bases of members' affiliation need not equate with criterial features of the subculture. This distinction is then used as a resource: because by making relevant the idea that subcultures are constituted through individual members, speakers are able to define the contemporary subculture through individualistic notions of personal tastes and preferences, and autonomy.

In the following extract, we can observe a further use of this distinction. In this extract, however, the speaker indicates that the meaning of the subculture is independent of (some) members' motivation for affiliation. He thereby elevates the ideological dimension of the subculture as criterial.

(6) 1P:M:T10SA [PC]

```
1     I:    PEople were talking about different reasons,
2           for: (.) being punk (.) do you think
3           there're different reasons
4           (3.2)
5     R:    PUNKS give one meaning (.) an' that's it
6           it means
7           (1.6)
8     R:    anti system (.) °an' that's it°
9           I mean there's not there's not any other
10          mean(ing) that's what punks all about (.)
11          anti system
12    I:    an' is that why: people, because they're
13          anti pu- anti:, system, become punks do you think
14          °or d'you think not°
15    R:    NAW: a lot of people jus:, sorta
16          like the. the hairstyles an'
17          the way the way they dress but tha- (.)
18          that is the right meaning
19          that's why it all started, (t-) shock people
20          and, rebel against society
21    I:    mmhm
22    R:    d'you know what I mean
```

It is interesting to note how the interviewer's questions constitute two attempts to elicit an account of members' motivation. She first produces a warrant for assuming that there is variability in the basis of individuals' affiliation: 'PEople were talking about different reasons, for: (.) being punk'. Her subsequent question, 'do you think there're different reasons' invites the respondent to affirm (or deny) this assumption. However, the respondent states that 'PUNKS give one meaning (.) an' that's it it means (1.6) anti system (.) °an' that's it°' (lines 5 to 8). The interviewer's subsequent question suggests that she is looking to see how this statement constitutes an answer to her prior question: 'an' is that why: people, because they're anti pu- anti:, system, become punks do you think °or d'you think not°'. This is dismissed and the respondent then provides an answer to the question of motivation which makes relevant a different basis for membership: 'NAW: a lot of people jus:, sorta like the. the hairstyles an' the way the way they dress' (lines 15 to 17). The implication is that despite members' varied and discrepant motivation for their membership, the subculture retains an anti-system ideology. Finally, he reinforces his claim that punk is anti-system, by stating that this is 'the right meaning that's why it all started, (t-) shock people and, rebel against society' (lines 18 to 20).

Therefore, we may suggest that the distinction between the subculture and its members may be used as a flexible resource in formulating the meaning of punk. In addition, we noted in relation to extracts (4) and (5) that built into the distinction between the subculture and individual members was a distinction between ideology and appearance; in extract (6) the speaker draws upon a similar distinction. But notice how respondents characterise members' appearance. In extract (6) the respondent says that 'a lot of people jus:, sorta like the. the hairstyles an' the way the way they dress'; and the speakers in extracts (4) and (5) refer to people who 'like dressing the way they do'. Characterising members' appearance in this way rather than, say, in terms of their preference for punk style addresses a sensitive inferential issue. Because if it is inferred that many members affiliate because they like the style, this could make relevant an alternative definition of the subculture as a style or image. This inference would in turn undermine the speakers' claim that being a punk depends on individual preferences and desires (extracts 4 and 5); and in extract (6), the availability of such inferences would undermine the speaker's claim that ideology is the primary meaning of the subculture.[2]

Portraying the diversity of the subculture's meanings

In the following extract, the speaker states explicitly that the subculture is hard to describe because there's so [many] different meanings about punks.

(7) 1P:F:T7SA [KR]

```
1      I:    ↑WHat's punk all about
2            (.)
3      R:    ·hhh e::r well I dunno i- (.) tch
4            it's har:d to descri:be 'cos er:,
5            there's so different meanings about punks
6            usually people think ·hh
7            (1)
8      R:    it's just destroying everything an h- hatred
9            an::: (.) all that
10           but I'm not really into:, fighting a:nd
11           war an' all that          ((laughing voice))
```

```
12      R:      I (.) I- I dunno if I'm a typical punk
13              in: th:at direction I- just w-
14              I'm more peaceful ⌈·hh
15      I:                       ⌊mmhm
16      R:      but, it's like mainly about anarchy
17              >do what you want do what you like<
18              (1.2)
19      I:      mmhm
20      R:      ·hh anti: government so no one:,
21              no one is for the government
22              no one likes Maggie Thatcher          ((laughing voice))
23              ·hhh HUH who does anyway
24              heh heh heh heh huh huh huh ·hhh
25              an' er (.) anti:, anti Chu:rch but ·hh
26              there're a few they're like, sort of:,
27              Christians but there're
28              not too many of them so most of them are
29              ↑anti Church as well ·hhh ju- it's mainly
30              do what you want do what you like
31              dress up what you like and don't give
32              a f:uck about anything ·hhh
33      I:      mmhm
```

In extract (7), the respondent lists attributes which may be considered as criterial or defining features of the subculture: nihilism and violence, anarchy, anti-church and so on. However, she goes on to undermine the validity of each of these criterial features. For example, she refers to other people's views of destructive and negative attributes of the subculture. But she then says that she does not personally endorse such attributes. Therefore it is implied that they are not necessary for being a punk. Second, she states that punk is 'anti-government' (line 20). But she then invokes the generality of this claim by asking the rhetorical question, 'who does [like Margaret Thatcher] anyway? (line 23).[3] An 'anti-government' position is thus characterised as being widespread throughout the population, and the speaker thereby establishes that it cannot be regarded as a criterial attribute of the punk subculture. Third, she produces the assertion that punk is 'anti-church' (line 25). Yet the categorical nature of this statement is undermined by her subsequent utterances in which she raises exceptions to this claim: punks who are also Christians. Billig (1985, 1987; Billig et al., 1988) too has noted that categorical statements are always open to challenge by particularised statements or exceptions to the rule. It seems that this is a common discursive strategy which may be employed to avoid making general, criterial claims about the meaning or constitution of social categories. It is, moreover, worth noting that this descriptive strategy rests on the way that social groups can also be characterised through their membership.

Nevertheless, in the final part of her account, the respondent does produce an unqualified summary assessment of the meaning of punk. But her assessment makes relevant individual desires and motivation, rather than any feature that is obviously or conventionally associated with the subculture. She says punk is all about doing 'what you want', and '[doing] what you like' (line 30). Again, she makes relevant the idea that the subculture is defined through individualistic notions, rather than subculture-specific features.

Similarly, in the following extract the respondent lists several definitions of punk, such as music and the behaviour of individual punks, before concluding that, in his opinion, a punk is someone who doesn't fit in.

(8) 2P:M:T18SA [B]

```
1     R:    depends what you mean by punk though like
2           i- i- if- if you take (.) 'hhh
3           if you take punk as a music
4           >especially which is just sort of<
5           a: a punk a sort of spiky haired, individual
6           drinking a can of beer and spitting at
7           at the camera an' that (y-) know
8           or if you take punk as something which is (.)
9           'hhh wh-wh- which is the way I take it
10          wh- is something whi- which could mean,
11          basically ANYthing as long as y'know
12          it doesn't have to be, a certain set
13          of values or a certain way of dress 'hhh
14          it's basically sort of like somebody who
15          jus doesn't (.) 'hhh 'hh somebody
16          who doesn't s- sort of f- a- a- fit in an' that
```

The implication is that *individual difference* is a more appropriate basis for defining membership than criterial attributes (for example 'a certain sort of values').

To summarise, in the extracts we have presented so far, we have seen that respondents mobilised a number of descriptive strategies which in various ways enabled them to avoid producing a consensual or criterial meaning of the contemporary subculture. For example, although speakers portrayed the contemporary meaning in terms of the diminution of past ideology, their verdicts were made contingent on their personal opinion. Second, in some accounts, we saw that the distinction between the subculture and its membership was used to characterise punk through individualistic rather than criterial attributes, or to question the criterial status of potentially relevant dimensions. Punk was therefore made contingent on its membership. Third, a number of respondents claimed that being a punk was partly about the expression of autonomy in appearance. So that, while punks' appearance was made relevant, their accounts of its significance were clearly different to those found in the sociological literature. New Subcultural theorists claimed that the ideological or political significance of the subculture was expressed through style; here we see a clear separation between these two dimensions of the subculture. Moreover, in their accounts, speakers make relevant the idea that appearance is based on individual autonomy, not collective or symbolic resistance.

Nevertheless, some respondents did attribute to the subculture an oppositional and rebellious significance. We have already seen that some respondents pointed to the meaning of the original subculture as anti-system. In the following section, we examine accounts in which such notions are made relevant in formulations of the contemporary subculture.

Oppositional narratives

In the following extract, for example, the speaker says that punk is about 'do[ing] what you want' and 'do[ing] your ain [own] thing'. These formulations are similar to the individualistic characterisations of the meaning of being a punk that we examined above. But he also describes the subculture in a way that resonates with themes made on behalf of the subculture in the sociological literature: 'just to screw the system up'.

(9) 1P:M:T6SB [KGR]

```
 1      I:    WHat's punk all ab↑out
 2            (.)
 3      R:    WHy?, er: what's it all about
 4            (.)
 5      I:    yeah
 6      R:    jus sortA (.) 'hhh screw the system u:p
 7            you know, and ER: (.) 'hhh
 8            do what you want (.) do your ain thing
 9            you know,
10      I:    mmhm=
11      R:    =jus:t (.) without having
12            (.6)
13            big brother looking (da) know: HUH
14            'hh huh ya still do tha
15      I:    mm what d'you mean by screw the system ↑up
16            (.8)
17      R:    we:ll you know no: s:- (.)
```

18		well we cannae screw the system up
19		obviously you know, becaus:e, huh hh
20		you'd just end up inside
21		(1.4)
22	R:	but it is just showing you know,
23		that you're against it sorta thing (.)
24	I:	mmhm
25	R:	y'know it's:: (.) tch a mess the way it is
26		(.2)
27	I:	mmhm

We can make two initial observations about the phrase 'just to screw the system up'. First, it is a formulaic or idiomatic characterisation of 'resistance'. Indeed such phrases have sometimes been cited in the sociological literature as poor but nevertheless supportive evidence for the symbolic message conveyed by the subculture. Second, the idea of *'screwing* the system up' implicates some form of activity in a way that, say, *being* against the system does not. Therefore, the interviewer's next question, 'what d'you mean by screw the system ↑up', may be treated as an invitation to the speaker to describe *how* punks attempt to accomplish this objective. He does not, however, provide this kind of answer. And this raises the analytic question, why should he decline the invitation to expand upon a feature of the subculture which he had initially introduced?

In a study of the interactional and sequential properties of idioms in ordinary conversation, Drew and Holt (1989) argue that these kinds of formulaic expressions are rarely treated as *factual* claims or statements of information. (For example, it is unlikely that the use of an idiom like 'Rome wasn't built in a day' would be followed by the question, 'well how long *did* it take?'.) Conventionally, then, in everyday conversational interaction, idiomatic expressions go unchallenged or unquestioned.

In extract (9) the interviewer's question (line 15) is designed to elicit a description of what exactly punks do to demonstrate their political and moral resistance to the status quo. But in so doing, it can be interpreted as an attempt to elicit the conventionally irrelevant factual basis of the formulaic expression 'screw up the system'. As such, it can be heard as a challenge to the use of that expression.

Similarly, in the following extracts we can observe the kinds of reactions that might be expected when respondents are asked to unpack formulaic expressions of the meaning of punk. In these extracts, however, the speakers do not use formulaic expressions. Instead, the interviewer's question embodies precisely the kinds of lay intuitions about subcultures portrayed by formulaic expressions: that punks are rebellious and anti-establishment and so on; for example, one speaker in extract (10) comments on the difficulty of unpacking the notion that punks are like this (line 15). In extract (11) the speaker produces two further questions, 'what do you want to know eh' and 'anti system and rebellious?' (lines 7 and 13). And in extract (10) one respondent indicates that 'that's about it you about summed it up heh a- a- anti establishment'.

(10) 2P:F:T2SB [CAM]

```
 1      I:      in the- in the media an' that (.) p- punks
 2              are often sort of looked upon as rebe:llious and
 3              anti establishment 'hh and so on
 4              d'you think that's accurate?
 5              (.)
 6      R1:     I think so, ┌yes
 7      R2:                 └°yeah° (.) yeah
 8      I:      c'n you tell me any more abou:t ┌°that°
 9      R2:                                     └e::rm
10              (.8)
11      ?       hhh (.) ·hh
12              (1.8)
13      ?       hmm
14              (1)
15      R2:     don't- don't know how to explain it °really°
16      R1:     you summed it up (there)
17      R2:     yeah heh heh ┌·hh
18      I:                   └sorry?
19      R1:     I said that's about it you about summed it up heh
20              a- a- anti establishment          ((laughing voice))
21              hh huh huh ·hh
22              (.2)
23      I:      an' how- how d'you think that you show
24              that (.) you're anti establishment
25      R1:     we don't really any more
26      R2:     no: (.) I mean apart from the way we loo:k
```

(11) 1P:M:T6SB [KGR]

```
 1      I:      w- punks are often portrayed in the media
 2              as being rebellious and anti establishment
 3              d'you think that's ↑accurate
 4      R:      yeah (.)
 5              huh heh heh heh hh hh huh
 6      I:      c- can you tell me something more?      ((laughing voice))
 7      R:      'hh 'hh ugh 'hh what do you want to know eh
 8              huh huh huh hh hh
 9      I:      how do you show it
```

10		(1.4)
11	R:	well
12		(2)
13	R:	err wi- <u>anti</u> system and re<u>bell</u>ious?
14		(.)
15	I:	hmm
16		(2)
17	R:	<u>dunno</u> just (.) huh huh huh huh ˙hhh just <u>do</u>
18	I:	mmhm
19		(.4)
20	R:	(mm) well you've got a <u>lot</u> of punks that
21		don't sign <u>on</u> an' that you know
22		<u>but</u> phew
23		(.2)
24	R:	because, 'cos of the <u>system</u> an', ˙hh things
25		you kno⌐w
26	I:	└who <u>don't</u> sign on=
27	R:	↓ye⌐↑ah=
28	I:	=└did you say?
29		(.)
30	I:	mmhm
31	R:	no for, ju<u>st</u> ˙hh wouldna <u>take</u> any money off
32		the Gove<u>rn</u>ment sort of thi<u>ng</u> (.) ˙hh
33		but (.) we all need <u>money</u> to sur<u>vive</u>
34		<u>anyway you know</u>
35	I:	mm
36	R:	so (.) beg steal or borrow hhh
37		huh huh huh huh

Thus, the interviewer's questions in extracts (9) to (11) can be seen as establishing a challenge by questioning the factual status of the kind of claims about the meaning of punk which are not normally open to question. Nonetheless, despite the inappropriateness of interrogating formulaic assessments of the subculture, the integrity of their initial claims is at stake. Subsequently, therefore, respondents do produce a version of punks' resistance.

Let us consider first extract (9). We can observe several features of the respondent's turn subsequent to the interviewer's question. First, he produces a *retraction*: 'we:ll you know no: s:- (.) well <u>we</u> cannae screw the system up <u>obviously</u>'. This retraction accomplishes two interactional tasks. It is a display of what the speaker has inferred to be the basis of the interviewer's challenge: that it is effectively impossible to change the status quo. But it also allows the speaker to align himself with the interviewer; that is, by characterising the unlikelihood of effective resistance as 'obvious', the speaker is 'doing agreement' with the prior challenge. Second, there is an *account* for the retraction:

'becaus:e, huh hh you'd just end up inside'. (We take it as uncontentious that in this context the speaker is referring to gaol when he says 'inside'.) Here, then, the speaker focuses on the personally damaging consequences of *actual* resistance to account for the *in-principle* impossibility of effective resistance. Third, the speaker then produces a *modified version* of his initial description of the oppositional meaning of punk. Specifically, 'screwing up the system' is amended to 'but it is just showing you know, that you're against it sorta thing'. Although a less strident formulation of active opposition, this description establishes the underlying relevance of some form of resistance. Finally the speaker refers to it [the system] as 'it's:: (.) tch a mess the way it is'. This negative reflection on civil life therefore stands as a *warrant* for the (now modified) claim that punk is about showing opposition and resistance.

In extracts (10) and (11), the interviewer produces a further question which invites the respondents to describe how they show that they are rebellious and anti-establishment. But the first speaker in extract (10) produces a retraction: she denies that the subculture remains rebellious (despite having affirmed that it is just some seconds earlier). The second respondent, however, invokes the punks' appearance as an indication of their continued oppositional position (echoing a central argument of the New Subcultural theories).

(from extract 10)

| 25 | R1: | we don't really any more |
| 26 | R2: | no: (.) I mean apart from the way we loo:k |

The implication is that in contrast to earlier manifestations of being anti-establishment, opposition is currently realised through a mundane aspect of their everyday lives: 'the way we look'. In extract (11), the speaker points to the way that some punks refuse to take state-provided financial entitlements as an instance of opposition.

(from extract 11)

20	R:	(mm) well you've got a lot of punks that
21		don't sign on an' that you know
22		but phew
23		(.2)
24	R:	because, 'cos of the system an', 'hh things
25		you know

Here, then, opposition is established through a passive activity: *not* accepting state benefits.[4]

The point is that when formulaic characterisations of punks' oppositional stance are challenged with an invitation to describe how their sentiments are made manifest, speakers do describe ways in which opposition can be

demonstrated by punks. But it is noticeable that in both cases the oppositional activities are not cases of direct action; their formulations are not
made contingent upon drastic public displays or avowedly rebellious
activities.[5] Instead, they invoke routine or mundane features of their everyday lives, or their abstention from conventionally expected and prescribed
courses of behaviour. A similar emphasis on the mundane can be observed
in the following extracts.

Extract (12) follows a long list of complaints: about the poll tax, restrictions
on the use of common land, police harassment, etc.

(12) Group discussion with punks: T11SB [RRF]

```
1     I:       you're saying you're against all this,
2              how- how do you show that
3     MR1:     how do I show it
4     I:       mmhm
5     ?        (              )
6     MR1:          ⌐I get arrested, every weekend
7              heh heh (.) ⌐hah hah heh
8                         ⌊((group laughter))
9     FR:      ˙hhh hh
10             (.)
11    MR1:     no (.) I mean you know huh ˙hh it's (.)
12             I've been in prison seven times right
13    I:       ahha
14    MR1:     the last sentence I done right
15             I sat in the block d'you know what the block is (.)
16             yeah? the block is:, you know (.)
17             I've forgotten the word, that they use
18             I only know it as the block (.) ˙hh
19             when you're on your own ˙hh
20             um isolation yeah
21    I:       ahha
22    MR1:     >I was in< an' I sa- I was there for
23             twenty seven days ˙hh an' I sat the whole time
24             like that ˙hh (.) smiling
25             (.8)
26             an' every time they looked through the
27             little thing[6] I was sat there (.) smiling at them
28             ˙hhh that's what I think of the system
29             hmm hmm BOllocks to it, it's a shit system you know
30             (.) I hope I can swear (again ah)
31             hhh hah ⌐(.) hah
32                     ⌊((group laughter))
```

Initially, the speaker reports frequent encounters with the law as a means of showing his opposition. However, it is not the speaker's claim to have been repeatedly imprisoned which forms the basis of his oppositional narrative; rather, he elects to display his opposition by reporting one feature of a recent incarceration. He describes his behaviour during a period of isolation: 'an' I sat the whole time like that 'hh (.) smiling'. The oppositional character of 'smiling' is in part affirmed by his detailed report of the length of time he spent in isolation (twenty-seven days) and the way he portrays the maximum possible case of smiling during this period. It is also affirmed through the inferences we may draw about the inappropriateness of this behaviour in the circumstances. These inferences are based on our cultural knowledge regarding the purpose and anticipated effects of isolation on the part of the prison authorities. That is, being put in isolation implicates fairly severe punishment, to which an appropriate or desired response might be penitence, or at the very least negative affect such as loneliness. It is through these descriptive strategies that the respondent accomplishes the status of his behaviour as resistance, or a display of 'what I think of the system'.

In the following extract, the respondent invokes a different form of interpersonal behaviour to characterise punks' rebellion.

(13) 1P:F:T7SA [KG]

```
1     I:    you ↑said befo:re that you thought,
2           some punks were rebe:llious:
3           how, do they (.) sh:ow that
4           (.6)
5     R:    tch
6           (.)
7     R:    e:rr hh like in doing different things
8           like everyone else ↑does (.) hh
9     I:    mmhm=
10    R:    =I mean
11          (1.4)
12    R:    e:r
13          (3)
14    R:    tch like just being different
15          not being polite 'cos er (.) THE:: (.)
16          the British race⁷ I think is very polite
17          they're always saying hh thank ↑you: and
18          they're queuing u:p and punks
19          they wouldn't do that you know 'hh
```

In this extract, the respondent formulates two ways in which punks demonstrate their rebellion. First, she claims that it is manifested in 'doing different things like everyone else ↑does'. The implication is that punks do not ascribe to conventional activities or forms of behaviour. Second, she produces a specific example of punks' difference: not being polite. This is warranted as an instance of rebellion by formulating politeness as a feature of the 'British race'. As in extract (11), it is noticeable that rebellion is formulated as abstention from or refusal to engage in socially expected behaviour, rather than through direct action.

In summary, we have examined several accounts of the ways that punks do or may exhibit opposition to the status quo. We observed in particular that these oppositional narratives do not invoke radical activities or public displays of resistance; rather, they are fashioned around the routine, the personal and the everyday. Moreover, like all narratives, they are mediated through communicative contingencies generated in the course of face-to-face interaction. For example, they are produced in response to an implicit challenge to formulaic expressions and hence threats to the integrity of respondents' claims that punk is about rebellion and being anti-establishment.

In Chapter 1, we noted that it was left to the sociologist to point to the (largely symbolic) meaning of the subculture because it was assumed that punks themselves were inarticulate. It was also considered unlikely that the members of the subculture would be aware of the symbolic significance of their style. There was no concerted attempt to ask punks themselves about the meaning of the subculture, nor about the forms their resistance took. But punks do have their own accounts of what the subculture means and of its social significance. For example, in the extracts we presented above, the subculture was characterised through reference to an ideological or political dimension such as being against the system or government; in addition, anarchy, nihilism and violence were invoked, as well as music and appearance. However, respondents also characterised the subculture through the bases of members' affiliation: individual preferences, desires and autonomy.

Clearly, then, our analysis questions the assumption that punk has a common meaning and that this revolves around a symbolic resistance to the social order. Indeed, in our analysis we identified several devices which were mobilised to avoid producing a unitary meaning or set of criterial attributes through which the subculture may be defined. For example, some respondents indicated that while a unitary or consensual meaning in terms of shared goals or values may be a feature of the original subculture, the contemporary meaning was a matter of personal opinion. In other extracts, respondents portrayed the diversity of meanings of punk as a warrant for the difficulty in specifying *the* meaning of the subculture. And even formulations of their appearance displayed a sensitivity to its potential criterial relevance.

One of the most interesting features of these accounts concerned respondents' orientation to the way that punk may be constituted both through shared goals, values and so on, and through individual members. The implicit distinction between these two characterisations of punk had related functional effects. It indicated that they are not necessarily equivalent, and this in turn enabled the respondent in extract (6) to preserve the ideological meaning of the subculture, while acknowledging many members' discrepant motivations. By contrast, in other extracts, the distinction was used to undermine the relevance of shared attributes; instead, punk was characterised through individualistic notions. On the one hand, respondents' orientation to individualism was not surprising given our observations in Chapters 7 and 8 about the kinds of problematic inferences that may be drawn if it is implied that members aspire to a collective identity through shared attributes. For example, collective identity implies a loss of individuality and consequently implicates self-inauthenticity. On the other hand, in earlier chapters, our focus was on *personal* accounts of membership and the significance of affiliation. In this chapter, we were concerned to elicit more *general* definitions of the meaning of the subculture: yet even here we have observed the use of similarly individualistic descriptive resources.

Moreover, these observations raise interesting issues to do with theoretical conceptualisations of subcultural groups: in particular, the 'problem' of group constitution. Remember that in Chapter 2 we described social scientists' efforts to reconcile claims that groups can be regarded as independent 'wholes' and as collections of individuals. Here, we begin to see that social scientists' problem is a resource used by respondents in portraying the meaning of the subcultural group.

However, individualistic narratives are not the only means available for formulating the meaning of punk. Indeed, some respondents' orientation to the political or ideological dimension of punk was obviously resonant with both the sociological and lay theorising about the meaning of the subculture. This is not surprising, for sociological interpretations have permeated the media and become part of our lay or common-sense knowledge about the meaning of subcultures; so that it is a culturally available assumption that punks are 'rebelling against society'.[8] These kinds of explanatory formulations for social behaviour are interpretative resources which both insiders and outsiders can draw upon in making sense of the subculture. Moreover, it is perhaps because of the availability of the sociological assessments of the subculture's meaning that respondents' descriptions of punks' rebellion often had the character of formulaic assessments.

This point has implications for the 'vexing issue of consciousness and intent' (S. Cohen, 1980: xiii). In one sense, respondents do display an awareness of what the subculture is supposed to mean: they formulated punk as rebellion or resistance and invoked the common-sense status of this meaning. On the other hand, with the exception of extract (10), speakers did not characterise resistance to the system by reference to appearance. And in some extracts we saw that they drew a clear distinction between ideological dimensions and appearance. So, we may argue that resistance through style is but one discursive strategy: it is not the case that 'being against the system' is inevitably expressed in style. Indeed, we also saw how oppositional narratives can be built into descriptions of mundane or routine features of everyday lives, or of abstention from anticipated or prescribed activities. Of course, it is not the case that activities like not signing on, not being polite and smiling in the isolation block are intrinsically rebellious; their significance as such is constituted in respondents' accounts. In other words, opposition is not an intrinsic feature of particular activities or of appearance; the oppositional significance of punks' activities and lifestyle is achieved through their descriptions of those activities and so on. Therefore, resistance is a discursive not a symbolic act.

The 'meaning' of the subculture is therefore a variable commodity. If we take this point seriously, we are liberated from the search for what exactly these phenomena mean (cf. S. Cohen, 1980). Rather than impose a rigid interpretation derived from largely theoretical academic explanations, it becomes more appropriate to address the variable meanings of the subculture as they inform members' accounts.

Notes

1. By restricting our analytic focus to accounts of the meaning of the punk subculture, we were able to ensure that analytic observations were based on a range of accounts of ostensibly the same phenomenon. Moreover, in contrast to the gothic and rocker subcultures, there is relatively extensive commentary on the punk subculture within New Subcultural Theories, so that we were able to re-examine sociological interpretations of punk alongside its members' own accounts.

2. Moreover, we saw in earlier chapters, that formulating subcultural style or image as a *motivation* for affiliation may be used to characterise the shallowness or inauthenticity of certain members. The phrase 'the way they dress', by contrast, does not have the same strongly negative connotations since it avoids making directly relevant a preference for *punk* style or image.

3. Margaret Thatcher was the Prime Minister when the interviews were conducted.

4. It is interesting that the respondent cites not signing on (claiming state benefits due to unemployment) as an instance of opposition. Claiming state benefits is conventionally regarded as an economic necessity; and the speaker acknowledges this when he states, in lines (33 to 34): 'but (.) we all need money to survive anyway you know so (.) beg steal or borrow'. Moreover, Marsh (1977) characterised punk as 'dole queue rock' and argued that punks emphasised their resistance to work by making themselves unemployable. So, for Marsh, signing on is anti-establishment insofar as it is a consequence of resistance to a system in which working is a conventionally prescribed activity. However, the respondent makes relevant a different interpretation of not signing on: '[they] wouldna take money off the Government'. He therefore implies that some punks are anti-establishment because they refuse to participate in a system of state benefits which makes them dependent upon the Government.

5. Indeed, the turn which follows R2's characterisation of punks' opposition through appearance implicates the relevance of this distinction to the participants. In this

turn, R1 invokes a distinction between routine and more active and direct forms of opposition.

2P:F:T2SB [CAM]

1	I:	<u>an</u>' <u>how</u>- <u>how</u> d'you think that you <u>show</u>
2		that (.) you're <u>an</u>ti es<u>tab</u>lishment
3	R1:	we don't really any <u>more</u>
4	R2:	<u>no:</u> (.) I mean apart from the way we <u>loo</u>:k
5		(.)
6	R1:	ye:ah (.) I mean there's some (.) like sort of
7		you get anarchist, t- type tramp punks
8	R2:	mm
9	R1:	the:y do a lot of <u>ma</u>rches about-
10		against the <u>ri</u>ch an' (.) <u>an</u>imal rights
11		and all this lot (.2) °<u>so</u>::° (.)
12		but <u>pun</u>ks don't
13		(.2)
14		we:ll I mean SOme of them <u>do</u>:
15		but a <u>lot</u> of them are just in for it
16		for the <u>mu</u>sic an' the <u>way</u> it ⌐is
17	R2:	└mhmm
18	R1:	the way you look (.) a lot of them,
19		just like the <u>mu</u>sic ˙hh

There are several interesting features of this account. The speakers describe and hence acknowledge different ways through which punks show they are anti-establishment: 'the way we <u>loo</u>:k' and 'do[ing] a lot of <u>ma</u>rches about against the <u>ri</u>ch an' (.) <u>an</u>imal rights and all this lot'. The second speaker thereby acknowledges that overt demonstrations of resistance do exist as an alternative means of realising anti-establishment sentiments. Nonetheless, she avoids making political activism a feature of the punk subculture or lifestyle. She attributes political activities to 'anarchist type tramp punks', thereby drawing a distinction between punks and activists. She also states that (most) punks don't go on marches. Finally, she states that 'a <u>lot</u> of [punks] are just in it for the <u>mu</u>sic an' the <u>way</u> it is the way you look'. She therefore builds an implicit contrast between different bases of affiliation: political concerns and activities, and music tastes and appearance. So, she denies political concerns as a primary motivating factor for most punks' affiliation with the subculture, and she thereby reinforces her earlier claim that political activism is not a feature of the subculture.

6. He is presumably here referring to the window in the cell door.
7. The speaker's use of the phrase 'the British *race*' indicates that she is not British. A slight accent suggested that she was of perhaps German origin. Despite the fact that she is therefore not a native speaker, we have included her in our analysis because of her fluency in English.
8. Indeed, this assumption informed the interviewer's question, in which she referred to media portrayals, and invited respondents to confirm, correct, celebrate this portrayal or whatever.

Chapter 10

SOCIAL SELVES IN ACTION

Our primary aims in this book were twofold. First, we wanted to address the hitherto neglected biographical level of subcultural analysis. Biography[1] encompasses several aspects of a person's involvement in a particular subculture: issues of identity and self-definition; the process of affiliation with and continued commitment to a particular subculture; and members' accounts of the meaning of the subculture (S. Cohen, 1980). Our analysis has addressed each of these aspects and, in the first part of this chapter, we summarise our main analytic conclusions and situate them in the context of the literature on social identity and subcultural groups.

Second, we wanted to make a contribution to more general contemporary debates about the relationship between individuals and social groups or society. Central in these debates were issues of the ontology, or the nature of the self, identity and action, human agency and social structure. In the second half of this chapter we discuss how the results from our analyses cast new light on these issues.

Subcultures and biography

It has not been our intention to crystallise subcultural identity and experience to produce a generalised account of members' biographies. Instead, we have focused on identifying the language strategies employed by respondents through which they formulate their identities, and discuss their involvement with subcultures. These devices are part of the stock of cultural communicative skills and competencies possessed by native members of a language community.

This analytic emphasis has yielded important methodological benefits. The kinds of discursive practices we have charted are not necessarily associated with specific social groups or collections of persons. Rather, they are part of the culturally available, tacit skills which all members possess by virtue of their integration within a natural language community. Therefore, our analytic claims may be relevant to a wider community of persons than those whose accounts are examined here.

We begin, then, with a review of the kinds of skills and strategies we have identified throughout. We will then point to several issues which permeate the accounting practices we have discussed.

Devices, descriptive strategies and communicative skills

The strategies we identified in the first three empirical chapters mobilised the relevance of ordinary identities, and minimised the relevance of subcultural identities. In Chapter 5, we saw how questions of clarification worked to avoid the subcultural self-definition which the interviewer's prior question was designed to elicit. Also, through these clarification questions, respondents established their identity as ordinary people. In Chapter 6, we observed how respondents characterised potentially evocative aspects of their appearance and behaviour in very mundane ways, thereby minimising the relevance of their subcultural identities for the interpretation of their appearance and activities.

In Chapters 7 and 8, we identified a range of descriptive strategies through which respondents accounted for group affiliation and the significance of being a member of a particular subculture. In Chapter 7, we described several ways in which respondents characterised their motivation for changing appearance and, by implication, for affiliation with a particular subculture. We observed, for example, how respondents ascribed their change in music tastes to the acquisition of personal knowledge. We saw too how changes in appearance were portrayed as a gradual realisation of a deeply held commitment to features of style, or of the expression of feelings or the true self. In these ways, participants ascribed the basis of their own change to individualistic forces. And we also examined some of the ways that respondents could characterise other members so as to highlight their comparative shallowness and insincerity.

Chapter 8 was an examination of discursive strategies through which respondents affirmed the significance of subcultural identity in such a way that this did not invoke the personal benefits or importance of that identity. For example, some respondents used minimal evaluative responses to portray importance as an irrelevant dimension for assessing the significance of identity; it was instead characterised as a 'just is' feature of their world. In other extracts respondents provided a measure of their involvement: their refusal to change despite personal costs. A third descriptive strategy concerned the way some respondents nominated and described features of categories which they claimed they couldn't be. Finally, we observed ways in which participants avoided the implication that the benefits derived from membership were also motivating factors for affiliation.

The final analytic chapter was concerned with the ways that participants formulated the meaning of the punk subculture. In particular, we identified several ways, both direct and indirect, through which participants avoided the production of a set of criterial or definitive attributes of punk. In some accounts the diversity of meanings was portrayed and warranted explicitly. More commonly, the contemporary meaning was made contingent on personal opinion or on members' desires, preferences and feelings. Moreover, the descriptive terms used to refer to appearance undermined the relevance of style as a criteria of the punk subculture. We showed how, in these ways, respondents characterised the meaning of punk in individualistic terms. Nevertheless, we also examined how respondents affirmed and substantiated its rebellious dimension; they used formulaic expressions to characterise the political significance of the subculture. But we also saw that, when such formulations were implicitly challenged, rebellion was warranted through descriptions of passive activities or personal actions within the context of individuals' mundane, everyday lives.

The devices and strategies we have examined have one feature in common: they are resources through which respondents accomplished resistance. The nature of this resistance, however, was not the kind of symbolic resistance to the social order embodied in New Subcultural theories; even characterisations of the rebelliousness of punk was accomplished through descriptions of mundane activities, rather than the subculture's symbolic message or by reference to overtly antagonistic actions. It is more accurate to see these accounting practices as accomplishing resistance at an inferential order: their accounts constituted resistance to the kinds of assumptions about subcultures, and the people who join them, which are enshrined in both lay and academic discourse.

It is assumed, for example, that subcultural identity is a key aspect of self-conception, and, therefore, that members will readily accept this categorical self-definition. But category ascriptions are also a form of social control: they are a means through which a person's identity and behaviour can be glossed, interpreted and characterised in terms of cultural knowledge about the category. Consequently, when, in the opening exchanges in the interviews, respondents resist the relevance of a subcultural categorisation, they minimise the likelihood that commonly held knowledge about those categories will be invoked to explain or account for their own behaviour and responses. And it is important to stress that this resistance is not due to interpersonal friction – that is, between them and the interviewer. Respondents are resisting the potential applicability of culturally available knowledge which is stored and distributed in society via social categorisations.

Furthermore, it is a common assumption that young people seek a meaningful identity and security through group membership; and that potential recruits have to learn to be members by participating in a process of initiation. Subsequently, it is believed that continued commitment to the subculture is a consequence of the investment of self in a subcultural identity and the benefits derived from membership. But the strategies we observed in Chapters 7 and 8 were designed to resist precisely these kinds of assumptions. For example, in Chapter 7, we examined several descriptive devices through which the potential relevance and influence of peers were both acknowledged and then undermined, for instance, in the ways that respondents portrayed their surprise at the discovery of similarly alternative others.

These empirical observations have significant implications. One central feature of the postmodern literature, for example, is the ascription of power to disembodied discourses (Gavey, 1989; Parker, 1992): power is manifest in discourses which inhabit texts. Power is therefore regarded as somehow 'speaking through' individual subjects and their talk. However, this focus obscures an important feature of the accounts we have presented here. Participants employ a range of devices and descriptive strategies to resist the kind of conventional knowledge about subcultural groups and their members. Indeed, it is arguable that an important aspect of subcultural biography is the acquisition of those communicative competencies by which to resist the kind of culturally available, inferential resources other people may draw upon. This observation resonates with two points Foucault (1981) made: first, that wherever there is power (or knowledge) there is resistance; second, that both are exercised in the most mundane, local contexts. We have argued that social interaction is the most basic and mundane context (see also Schegloff, 1991) and the communicative skills exercised in conversations are vehicles for resistance. While interviews, however informal, are unlikely to be common features of everyday life, and therefore they are not mundane, we noted in Chapter 3 that they nevertheless function to elicit the kinds of discursive practices which are a feature of everyday communication.

Motivation, individuality and authenticity

The analyses have also shown why respondents resist conventional knowledge about subcultural groups and the individuals who join them. Common assumptions, enshrined in academic discourse and media examinations of subcultures, are largely negative: they tend to characterise members as shallow creatures who are passing through adolescent phases, or simply following fashionable trends and fads. Consequently, it is no surprise to detect a sensitivity to issues of motivation, individuality and authenticity in the respondents' biographical accounts.

Of course, these issues are not only participants' concerns; they have featured prominently in some areas of academic research and theorising. However, what we have tried to do throughout is to demonstrate the utility of addressing these issues as participants' concerns which are made relevant within and to their accounting practices. In this section, we want to clarify points of divergence and commonality and thereby point to the ways that common cultural concerns may be dealt with differently by academics and members. Later in this chapter, we shall argue that without due attention to the ways that issues of motivation, authenticity and individuality are live concerns, social scientists cannot appreciate the role they play in social life.

The concepts of sincerity and authenticity and their relation to notions of self have largely been examined through historical, literary and conceptual analyses (see, for example, Lyons, 1978; Trilling, 1972; and Silver and Sabini, 1985, respectively). These analyses reveal a range of interpretations of what it means to be a sincere person. What is common to these writings is the idea that sincerity necessitates resistance to the hypocritical demands and pressures imposed by society and its conventions.[2] Not surprisingly, this cultural assumption also permeates the accounts presented in this book insofar as the achievement of self-authenticity is partly dependent on warranting claims not to have been influenced by others, subject to peer pressure or conformity.

Of course, there are parallel concerns about sincerity and the self in social scientific accounts. Three broad theories of self can be identified in the mainstream literature: the trait self, the role self and the humanist self (Potter *et al.*, 1984). In order to show that, and how our analyses offer an alternative conceptualisation of these issues, based on participants' concerns, it is useful to outline the main features of these models of self, and show how they are relevant to theories specifically about identity and group membership.

Trait theory is based on the idea that people have essential qualities or traits. The theory implies that the person is authentic if acting according to these traits (for example, Eysenck, 1970). Gergen (1968), however, argues that the assumption of behavioural consistency on which trait theory depends is a cultural imperative which is maintained through the imposition of ethical sanctions; one such sanction is the charge of authenticity. Role theories embody the understanding of self as an actor performing social roles. The self is thus portrayed as a chameleon-like character without a central core. The role self has been criticised on the grounds that it is insincere; the self is simply a facade, hiding behind a mask (see Potter and Wetherell, 1987). It is not the case, however, that role theorists ignore issues of authenticity. In particular, it is argued that sincerity is an important part of one's performance, designed to generate social approval (Goffman, 1959). Nevertheless, the objection to this position is that it fits uncomfortably with cultural assumptions of sincerity as based on a real self. Finally, humanist accounts of selves are based on the idea that humans '[possess] within themselves the "potential" for an authentic inner self' (Shotter, 1993:192), the emergence of which is constrained by society. The acknowledgement and expression of feelings and desires are seen as the basis for achieving an authentic inner life.

Each of these theories of self has some relevance in accounting for self-identity and subcultural group affiliation; for example, Brake's (1985) analysis of membership and the construction of a self-image draws on role theory. He discusses the importance of staging a convincing performance by learning the appropriate performance skills through which to wear the 'costume' and project the image with sincerity. Nonetheless, however sincerely the image is projected, the idea that it is an image remains a problem in the context of cultural notions of the attachment of sincerity to a real, unique self.

The concept of social identity embodied in the Social Identity approach is more authentic insofar as social roles are not just performances, they are internalised and become part of the self-concept. Moreover, this approach assumes a perceiving agent who makes judgements about the appropriateness and performance of particular social identities. There is thus some notion of a core self lying beneath the act. The concept of social identity, however, constitutes a different kind of threat to self-authenticity. In particular, social identity implies a consequent, if temporary, loss of individuality or personal identity. This idea is encapsulated in the theoretical concept of depersonalisation in Self-Categorisation Theory (Turner *et al.*, 1987). This is the process whereby individuals self-stereotype and thereby come to perceive themselves as interchangeable exemplars of a social category. But in everyday terms, and in terms of the existentialist notion of authenticity, the idea of depersonalisation, self-stereotyping and acting in terms of a social category can be regarded as a threat to a person's integrity (Greenwood, 1994).[3] Role and Social Identity theories are therefore based on an understanding of selves and social identities which is inauthentic. Insofar as these theories are applied to members of subcultures, the implication is that subcultural identity is not sincere.

Claims made by respondents regarding the genuine nature of their identity and affiliation with subcultures resonate with the humanist understanding of self in which it is suggested that self-authenticity is accomplished through realising and expressing an inner self while resisting social pressures. But in the accounts presented here, it is not the constraints of social conventions that constitute the primary threat to the achievement of individuality; rather, it is the respondents' simultaneous visibility as members of subcultures. It is within the context of this way of being categorised, and the inferential implications it entails, that members negotiate the authenticity of self-identity. A key feature of this negotiation (and one which is absent in the humanist account) are respondents' formulations of personal motives. The authentic individual (or group affiliate) made relevant in these accounts is one who has the right grounds for being who he or she claims to be. Authenticity, then, is a primarily moral concern to do with issues of accountability in terms of one's motives for self-identity (Garfinkel, 1967). Shotter's (1993) account of authentic personhood similarly emphasises accountability. He proposes that

> To be a person and to qualify for certain rights as a free, self-determining, autonomous person with one's own identity, one must be able to show in one's actions certain social competencies, i.e. fulfil certain duties and to be *accountable* to others in the sense of being able to justify one's actions to them. (Shotter, 1993:193; original emphasis)

This emphasis is markedly different to current formulations of the relationship between identity and motivation, in which motivation is characterised as having a mediating role in identity-related action. Markus and Nurius (1987), for example, propose that motives are contained within our cognitive representations of possible selves. Thus, motivation is tied to the realisation through action of possible selves. Similarly, Greenwood (1994) regards motives as intrinsic to the pursuit of the identity projects (or moral careers) to which we are committed. Abrams and Hogg (1990) provide a different account of motivation; they argue that the desire for self-knowledge and the search for coherence and meaning are fundamental human motives because it is through the imposition of meaning or order that we are able to predict and control the social world. For Abrams and Hogg the establishment of order is essentially a perceptual phenomenon; it is achieved by imposing meaningful categories upon the diverse array of sensory experiences with which we are confronted. Our motives thus influence the accessibility of certain categories including self-categories or identities. For them, the accompanying activity and self-evaluation which is the behavioural manifestation of the self-category depend upon socio-cultural and contextual factors. In this account, then, the emphasis is on rationality: motives are part of our psychological make-up and tied to a rational search for meaning and control, or to our decisions to act.

The empirical approach exemplified in the analytic chapters invokes a very different view, in that it suggests that it is more useful to regard motivation as a discursive resource and accomplishment, rather than an internal construct. In this discussion we have focused upon its use in warranting the authenticity of self-identity. But the analysis has also shown how motivation is used to distinguish genuine and shallow members (Chapter 7), to undermine the reasonableness of others' actions (Chapter 6) and to define the subculture (Chapter 9). In all these instances, negotiation of motives was used to account for identity and action. In this sense, motivation can be regarded as a real, practical and moral concern to do with accountability.

Social identities and social groups

We have until now been concerned primarily with issues of self and identity: for example, the implications of social identities for individual integrity. We have not yet examined the relationship between social identity and the social group. Nor have we considered the debates surrounding the nature of social groups and social categories.

It is widely assumed that subcultural or indeed any social identity depends upon membership of a social group or category. Tajfel (1972), for example, defined social identity as the awareness of belonging to a group, together with the emotional and evaluative significance of that group membership. Several measures of the strength of social identity operationalise this definition by asking people to assess cognitive, evaluative and affective aspects of group membership (for example, Brown *et al.*, 1986; Hinkle *et al.*, 1989; Karasawa, 1991). Conversely, the social group is defined in psychological terms as a collection of people who share a common social identity (Turner, 1982) and who are defined by others as a group (Brown, 1988).

At the same time, the social reality of social groups is taken for granted. Society is understood in structuralist-functionalist terms as 'hierarchically structured into discrete social categories which stand in power, status and prestige relations to one another' (Hogg and Abrams, 1988:18). Within this arrangement, social groups are historically and culturally constructed, along with the attributes which differentiate them from each other (Turner et al., 1987; Turner and Oakes, 1986). Explaining the emergence of social groups is regarded as the province of sociology, economics, history and politics; social psychologists' concern is with the psychological reality of social groups. More-over, it is argued that the advantage of conceptualising social identity as the basis for the group is that the definition – and hence the theoretical claims based upon it – will apply to the whole range of groups or social categories with which people affiliate or through which their identities are ascribed (for example, Hogg, 1987). Therefore, nationality, political positions, arts students and artificially created groups are used interchangeably in exemplifying theoretical claims (see Oakes et al., 1994).

A number of critics have, however, argued that it is important that we attend to the nature of the groups under consideration because different kinds of groups are likely to have different implications for members' identities. Rabbie and Horwitz (1988), for example, argue for a distinction between social groups which are characterised by perceived interdependence amongst members, and social categories whose members share at least one attribute in common (see also Bornewasser and Bober, 1987). Greenwood (1994) draws a distinction between social collectives whose members are involved in sets of arrangements, conventions and agreements (for example, populations of bankers, or Hell's Angels) and what he calls derivatively social groups. These are aggregate groups comprised of populations who share one or more com-mon properties which are socially significant (for example, men, women, blacks). Greenwood argues that although derivatively social groups are sig-nificant and emotionally potent, they do not in themselves constitute identi-ties because they do not provide practical or conceptual resources for the formation and maintenance of identity. Instead, he argues that they provide a basis for social and self-labelling and social comparison. Moreover, the social dynamics of such labelling are powerful in determining the possibilities of entry into, and the outcome of, the socially available moral careers (or iden-tity projects) that are constitutive of identity. It is through the restraints on the moral careers of some and the facilitation of others that social labelling has a socio-political function. In addition, the emotional potency of such labelling may be derived from the way that it can encourage feelings of communion, harmony or solidarity.

Within the literature on adolescent peer groups, a number of researchers have distinguished between crowds which are based primarily on stereotypes and reputations, and cliques which are small, interacting groups based around shared and regular activities or interests. The former are said to be important in identity formation and role experimentation; the latter plays a primarily supportive role in the achievement of developmental tasks (Steinberg, 1993).

These kinds of distinctions are also relevant to youth subcultures; that is, sometimes youth subcultures are conceptualised according to the idea of social categories or derivatively social groups. In this sense, they are seen as a constellation of cultural values and attributes which members share in common and which differentiate them from outsiders. Clarke *et al.* (1976:14), for example, define subcultures through the

> peculiar dress, style, focal concerns, milieux, etc. [which] set them off, as distinctive groupings, both from the broad patterns of working-class culture as a whole, and also from the more diffused patterns exhibited by 'ordinary' working-class boys (and, to a more limited extent, girls).

This concept is invoked in discussions of the hegemonic processes through which subcultures come into existence. It is also the notion made relevant in Brake's (1985) argument that subcultures provide cultural resources for the construction of identities.

Nevertheless, it is also recognised that subcultural groups emerge within the local neighbourhood. In this sense, subcultures are conceptualised as collections of like-minded individuals who come together, interact in terms of a common identity, and engage in social activities together. This kind of group is the focus of ethnographic studies, and made relevant in Brake's (1985) proposition that subcultures provide a meaningful way of life during leisure.

Both kinds of conceptualisations were made relevant, implicitly or explicitly in our interviews. For example, respondents characterised shallow membership in terms of a group of friends who decide to change their image overnight; they also talked of how some people equate membership and hence the subculture with prototypical attributes (see Chapter 7). But consider what happened when we asked respondents to account for their own initial and continued affiliation with the subculture. With a few exceptions (most notably accounts of shallow members), their responses provided little sense of subcultures as groups which they joined. Likewise, in their formulations of the significance of being a member, they did not invoke a sense of shared identity, nor the benefits of affiliation with like-minded others. Characterisations of the punk subculture as a cultural category similarly gave the impression of its elusiveness. So, in Chapter 9 we noted the employment of a variety of descriptive resources and strategies to avoid the provision of criterial and consensual attributes through which to define the subculture. Moreover, by portraying explicitly the subculture's diverse meanings, some respondents avoided its reification. Thus, respondents do not provide a sense of attributes shared by virtue of common category membership. Indeed, in all bar one extract we presented in Chapter 9, individualistic notions were the only kinds of claims about being a punk that were uncontested in the accounts; for example, punk was characterised as individuals acting autonomously.

The orientation towards the elusiveness of the concept of social groups is not, however, confined to the participants in our study. We noted in Chapter 8 that the ontological status of social groups has been a long-standing matter of controversy throughout the social sciences (see Turner et al., 1987; also Durkheim, 1895; Weber, 1922; and Greenwood's commentary, 1994). The key difference between our position and these social theorists is that they see the social group as a problem to be resolved theoretically; we regard the very nebulousness of the concept to be a significant cultural resource in interaction and social and practical activities.

In this, we are sympathetic to the more radical critique of the taken-for-granted existence of social groups offered by Wetherell and Potter (1992; see also Potter and Wetherell, 1987). They argue that especially when social categorisations are reified as independent variables, there is a confusion of the descriptive with the ontological status of categorisations; that is, the act of describing someone as a Maori is taken to be a description of the person's essence. But there is nothing natural about national, racial or cultural distinctions; these categorisations are 'discursive orderings with traceable historical origins' (Wetherell and Potter, 1992:146). It is important to emphasise that discursive constructions of social groups are both integral to and facilitate material, economic and political forces from which they cannot be disentangled. Wetherell and Potter (1992: Chapter 5) provide an empirical example of the flexible construction of the Maori people as a nation, race and culture. Similar conclusions have been derived from the search for the essence of Scottishness (see McCrone, 1992; Nairn, 1988). It should be no surprise therefore that 'once we look closely at [categories] we see that they themselves are not solid and defined, but have to be moulded in discourse for use in different accounts' (Potter and Wetherell, 1987:137).

Wetherell and Potter (1992) conclude that the study of the discursive processes through which social groups are constituted and made real is a crucial social psychological and sociological topic. Analysis should moreover include the processes of negotiation and active constitution of group characteristics in changing social circumstances, together with the means through which subjectivity is implicated and constructed in the process. Our analysis is a step in this direction in that we have seen how particular construction of subcultural groups implicates their basis in individual autonomy.

There is a final point we need to make, because it was not the case that respondents avoided all reference to like-minded others. But when they did so, they did not make relevant conceptions of social groups or categories. Instead, we noted occasions on which our respondents drew upon notions of community and kinship in describing bonds between members. Similarly, a number of social scientists have shifted their emphasis from social groups to the concept of community (for example, Shotter, 1993). The social anthropologist A. Cohen (1985) argues that the character of communities 'is sufficiently malleable that it can accommodate all of its members' selves without them feeling their individuality to be overly compromised' (*op. cit.*:109). This is partly because our understanding of communities is such that they do not have an articulate and inherent character; they are not objective entities but subjective constructs. Thus, the notion of community 'becomes an eloquent and collective emblem of their social selves' (*op. cit.*:114). Willis (1990) similarly recommends a shift in thinking from distinctive subcultural groups to the idea of 'proto-communities'. These are loosely based networks of people who may not be recognised by outsiders as a collectivity. They arise through contingency, fun, shared desires and accidents; and their formation is a result of unplanned, unorganised, spontaneous patterns of shared 'symbolic work' and creativity.

In summary, at the very least, social scientists need to examine the hitherto largely taken-for-granted concept of the social group. If, moreover, their theories aim to represent or explain collective relationships, they must be formulated with a sensitivity to the elusiveness of and problems engendered by certain ways of understanding communal existence. Moreover, instead of treating subcultural groups as given, and the centre of the constellation of cultural artefacts and practices, a more flexible approach to the creation and use of culture in practical activities, and the discursive and non-verbal resources made available through which individuals construct identities within collectives, may be the more profitable way to proceed (Willis, 1990; see also Brake, 1985:186–7).

Social selves

At this point, it is useful to draw together and clarify the understanding of selves and identities implicated in our analytic approach. We also need to ask whether our approach enables us to overcome individual-social dualism without denying human agency. Finally, we will consider the kinds of benefits that may accrue from a pragmatic understanding of selves and social identities in contrast to the various conceptual resolutions we discussed in Chapter 2.

Identity and the procedural self

In our analyses, we have sought to describe some of the ways in which specific characterisations of self, or identities, become relevant, modified and exploited to address contingencies which emerge in the course of verbal interaction. Consequently, we have begun to see identity as a fluid accomplishment, instantiated in the procedural flow of verbal interaction. Our claim is therefore that identity is an active, practical and situated accomplishment, and our analytic approach is based upon and substantiates this claim. First, our analytic observations are contingent on a prior description of what participants were doing verbally. So, our attention to the details of how identities are actually mobilised in language use is an explicit attempt to show the active accomplishment of identities. Second, identities are mobilised for some purpose which is understood within the interactional sequences of which identities are a part; therefore identities are practical achievements. Finally, identity accomplishment or resistance is situated in the back-and-forth flow of conversation. Therefore, identity is not the achievement of an individual; instead, identities are products of joint action and the intersubjective organisation of verbal interaction. In other words, their production is contingent on negotiated, publicly displayed and shared understanding. Consequently, identities cannot be regarded merely as impositions or ascriptions related to a person's social location or biological composition.

We noted above that identities are characterisations of self. But what kind of self is implicated in our approach? It is useful to distinguish two kinds of answers to these questions which refer in part to different aspects of the research process. The pragmatic response is that the conversations we analyse here actually took place; they were not free-floating conversations, but embodied in the participants in these interactions. Social life and interaction could not be sustained unless we treated each other as generally competent persons who exercise some degree of choice over our verbal and non-verbal actions. The second kind of answer relates to the analytic approach we have adopted. Our analytic aim was to provide a systematic account of the discursive production of selves and identities in action. The understanding of self that we have been developing may therefore be characterised as a procedural self. It represents an attempt to substantiate theoretical claims through analytic practices: for example, that selves cannot be disentangled from social activities (Burkitt, 1991; Mead, 1934), and that the focus of analytic and theoretical attention should be selves-in-relationships (Gergen, 1987); selves-in-joint-activities (Shotter, 1989); or selves-in-conversation (Harré, 1987, 1989; see also Chapter 4). Thus, we have harnessed the conceptual benefits of postmodern and other shifts in thinking to analytic approaches which provide rigorous methodological guidelines for the examination of details of language use, speakers' competencies and the products of interaction.[4]

Our focus on selves in interaction ensures that our approach does not assume an isolated self-contained individual. Our emphasis on the situated relevance of identities, intersubjectivity and joint conversational action provides an understanding of social selves, and of our embeddedness in social life. Moreover, through our attention to the actions accomplished in talk, agency is thoroughly implicated in our analytic observations, without locating agency in self-conscious intentionality, cognitive process, or in abstract discourses. Therefore, this kind of approach enables us to overcome dualistic assumptions without denying human agency. Finally, we argued that social structures are effective and reproduced through the mundane activities of interacting individuals (Schegloff, 1991; see also Giddens, 1979), and we have shown that interaction is also the site for accomplishing resistance. This focus therefore promises a concrete and practical appreciation of the relationship between agency and structure.

The idea of procedural selves engaged in ongoing activities yields certain benefits in comparison to alternative resolutions which we have discussed throughout this book.

Motives, mechanisms and the thinking self

Consider, for example, Self-Categorisation Theory which is the most explicit attempt to address the individual–society issue within mainstream social psychology. Turner and Oakes (1986) characterise this as an interactionist perspective in that individuals' psychological processes continually interact with and are implicated in social processes. Individuals construct categories in ways that are sensitive to changing social circumstances. They represent and judge reality, and their perceptual judgements are selectively and constructively mediated by internal cognitive structures such as attitudes, beliefs and categories. In the process of actively making sense of social reality by constructing perceptually and motivationally appropriate categories (Oakes *et al.*, 1994), they construct subjectivity or identity for self and others. For example, when we see others as groups or as group members rather than as individuals, the self becomes transformed or depersonalised through the same judgemental processes. This in turn leads to collective or group-based action, the products of which (for example, norms, values and stereotypes) cannot be reduced to individual activity. These collective products may become part of the background knowledge which subsequently helps to guide individual judgement.

But at the heart of this model is a solitary observer who does not engage directly with the others who constitute the social world (Wetherell and Potter, 1992). The social world becomes a perceptual field rather than an interactive one, which is only effective through its psychological representation (for example, Hogg and McGarty, 1990:24). Engagement with others is only possible via the mediation of their internal representation and the interposition of cognitive operations (cf. Parker, 1992). Thus, concrete social interactions are apprehended through their inner mental representations (Oakes *et al.*, 1994:204), not by virtue of our participation in them.[5]

Moreover, Self-Categorisation Theory is constrained in its attempt to produce an understanding of how individuals and groups (society) are inseparable because its basic premise is that psychological processes reside only in individuals (Turner, 1987a) and should be the focus of research. Locating psychological processes of perceiving, categorising, judging and so on as mental operations in individuals' minds implicates the detachment of the individual from the external landscape (Wetherell and Potter, 1992). In addition, the assumption that they reside in individuals only makes sense if a division between the social and individual is maintained. Thus, this theory, with its focus on cognitive and perceptual processes which inhere in individuals, fails to provide an adequate appreciation of the way we are inseparable from the society in which we act.

Furthermore, it is important to remember that cognitive processes are hypothetical constructs, despite the tendency to treat them as if they had ontological (possibly neurological) status. Indeed, some critical social psychologists have taken as their topic of study the ways that psychologists have constructed the epistemological reality of cognitive processes. This is accomplished primarily within the essentially intertextual practice of scientific psychology (for example, Bowers, 1991; Shotter, 1991). (Put simply, psychology depends on texts, and simply writing about a phenomenon gives it the status of a linguistic and epistemological reality.)

Adherence to cognitive processes is further ensured by the belief in their explanatory utility. This in turn seems to derive from an inability to regard thinking in terms other than as cognitive processes. Yet, many years ago Wittgenstein (1953) marvelled at the way that cognitive processes had assumed such a taken-for-granted status. He did not deny that there is any process at all involved in thinking and remembering, but he questioned the idea that everything intelligent we do involves a cognitive process working in terms of inner mental representations of the external world.

> Why must something or other, whatever it may be, be stored up [in one's nervous system] in any form? Why must a trace have been left behind? Why should there not be a psychological regularity to which no physiological regularity corresponds? If this upsets our concepts of causality then it is high time they were upset. (Wittgenstein, 1981: no. 610) (Cited in Shotter, 1993:84)

There is moreover a history of thought in psychology which argues that cognitive processes are not intrinsic to individuals' minds. Instead, social activity should be viewed as logically prior to the individual mind (for example, Mead, 1934; Vygotsky, 1978, 1981; Wertsch, 1991). In this way, we avoid starting from problematic dualistic assumptions.

Similarly, our analytic approach is not insensitive to issues of understanding, thinking, reasoning and so on. We also do not conceive of these concepts in terms of an underlying cognitive apparatus which facilitates particular mental or social events. Instead, we emphasise the notion of practical reasoning, and seek to describe how understanding, reasoning, etc., are intrinsic to, and embedded in, social actions. Thus, we reject a distinction between cognitive predispositions or processes, as defined in terms of mentalistic phenomena, and the actions which are deemed to spring from them. This reconceptualisation ensures that processes which are traditionally taken to be hidden, hypothetical and deterministic, are exposed as visible, publicly available and organisational resources for human conduct (cf. Coulter's 1979, 1989 discussion of an ethnomethodological conception of cognition and cognitive processes). Thinking from this perspective is intrinsic to pragmatic, communicative and linguistic practices not the cause of them (see also Billig, 1987; Edwards, 1991; Edwards and Potter, 1992; Middleton and Edwards, 1990). Finally, agency is thoroughly ingrained in this approach in several ways without equating it with universal underlying processes which produce discrete acts. It is, for example, built into the analysis, and it is also addressed through the ways that agency is a participants' concern; that is, agency is drawn upon as a resource in managing membership, and in accounting for and assessing actions. Agency is thus both a built-in component of our analytic approach and assumptions and an accounting resource. Finally, agency is implicated in our emphasis on social activity as an ongoing and continuous process within which subsequent acts are enabled and given impetus by prior acts.

The point is that an understanding of social selves is more fruitfully pursued within an approach which takes as its starting point direct engagement in social interaction rather than the transformation of internalised processes of the mute and solitary observer.

Selves and subjectivity: some postmodern dilemmas

There is a closer relationship between the approach we have adopted in this book, and the variety of approaches which are characterised as postmodern or poststructuralist. We share, for example, a common concern with the ways that the self is constituted through language, and we drew partly upon the postmodern literature in warranting this turn to language. There is a crucial difference, however. Whereas postmodern thought utilises the notion of discourses, and the metaphor of the text, we have focused on language use in interaction as the primary site in which selves are constituted, negotiated and resisted. In Chapter 3, we discussed some problems engendered when the postmodern view of language is used to inform an analytic approach. Here we shall be concerned with a number of conceptual dilemmas centred on the understanding of selves which are at least partly a consequence of this view of language. We will then suggest that the kind of approach exemplified in the analytic chapters allows researchers to circumvent these dilemmas and hence the further difficulties raised by attempts to deal with them.

The dilemmas arise from postmodern efforts to accomplish the 'death of the subject'. That is, the death, more specifically, of the unified, reified, essentialised self: the rational, agentic and self-contained concept of self which, it is assumed, is central in Western academic and lay thinking. This has been achieved primarily through a shift away from intrapsychic terminology to metaphors of text, discourse and conversations. Thus, the postmodern self has become a by-product of the concern with specifying discourses, their historical and cultural emergence, the power relations and institutions in which they are invested. Consequently, selves are regarded as positions in often contradictory, multiple, and shifting discourses. Often, however, the focus of theory and research is on identity, not the self, because the concept of identity captures nicely ideas of both agency and structure and their interrelationship while avoiding the idea of a core or authentic self. At times, however, it seems that the shift has simply involved a change in terms so that the terms 'identity' and the individual are used instead of the self (Bhavnani and Phoenix, 1994:9). The terms used are, however, less important than considerations of the political implications of the ways in which identities are experienced and theorised, and how collective identities are implicated in political action (see the collection of papers in Bhavnani and Phoenix, *op. cit.*, for examples).

Other theorists have been more critical of the fractured, fragmented and schizoid self (Lather, 1992) (or individual) assumed in many postmodern accounts. Criticisms levelled at this vision of selves are related to existential, moral and political dilemmas it has generated. The existential dilemmas revolve partly around the incompatibility between the theoretical absence of a core self and the everyday sense of a self, with a unique identity which is continuous throughout personal history (see Henriques *et al.*, 1984; Hollway, 1989). The moral dilemmas relate to the apparent denial of moral virtues such as authenticity, autonomy and intentionality (for example, Løvlie, 1992). Finally, the political dilemmas arise because it seems that denying a self-determining agent predicates the impossibility of social and political change and resistance (for example, Henriques *et al.*, 1984; Hollway, 1989).

In the light of these dilemmas, if not always in direct response to them, we can identify three conceptual developments. Some theorists refer explicitly to a new *concept* of self. We have already discussed metaphors of selves in conversations and joint action; Gergen (1991) similarly talks of a 'saturated self' which exists through relations with others (see also Kvale, 1992). Lather (1992) invites us to assume a 'provisional, contingent, strategic, constructed subject which, while intelligible, is not essentialised' (Lather, 1992:103) .

Second there have been several attempts to develop (or call for) new theories of subjectivity because it is argued that without an explicit theory of the subject, attempts could be made to reinstate an underlying cognitive apparatus and thereby jeopardise the efforts to overcome dualism (see Parker, 1992). The resulting theoretical developments have drawn heavily on psychoanalytic concepts (for example, Henriques *et al.*, 1984; Hollway, 1989; Parker, 1992; but see Løvlie (1992) for an alternative approach which draws upon de Saussure).

A third strategy has been to reject postmodernism on the grounds that the 'death of the subject' is not a useful accomplishment. Moreover, the practical production of language by humans is ignored, and instead concentration is focused on the discursive production of individuals by language (Burkitt, 1991:100). And because language is treated as a disembodied, abstract and coercive system, postmodern accounts seem to imply discursive determinism. Therefore, Burkitt (1991) argues that issues of identity and subjectivity are most usefully pursued within the cultural-historical schools of thought exemplified by Mead (1934), Vygotsky (for example, 1978, 1981), Leontyev (for example, 1978, 1981), Luria (1981) and Wertsch (1985). Burkitt's (1991) theory of social selves is formulated and warranted by integrating aspects of these theories. His emphasis is on the ways that self and self-consciousness are formed and embodied in practical activity such as labour, social structure and language.

We have suggested above that these responses are partly aimed at overcoming problems engendered by the absence of a subject. However, the purpose of this theoretical activity is actually more ambiguous than we have suggested; that is, sometimes, theoretical developments seem to be informed by a desire to push self-conceptions (and social science) in politically and morally desirable directions (for example, Parker, 1992). In this sense, theories claim to be about *constructing new possibilities* for understanding subjectivity which will emancipate people (for example, Hollway, 1989) while preserving valued aspects of contemporary subjectivity. But it is also argued that social science should be producing more local, practical and everyday knowledge (Shotter, 1992; see also Kvale, 1992)[6] and theoretical formulations are apparently oriented towards describing the way we really are (and have been all along, if only we realised it). This orientation is especially evident when theorists appeal to ideas of the historical and ontological origins of selves to warrant their theoretical arguments (Shotter, 1993; Burkitt, 1991). Put simply, if rather crudely, it is often not clear whether the theoretical aims are primarily reconstruction or explanation.

The ambiguity is further compounded by the abstract, often metaphorical, and intratextual nature of theoretical solutions regarding the nature of selves; that is, they are developed with reference to and the integration of other theories. The irony here is that the intralinguistic practice of mainstream social psychology has been central in the critique mounted against it (see Parker and Shotter, 1990). In particular, it is argued that the creation of psychological facts, together with their meaning and sense, depend on the thoroughly textual nature of the discipline and this is how psychologists are able to construct and preserve 'fictions of their own making' (*op. cit.*:2). New theories of subjectivity are similarly in danger of growing 'out of touch with the world they seek to comment on' (Marcus and Fischer, 1986; see Lather, 1992). This in turn imposes constraints upon their explanatory utility.

Likewise, the complexity of theory and the opacity of the conceptual terms used in constructing new theories of subjectivity make the aim of thereby empowering people unrealistic; this is because they are largely inaccessible to people outside the disciplines within which they are constructed (see Burman, 1990; Widdicombe, 1992). There is, then, a danger of simply replacing scientific with intellectual elitism. Moreover, if it is to be socially and politically useful, it makes sense to ground social scientific practices in an understanding of everyday social life and activity. In this way, its products are rendered accessible as resources for resistance and hence social change.

Therefore, we suggest that the approach we are advocating here not only avoids the problems outlined above, it also constitutes a more fruitful direction from which to pursue the aims above. First, through our focus on social interaction, and on selves embedded and constituted in ongoing social and practical activities, we have begun to produce an understanding of our inherently social nature and of what we do rather than how (theoretically) we do things. Second, we already have numerous conceptual tools at our disposal for justifying (academically) a focus on the discursive production of selves and for the shift away from an understanding of selves whose participation with others in social life is mediated by cognitive processes located within individuals' minds. Our task now is to understand selves in practice. Therefore, rather than become embroiled in constructing theories of what the self is, 'the important consideration is that people for the most part orient themselves *as if* they had discoverable and ultimately characterizable selves . . .' (R. Turner, 1987:123; original emphasis). In other words, it is the availability in our culture of a folk concept of self that is significant in enabling social, moral and political activity. Shotter (1993) similarly argues that the sense of having real selves does not depend on their location in space, time, or people's heads. Instead, selves like roles, identities and individuals have real attributes by virtue of their functioning in people's actions and joint activities. Selves subsist in people's practices because they matter practically in terms of the difference they make to people's lives and in making forms of life possible (see Shotter's discussion of the imaginary, 1993).[7]

Our focus on selves in action constitutes a step in this direction and leads to the final issue we want to discuss: the relation between social science and everyday accounts of selves, identities and social action.

Accounts of social action and accounts in social action

Social scientific research on youth subcultures has tended to ignore the accounts produced by members of those subcultures.[8] Instead, they have provided explanations of aspects of the behaviour of subcultures and their members. For example, sociologists have examined the ways in which subcultural membership constitutes resistance to the prevailing social order; and social psychologists have looked at why young people are attracted to subcultural groups. These analytic accounts are forms of explanation: they seek to explain aspects of the members' involvement in their subcultures.

In this book we have not been content merely to furnish another set of analytic accounts; instead we have emphasised the importance of studying accounts produced by the members themselves. One of the overriding findings from this has been the extent to which the kinds of concerns addressed in the social science literature also inform the members' accounts. Conformity, authenticity, the political dimension of membership, categorisation, the relationship between the individual and the group, the identity of self and the constitution of the group: all these matters are addressed in interviews conducted with our respondents. Sometimes they are raised explicitly, but frequently the relevance of these issues is to be found in the degree to which they infuse the accounts being produced. Initially, then, there appears to be a symmetry, in that the concerns addressed in professional social science accounts are mirrored in the discourse of the members themselves.

There is, however, a crucial difference. In social scientific accounts, these kinds of issues are either produced as part of the explanation for social life, or are a feature of that aspect of behaviour which is to be explained. But in the discourse of the members' own accounts these issues are resources for discursive social action. Consider, for example, the issue of social identity. In Chapter 6 we examined how speakers designed complaints about the ways in which they were treated by other groups (landlords and the police). In each case the social identity of the speaker was produced as a resource to substantiate the legitimacy of the complaint. So, for members themselves, issues such as self-categorisation, social identity and its relationship to social action, and authenticity of membership are not dry intellectual concerns: they are deeply enmeshed in the ways that the members address and negotiate specific discursive actions which become relevant in verbal interaction.

There is a further distinction between academic and lay accounts. Consider how social identity theorists characterise the way in which an individual develops a commitment to a particular subculture. It is assumed that the individual first defines him or herself as a member of a social category; for example punk or gothic. The theoretical claim is that adolescents then adopt what they regard as criterial features because this is the way that they can achieve their social identity as a group member (for example, Reicher, 1987). The issue here is conformity: the individual becomes a member of a group by conforming to criterial attributes. However, in this analytic account conformity has no positive or negative connotations: it is simply a neutral term. However, in the accounts produced by members themselves, conformity has very different implications: being seen to conform to the criterial features of a subcultural group is taken to be a sign of inauthenticity. In members' own accounts, then, issues such as conformity are not neutral: they have inferential consequences. The ascription or denial of conformity is therefore a live interactional concern for members. Similar arguments can be made for issues of social identity, the self, individuality and the social group. Moreover, social scientists' dilemmas such as the relationship between the individual and group, upon which they erect their theories, are also everyday dilemmas, which are both resources for action and practically resolved.

The kinds of issues which permeate the social scientific literature also inform the accounts of members themselves. In the rarefied atmosphere of academic debate, however, these issues are arid and lifeless; yet in the accounts of members, they have a vitality in that they are deeply relevant to real-life interactional and inferential concerns. Instead of trying to explain the behaviour of young people by utilising common sense or intuitive ways of accounting for behaviour, it seems more appropriate to begin with the examination of how those common-sense accounts inform the discursive actions produced by young people themselves, for it is in this domain that such accounts have a crucial significance.

Notes

1. We do not, of course, claim to cover all aspects of a person's biography. Clearly, this would be beyond the scope of this book. The biographical features with which we have been concerned are those specific to identity and membership of youth subcultures.
2. It is worth noting that when the term 'sincerity' first appeared in the English language in the early part of the sixteenth century, it meant pure or unmixed and was used to refer to inanimate objects like wine. Its more common use, and exclusive application to people in the late sixteenth and early seventeenth century occurred alongside the more frequent use of the term 'society' which, Trilling (1972) observes, was probably not coincidental.
3. To some extent, there has been some recognition of the problematic implications of this model. Breakwell (1986), for example, argues that social and personal identities are indistinguishable: social identities are personal. Abrams (1994) argues that they are not conceptually distinct because the same trait, intellectual for example, can be used to identify a person as a member of a collective or it can be regarded as an individual trait. And Greenwood (1994) argues that the possession of particular traits is not equivalent to notions of individuality. Moreover, even these modifications fail to address the issue of authenticity as central in the issue of individuality and social identities. Consequently, it has been argued that the issue of individuality and social identity should be regarded as an everyday dilemma or paradox (Billig *et al.*, 1988) which people deal with in ways that are functionally adequate for the circumstances (see Widdicombe, 1993).
4. Approaches which provide the analytic tools with which to understand selves-in-conversation, such as conversation analysis and ethnomethodologically based discourse analysis, are informed by a reconceptualisation of language as a practical tool, not a concern to produce visions of social selves. Even within social psychology, attempts to reconceptualise specific psychological concepts have not generally been accompanied by conceptual shifts in understanding selves and trying to overcome dualism (see Potter and Wetherell, 1987). This is why it was necessary for us to integrate the two approaches.
5. The theoretical and empirical detachment of the individual and the social is perhaps clearest in the discussion of the social validation of group attributes (Oakes *et al.*, 1994). Validating social knowledge depends on discussion, argument and the exchanging of views with like-minded others; these processes are only made possible, however, through the prior categorisation of self and others as the same. Since the aim is to produce consensual knowledge, disagreement may lead to the recategorisation of self and others as different. Social validation therefore appears to be a self-fulfilling prophecy; my perception will always be sustained if disagreement

results in those who disagree being recategorised as not relevant for socially validating my views. This problem is avoided by Oakes *et al.*, however, because their emphasis is on the underlying categorisation processes which they argue are precursors to argument and debate. By contrast, we regard debate as central to social life, and our approach makes the essentially interactive processes of discussion the focus of research. Moreover, categorisations are more usefully regarded as a type of discursive action (Edwards, 1991) which are made interactionally relevant to accomplish rhetorical ends rather than as precursors to argument (see also Billig, 1987).

6. Polkinghorne (1992) makes a similar point in relation to psychotherapy and its practice. He cites studies which show that in their practice, psychotherapists rely not on psychological research but on a second body of knowledge which is largely oral, dynamic and context-dependent. In other words, they rely on practical, local knowledge of the kind that Shotter recommends. This, for Polkinghorne, is truly postmodern knowledge in that it is without foundations, fragmentary and constructed.

7. Shotter (1993) provides a useful analogy with the imaginary numbers like $\sqrt{(-1)}$, which are used as a source of mathematical research, and in bridging positive and negative in electrical engineering:

> although they cannot exist as mathematical objects, they none the less play a 'real' part in mathematical procedures; not in the sense of correspondence with reality, but in the sense of achieving reproducible results by the use of socially sharable (mathematical) procedures . . . (Shotter, 1993:200)

8. Of course, not all sociologists of youth have overlooked accounts; ethnographers such as Willis (1977) collected and drew upon the 'lads'' accounts. However, the accounts he collected were treated as sources of information about their lives rather than the focus of his analysis. Moreover, they were subsequently interpreted and used to support a pre-established sociopolitical perspective (see Chapter 1).

APPENDIX
Data collection and transcription

Data sources

Interviews were conducted in August 1987 and August 1989 at the following locations: Camden Market, London [CAM]; King's Road, London [KR]; Kensington High Street, London [KHS]; The Reading Rock Festival [RRF]; Finsbury Park, London [FP]; Hammersmith, London [H]; and Bristol [B]. Thirty-eight interviews were conducted, and eighty-five people were interviewed, either separately or in group interviews.

Transcription

The transcription symbols used here are common to conversation analytic research, and were developed by Gail Jefferson. The following symbols are used in the data.

.	A full stop indicates a stopping fall in tone. It does not necessarily indicate the end of a sentence.
,	A comma indicates a continuing intonation.
?	A question mark indicates a rising inflection. It does not necessarily indicate a question.
(.3)	The number in brackets indicates a time gap in tenths of a second.
(.)	A dot enclosed in a bracket indicates a pause in the talk of less than two-tenths of a second.
(( ))	A description enclosed in a double bracket indicates a non-verbal activity. For example ((*banging sound*))
-	A dash indicates the sharp cut-off of the prior word or sound.
:	Colons indicate that the speaker has stretched the preceding sound or letter. The more colons the greater the extent of the stretching.
( )	Empty parentheses indicate the presence of an unclear fragment on the tape.

(guess)	The words within a single bracket indicate the transcriber's best guess at an unclear fragment.
˙hh	A dot before an 'h' indicates speaker in-breath. The more h's, the longer the inbreath.
hh	An 'h' indicates an out-breath. The more 'h's the longer the outbreath.
*	An asterisk indicates a 'croaky' pronunciation of the immediately following section.
<u>Under</u>	Underlined fragments indicate speaker emphasis.
↑ ↓	Pointed arrows indicate a marked falling or rising intonational shift. They are placed immediately before the onset of the shift.
CAPITALS	With the exception of proper nouns, capital letters indicate a section of speech noticeably louder than that surrounding it.
° °	Degree signs are used to indicate that the talk they encompass is spoken noticeably quieter than the surrounding talk.
Thaght	A 'gh' indicates that the word in which it is placed had a guttural pronunciation.
> <	'More than' and 'less than' signs indicate that the talk they encompass was produced noticeably quicker than the surrounding talk.
=	The 'equals' sign indicates contiguous utterances.
[ ]	Square brackets between adjacent lines of concurrent speech indicate the onset and end of a spate of overlapping talk. For example:

```
1      I:     RIght how would you describe your sty:le,
2             (.6)
3      R:     how would I describe ⌈the s⌉tyle
4      I:                          ⌊yeah ⌋
```

REFERENCES

Abelson, R. P. (1981), 'Psychological status of the script concept', *American Psychologist*, **36**, 715–29.

Abrahams, R. D. (1974), 'Black talking on the streets', in R. Bauman and J. Sherzer (eds), *Explorations in the Ethnography of Speaking*, London: Cambridge University Press.

Abrams, D. (1990), 'How do group members regulate their behaviour? An integration of Social Identity and Self-awareness theories', in D. Abrams and M. A. Hogg (eds), *Social Identity Theory: Constructive and Critical Advances*, Hemel Hempstead: Harvester Wheatsheaf.

Abrams, D. (1994), 'Collective and private selves: two baskets or one?', paper presented at the Annual Conference of the British Psychological Society, Brighton.

Abrams, D. and Hogg, M. A. (eds) (1990), *Social Identity Theory: Constructive and Critical Advances*, Hemel Hempstead: Harvester Wheatsheaf.

Allport, F. H. (1924), *Social Psychology*, Boston, Mass.: Houghton Mifflin.

Atkinson, J. M. (1984a), *Our Masters' Voices: The Language and Body Language of Politics*, London: Methuen.

Atkinson, J. M. (1984b), 'Public speaking and audience responses: some techniques for inviting applause', in J. M. Atkinson and J. Heritage (eds), *Structures of Social Action: Studies in Conversation Analysis*, Cambridge: Cambridge University Press.

Atkinson, J. M. and Drew, P. (1979), *Order in Court: The Organisation of Verbal Interaction in Judicial Settings*, London: Macmillan.

Atkinson, J. M. and Heritage, J. (eds) (1984), *Structures of Social Action: Studies in Conversation Analysis*, Cambridge: Cambridge University Press.

Austin, J. L. (1962), *How to do Things with Words*, Oxford: Oxford University Press.

Barker, P. and Little, A. (1964), 'The Margate offenders: a survey', *New Society*, **4**, no. 96, 6–10.

Baron, R. A., Byrne, D. and Griffitt, W. (1974), *Social Psychology: Understanding Human Interaction*, Boston, Mass.: Allyn and Bacon.

Barthes, R. (1971), 'Rhetoric of the image', *Working Papers in Cultural Studies 1*, Centre for Contemporary Cultural Studies, University of Birmingham.

Bass, B. M. (1960), *Leadership, Psychology and Organizational Behavior*, New York: Harper.

Bauman, R. and Sherzer, J. (eds) (1974), *Explorations in the Ethnography of Speaking*, London: Cambridge University Press.

Bhavnani, K-K. (1990), 'What's power got to do with it? Empowerment and social research', in I. Parker and J. Shotter (eds), *Deconstructing Social Psychology*, London: Routledge.

Bhavnani, K-K. (1991), *Talking Politics: A Psychological Framing for Views from Youth in Britain'*, Cambridge: Cambridge University Press.

Bhavnani, K-K. and Phoenix, A. (1994), 'Shifting identities shifting racisms: an introduction', in K-K. Bhavnani and A. Phoenix (eds), *Shifting Identities Shifting Racisms: A Feminism and Psychology Reader*, London: Sage.

Billig, M. (1985), 'Prejudice, categorisation and particularisation: from a perceptual to a rhetorical approach', *European Journal of Social Psychology*, **15**, 79–103.

Billig, M. (1987), *Arguing and Thinking: A Rhetorical Approach to Social Psychology*, Cambridge: Cambridge University Press.

Billig, M., Condor, S., Edwards, D., Gane, M., Middleton, D. and Radley, A. (1988), *Ideological Dilemmas: A Social Psychology of Everyday Thinking*, London: Sage.

Bonner, H. (1959), *Group Dynamics: Principles and Applications*, New York: Ronald Press.

Bornewasser, M. and Bober, J. (1987), 'Individual, social group and intergroup behaviour. Some conceptual remarks on the Social Identity Theory', *European Journal of Social Psychology*, **17**, 167–76.

Bowers, J. M. (1991), 'Time, representation and power/knowledge: towards a critique of cognitive science as a knowledge-producing practice', *Theory and Psychology*, **1** (Special Issue, Cognitivism and its Discontents), 543–69.

Brake, M. (1985), *Comparative Youth Culture: The Sociology of Youth Culture and Youth Subcultures in America, Britain and Canada*, London: Routledge and Kegan Paul.

Breakwell, G. (1986), *Coping with Threatened Identities*, London: Methuen.

Brown, B. B., Eicher, S. A. and Petrie, S. (1986), 'The importance of peer group ('crowd') affiliation in adolescence', *Journal of Adolescence*, **9**, 73–95.

Brown, G. and Yule, G. (1983), *Discourse Analysis*, Cambridge: Cambridge University Press.

Brown, R. J. (1988), *Group Processes: Dynamics Within and Between Groups*, Oxford: Basil Blackwell.

Brown, R. J., Condor, S., Mathews, A., Wade, G. and Williams, J. A. (1986), 'Explaining intergroup differentiation in an industrial organisation', *Journal of Occupational Psychology*, **59**, 273–86.

Bruner, J. S. and Goodman, C. D. (1947), 'Value and need as organising factors in perception', *Journal of Abnormal and Social Psychology*, **42**, 33–44.

Burkitt, I. (1991), *Social Selves: Theories of the Social Formation of Personality*, London: Sage.

Burman, E. (1990), 'Differing with deconstruction: a feminist critique', in I. Parker and J. Shotter (eds), *Deconstructing Social Psychology*, London: Routledge.

Burman, E. and Parker, I. (eds) (1993a), *Discourse Analytic Research: Repertoires and Readings of Texts in Action*, London: Routledge.

Burman, E. and Parker, I. (1993b), 'Introduction – discourse analysis: the turn to the text', in E. Burman and I. Parker (eds), *Discourse Analytic Research: Repertoires and Readings of Texts in Action*, London: Routledge.

Campbell, A. (1981), *Girl Delinquents*, Oxford: Blackwell.

Cashmore, E. E. (1984), *No Future*, London: Heinemann.

Chaikra, E. (1982), *Language: The Social Mirror*, Rowley, Mass.: Newbury.

Clarke, D. (1980), 'The state of cultural theory', *Alternate Routes*, **4**, 106–56, Carleton University, Ottawa.

Clarke, J. (1976), 'Style', in S. Hall and T. Jefferson (eds), *Resistance through Rituals: Youth Subcultures in Post-War Britain*, London: Hutchinson.

Clarke, J., Hall, S., Jefferson, T. and Roberts, B. (1976), 'Subcultures, cultures and class: a theoretical overview', in S. Hall and T. Jefferson (eds), *Resistance through Rituals: Youth Subcultures in Post-War Britain*, London: Hutchinson.

Cloward, R. and Ohlin, L. E. (1960), *Delinquency and Opportunity*, New York: Free Press of Glencoe.

Cohen, A. K. (1955), *Delinquent Boys: The Subculture of the Gang*, London: Collier Macmillan.

Cohen, A. P. (1985), *The Symbolic Construction of Community*, London: Routledge.

Cohen, P. (1972), 'Subcultural conflict and working class community', in *Working Papers in Cultural Studies 2*, Centre for Contemporary Cultural Studies, University of Birmingham.

Cohen, S. (1972), *Folk Devils and Moral Panics: The Creation of the Mods and Rockers*, London: MacGibbon and Kee.

Cohen, S. (1980), 'Symbols of trouble: introduction to the new edition', of S. Cohen (1972), *Folk Devils and Moral Panics: The Creation of the Mods and Rockers*, London: Martin Robertson.

Coleman, J. C. and Hendry, L. (1990), *The Nature of Adolescence*, 2nd edition, London: Routledge.

Coleman, J. S. (1961), *The Adolescent Society*, New York: The Free Press.

Condor, S. (1989), ' "Biting into the future": social change and the social identity of women', in S. Skevington and D. Baker (eds), *The Social Identity of Women*, London: Sage.

Corrigan, P. (1979), *Schooling the Smash Street Kids*, London: Macmillan.

Coulter, J. (1979), *The Social Construction of Mind*, London: Macmillan.

Coulter, J. (1989), *Mind in Action*, London: Macmillan.

Davis, B. and Harré, R. (1990), 'Positioning: the discursive production of selves', *Journal for the Theory of Social Behaviour*, **20**, 43–63.

Davis, J. (1990), *Youth and the Condition of Britain: Images of Adolescent Conflict*, London: The Athlone Press.

Deutsch, M. (1949), 'A theory of co-operation and competition', *Human Relations*, **2**, 129–52.

Deutsch, M. (1973), *The Resolution of Conflict*, Newhaven, Conn.: Yale University Press.

Dorn, N. and South, N. (1982), 'Of males and markets: a critical review of youth culture theory', *Research Papers*, no. 1, Middlesex Polytechnic, Enfield.

Downes, D. (1966), *The Delinquent Solution*, London: Routledge and Kegan Paul.

Drew, P. (1987), 'Po-faced receipts of teases', *Linguistics*, **25–1**, 219–53.

Drew, P. (1994), 'Conversation analysis', *The Encyclopaedia of Language and Linguistics*, Two volumes, Pergamon Press and Aberdeen University Press; vol. 2, 749–54.

Drew, P. and Holt, E. (1989), 'Complainable matters: the use of idiomatic expressions in making complaints', *Social Problems*, **35**, 501–20.

Drew, P. and Wootton, A. (1988), 'Introduction', in P. Drew and A. Wootton (eds), *Erving Goffman: Exploring the Interaction Order*, Cambridge: Polity Press.

Durkheim, E. (1895), 'The rules of sociological method', translated by W. D. Halls, in S. Lukes (ed.), *Durkheim: The Rules of Sociological Method and Selected Texts on Sociology and its Method*, New York: Macmillan (1982).

Durkheim, E. (1969), 'Individualism and the intellectuals', translated by S. and J. Lukes, *Political Studies*, **XVII** (1), 14–30.

Edwards, D. (1991), 'Categories are for talking: on the cognitive and discursive bases of categorisation', *Theory and Psychology*, **1** (Special Issue on Cognitivism and its Discontents), 515–42.

Edwards, D. and Potter, J. (1992), *Discursive Psychology*, London: Sage.

Edwards, J. (1985), *Language, Society and Identity*, Oxford: Basil Blackwell.

Eiser, J. R. (1986), *Social Psychology: Attitudes, Cognition and Social Behaviour*, Cambridge: Cambridge University Press.

Eiser, J. R. and van der Pligt, J. (1988), *Attitudes and Decisions*, London: Routledge.

Elias, N. (1978), *The History of Manners: The Civilizing Process*, vol. 1, Oxford: Basil Blackwell.

Elias, N. (1982), *State Formation and Civilization: The Civilizing Process*, vol. 2, Oxford: Basil Blackwell.

Erikson, E. (1956), 'The problem of ego identity', *Journal of American Psychoanalytic Association*, **4**, 56–121.

Eysenck, H. J. (1970), *Crime and Personality*, London: Routledge and Kegan Paul.

Farr, R. M. (1990), 'Waxing and waning of interest in societal psychology: a historical perspective', in H. T. Himmelweit and G. Gaskell (eds), *Societal Psychology*, London: Sage.

Farr, R. M. and Moscovici, S. (eds) (1984), *Social Representations*, Cambridge: Cambridge University Press.

Festinger, L. (1950), 'Informal social communication', *Psychological Review*, **57**, 271–82.

Festinger, L. (1954), 'A theory of social comparison processes', *Human Relations*, **7**, 117–40.

Fishbein, M. and Ajzen, I. (1975), *Belief, Attitude, Intention and Behavior: An Introduction to Theory and Research*, Reading, Mass.: Addison-Wesley.

Foote, N. (1951), 'Identification as the basis for a theory of motivation', *American Sociological Review*, **16**, 14–21.

Foucault, M. (1977), *Discipline and Punish: The Birth of the Prison*, translated by Alan Sheridan, Harmondsworth: Penguin.

Foucault, M. (1981), *The History of Sexuality: Vol. 1. An Introduction*, translated by Robert Hurley, New York: Vintage/Random House.

Fox, K. J. (1987), 'Real punks and pretenders: the social organisation of a counterculture', *Journal of Contemporary Ethnography*, **16**, 344–70.

Freud, S. (1921), 'Group psychology and the analysis of the ego', in J. Strachey (ed.) (1953), *The Standard Edition of the Complete Psychological Works of Sigmund Freud*, London: Hogarth.

Frith, S. (1978), *The Sociology of Rock*, London: Constable.

Frith, S. (1983), *Sound Effects: Youth, Leisure, and the Politics of Rock'n'Roll*, London: Constable.

Fyvel, T. R. (1963), *The Insecure Offenders: Rebellious Youth in the Welfare State*, Harmondsworth: Penguin.

Garfinkel, H. (1967), *Studies in Ethnomethodology*, Englewood Cliffs, N.J.: Prentice-Hall.

Gaskell, G. and Smith, P. (1986), 'Group membership and social attitudes of youth: an investigation of some implications of Social Identity Theory', *Social Behaviour*, **1**, 67–77.

Gavey, N. (1989), 'Feminist poststructuralism and discourse analysis: contributions to feminist psychology', *Psychology of Women Quarterly*, **13**, 459–75.

Geertz, C. (1979), 'From the native's point of view: on the nature of anthropological understanding', in P. Rabinow and W. M. Sullivan (eds), *Interpretative Social Science*, Berkeley, Calif.: University of California Press.

Gergen, K. J. (1968), 'Personal consistency and the presentation of self', in C. Gordon and K. J. Gergen (eds), *The Self in Social Interaction*, New York: John Wiley and Sons.

Gergen, K. J. (1971), *The Concept of Self*, New York: Holt, Rinehart and Winston.

Gergen, K. J. (1985), 'Social pragmatics and the origins of psychological discourse', in K. J. Gergen and K. E. Davis (eds), *The Social Construction of the Person*, New York: Springer-Verlag.

Gergen, K. J. (1987), 'Toward self as relationship', in K. Yardley and T. Honess (eds), *Self and Identity: Psychosocial Perspectives*, Chichester: John Wiley and Sons.

Gergen, K J. (1989), 'Warranting voice and the elaboration of the self', in J. Shotter and K. J. Gergen (eds), *Texts of Identity*, London: Sage.

Gergen, K. J. (1991), *The Saturated Self: Dilemmas of Identity in Contemporary Life*, New York: Basic Books.

Giddens, A. (1979), *Central Problems in Social Theory: Action, Structure and Contradiction in Social Analysis*, London: Macmillan.

Giddens, A. (1993), *Sociology*, 2nd edition, Cambridge: Polity Press.

Gilbert, N. and Mulkay, M. J. (1984), *Opening Pandora's Box: A Sociological Analysis of Scientists' Discourse*, Cambridge: Cambridge University Press.

Giles, H. and Coupland, N. (1991), *Language: Contexts and Consequences*, Milton Keynes: Open University Press.

Giles, H. and St. Clair, R. (eds) (1979), *Language and Social Psychology*, Oxford: Basil Blackwell.

Goffman, E. (1959), *The Presentation of Self in Everyday Life*, New York: Doubleday Anchor.

Goffman, E. (1974), *Frame Analysis: An Essay on the Organization of Experience*, New York: Harper and Row.

Goffman, E. (1981), *Forms of Talk*, Oxford: Basil Blackwell.

Goffman, E. (1983), 'The interaction order', *American Sociological Review*, **48**, 1–17.

Gramsci, A. (1971), Selections from the *Prison Notebooks*, in Hoare and Newell Smith, London: Lawrence and Wishart, 323.

Graumann, C. F. (1988), 'Introduction to a history of social psychology', in M. Hewstone, W. Stroebe, J-P. Codol and G. M. Stephenson (eds), *Introduction to Social Psychology: A European Perspective*, Oxford: Basil Blackwell.

Greenwald, A. G. (1980), 'The totalitarian ego: fabrication and revision of personal history', *American Psychologist*, **35**, 603–18.

Greenwood, J. D. (1994), *Realism, Identity and Emotion: Reclaiming Social Psychology*, London: Sage.

Grice, H. P. (1975), 'Logic and conversation', in P. Cole and J. L. L. Morgan (eds), *Syntax and Semantics 3: Speech Acts*, New York: Academic Press.

Gumperz, J. J. (ed.) (1982), *Language and Social Identity*, Cambridge: Cambridge University Press.

Gumperz, J. J. and Hymes, D. (1972), *Directions in Sociolinguistics: The Ethnography of Communication*, New York: Holt, Rinehart and Winston.

Hall, S. (1991), 'Ethnicity: identity and difference', *Radical America*, **23**, 9–20.

Hall, S. and Jefferson, T. (1976), *Resistance through Rituals: Youth Subcultures in Post-War Britain*, London: Hutchinson.

Hargreaves, D. H. (1967), *Social Relations in a Secondary School*, London: Routledge and Kegan Paul.

Harré, R. (1979), *Social Being: A Theory for Social Psychology*, Oxford: Basil Blackwell.

Harré, R. (1983), *Personal Being: A Theory for Individual Psychology*, Oxford: Basil Blackwell.

Harré, R. (1987), 'The social construction of selves', in K. Yardley and T. Honess (eds), *Self and Identity: Psychosocial Perspectives*, Chichester: John Wiley and Sons.

Harré, R. (1989), 'Language games and the texts of identity', in J. Shotter and K. J. Gergen (eds), *Texts of Identity*, London: Sage.

Hayes, N. (1993), *Principles of Social Psychology*, Hove, UK: Lawrence Erlbaum.

Hebdige, D. (1976), 'The meaning of mod', in S. Hall and T. Jefferson (eds), *Resistance through Rituals: Youth Subcultures in Post-War Britain*, London: Hutchinson.

Hebdige, D. (1979), *Subculture: The Meaning of Style*, London: Methuen.

Hebdige, D. (1987), *Cut'n'mix: Culture, Identity and Caribbean Music*, London: Comedia.

Heidegger, M. (1927), *Being and Time*, translated by J. Macquarrie and E. Robinson, Oxford: Basil Blackwell (1962).

Heider, F. (1958), *The Psychology of Interpersonal Relations*, New York: Wiley.

Heiss, J. (1981), 'Social roles', in M. Rosenberg and R. H. Turner (eds), *Social Psychology: Sociological Perspectives*, New York: Basic Books.

Henriques, J., Hollway, W., Urwin, C., Venn, C. and Walkerdine, V. (1984), *Changing the Subject: Psychology, Social Relations and Subjectivity*, London: Methuen.

Heritage, J. (1984), *Garfinkel and Ethnomethodology*, Cambridge: Polity Press.

Heritage, J. and Greatbatch, D. (1986), 'Generating applause: a study of rhetoric and response at party political conferences', *American Journal of Sociology*, **92**(1), 110–57.

Heritage, J. and Watson, R. (1979), 'Formulations as conversational objects', in G. Psathas (ed.), *Everyday Language: Studies in Ethnomethodology*, New York: Irvington.

Hinkle, S., Taylor, L. A. and Fox-Cardamone, D. L. (1989), 'Intragroup identification and intergroup differentiation: a multicomponent approach', *British Journal of Social Psychology*, **28**, 305–17.

Hogg, M. A. (1987), 'Social identity and group cohesiveness', in J. C. Turner, M. A. Hogg, P. J. Oakes, S. D. Reicher and M. S. Wetherell, *Rediscovering the Social Group: A Self-Categorization Theory*, Oxford: Basil Blackwell.

Hogg, M. A. (1992), *The Social Psychology of Group Cohesiveness*, Hemel Hempstead: Harvester Wheatsheaf.

Hogg, M. A. and Abrams, D. (1988), *Social Identifications: A Social Psychology of Intergroup Relations and Group Processes*, London: Routledge.

Hogg, M. A. and Abrams, D. (1990), 'Social motivation, self-esteem and social identity', in D. Abrams and M. A. Hogg (eds), *Social Identity Theory: Constructive and Critical Advances*, Hemel Hempstead: Harvester Wheatsheaf.

Hogg, M. A. and McGarty, C. (1990), 'Self-categorisation and social identity', in D. Abrams and M. A. Hogg (eds), *Social Identity Theory: Constructive and Critical Advances*, Hemel Hempstead: Harvester Wheatsheaf.

Holland, R. (1977), *Self and Social Context*, London: Macmillan.

Hollway, W. (1989), *Subjectivity and Method in Psychology: Gender, Meaning and Science*, London: Sage.

James, W. (1890), *Principles of Psychology*, New York: Holt.

Jefferson, G. (1984), ' "At first I thought": A normalizing device for extraordinary events', unpublished manuscript, Katholieke Hogeschool, Tilburg.

Jefferson, G. (1991), 'List construction as a task and resource', in G. Psathas (ed.), *Interaction Competence*, Hillsdale, N.J.: Lawrence Erlbaum.

Jones, E. E. and Pittman, T. S. (1982), 'Toward a general theory of strategic self-presentation', in J. Suls (ed.), *Psychological Perspectives on the Self*, vol. 1, Hillsdale, N.J.: Lawrence Erlbaum.

Karasawa, M. (1991), 'Toward an assessment of social identity: the structure of group identification and its effects on in-group evaluations', *British Journal of Social Psychology*, **30**, 293–307.

Kelly, J. R. (1983), *Leisure Identities and Interactions*, London: Allen and Unwin.

Khleif, B. B. (1979), 'Language as an ethnic boundary in Welsh–English relations', in P. Lamy (ed.), *International Journal of the Sociology of Language*, Special Issue on Language Planning and Identity Planning, 59–74.

Kitwood, T. (1980), *Disclosures to a Stranger: Adolescent Values in an Advanced Industrial Society*, London: Routledge and Kegan Paul.

Kitwood, T. (1983), 'Self-conception among young British-Asian Muslims: confutation of a stereotype', in G. Breakwell (ed.), *Threatened Identities*, Chichester: John Wiley and Sons.

Kvale, S. (ed.) (1992), *Psychology and Postmodernism*, London: Sage.

Laing, D. (1978), 'Interpreting punk rock', *Marxism Today*, 123–8.

Lather, P. (1992), 'Postmodernism and the human sciences', in S. Kvale (ed.), *Psychology and Postmodernism*, London: Sage.

Latour, B. and Woolgar, S. (1986), *Laboratory Life: The Social Construction of Scientific Facts*, 2nd edition, Princeton, N.J.: Princeton University Press.

Le Bon, G. (1895), *Psychologie des foules*, Paris: Alcan (English translation, *The Crowd*, London: Unwin, 1903).

Lee, D. (1987), 'The semantics of *just*', *Journal of Pragmatics*, **11**, 377–98.

Lee, J. R. (1991), 'Language and culture: the linguistic analysis of culture', in G. Button (ed.), *Ethnomethodology and the Human Sciences*, Cambridge: Cambridge University Press.

Leontyev, A. N. (1972), 'The problem of activity in psychology', *Soviet Psychology*, **9**, 4–33.

Leontyev, A. N. (1981), *Problems of the Development of the Mind*, Moscow: Progress Publishers.

Le Page, R. B. and Tabouret-Keller, A. (1985), *Acts of Identity: Creole-Based Approaches to Language and Ethnicity*, Cambridge: Cambridge University Press.

Levinson, S. C. (1983), *Pragmatics*, Cambridge: Cambridge University Press.

Lewin, K. (1948), *Resolving Social Conflicts*, New York: Harper.

Leyens, J-P. and Codol, J-P. (1988), 'Social cognition', in M. Hewstone, W. Stroebe, J-P. Codol and G. M. Stephenson (eds), *Introduction to Social Psychology: A European Perspective*, Oxford: Basil Blackwell.

Litton, I. and Potter, J. (1985), 'Social representations in the ordinary explanation of a "riot" ', *European Journal of Social Psychology*, **15**, 371–88.

Logan, R. D. (1987), 'Historical change in prevailing sense of self', in K. Yardley and T. Honess (eds), *Self and Identity: Psychosocial Perspectives*, Chichester: John Wiley and Sons.

Lott, A. J. and Lott, B. E. (1961), 'Group cohesiveness, communication level and conformity', *Journal of Abnormal and Social Psychology*, **62**, 408–12.

Lott, A. J. and Lott, B. E. (1965), 'Group cohesiveness as interpersonal attraction: a review of relationships with antecedent and consequent variables', *Psychological Bulletin*, **64**, 259–309.

Løvlie, L. (1992), 'Postmodernism and subjectivity', in S. Kvale (ed.), *Psychology and Postmodernism*, London: Sage.

Luria, A. R. (1981), *Language and Cognition*, New York: John Wiley.

Lyons, J. O. (1978), *The Invention of the Self*, Carbondale, Ill.: Southern Illinois Press.

Maltz, D. N. and Borker, R. (1982), 'A cultural approach to male–female communication', in J. J. Gumperz (ed.), *Language and Social Identity*, Cambridge: Cambridge University Press.

Marcus, G. and Fischer, R. (1986), *Anthropology as Cultural Critique: An Experimental Moment in the Human Sciences*, Chicago: University of Chicago Press.

Marin, L. (1983), 'Discourse of power – power of discourse: Pascalian notes', in A. Montefiore (ed.), *Philosophy in France Today*, Cambridge: Cambridge University Press.

Marks, D. (1993), 'Case-conference analysis and action research', in E. Burman and I. Parker (eds), *Discourse Analytic Research: Repertoires and Readings of Texts in Action*, London: Routledge.

Markus, H. (1977), 'Self-schemata and processing information about the self', *Journal of Personality and Social Psychology*, **35**, 63–78.

Markus, H. and Nurius, P. (1987), 'Possible selves: the interface between motivation and the self-concept', in K. Yardley and T. Honess (eds), *Self and Identity: Psychosocial Perspectives*, Chichester: John Wiley and Sons.

Markus, H. and Zajonc, R. B. (1985), 'The cognitive perspective in social psychology', in G. Lindzey and E. Aronson (eds), *Handbook of Social Psychology*, New York: Random House.

Marsh, P. (1977), 'Dole queue rock', *New Society*, 20th January.

Matza, D. and Sykes, G. (1961), 'Juvenile delinquency and subterranean values', *American Sociological Review*, **26**, 712–19.

McCall, G. J. (1987), 'The structure, content, and dynamics of self: continuities in the study of role-identities', in K. Yardley and T. Honess (eds), *Self and Identity: Psychosocial Perspectives*, Chichester: John Wiley and Sons.

McCall, G. J. and Simmons, J. L. (1982), *Social Psychology: A Sociological Approach*, New York: Free Press.

McCrone, D. (1992), *Understanding Scotland: The Sociology of a Stateless Nation*, London: Routledge.

McDougall, W. (1920), *The Group Mind*, Cambridge: Cambridge University Press.

McRobbie, A. (1980), 'Settling accounts with subcultures: a feminist critique', *Screen Education*, Spring, **34**.

McRobbie, A. and Garber, J. (1976), 'Girls and subcultures: an exploration', in S. Hall and T. Jefferson (eds), *Resistance through Rituals: Youth Subcultures in Post-War Britain*, London: Hutchinson.

Mead, G. H. (1910), 'Social consciousness and the consciousness of meaning', in A. J. Reck (ed.), *Selected Writings: George Herbert Mead*, Chicago: Chicago University Press.

Mead, G. H. (1934), *Mind, Self and Society: From the Standpoint of a Social Behaviorist*, Chicago: Chicago University Press.

Middleton, D. and Edwards, D. (1990), *Collective Remembering*, London: Sage.

Miller, W. B. (1958), 'Lower class culture as a generating milieu of gang delinquency', *Journal of Social Issues*, **14**, 5–19.

Mischel, W. (1976), *Introduction to Personality*, 2nd edition, New York: Holt, Rinehart and Winston.

Moghaddam, F. M., Taylor, D. M. and Wright, S. C. (1993), *Social Psychology in Cross-Cultural Perspective*, New York: W. H. Freeman and Company.

Moreland, R. L. and Levine, J. M. (1982), 'Socialisation in small groups: temporal changes in individual–group relations', in L. Berkowitz (ed.), *Advances in Experimental Social Psychology*, **15**, New York: Academic Press.

Morgan, D. L. and Schwalbe, M. L. (1990), 'Mind and self in society: linking social structure and social cognition', *Social Psychology Quarterly*, **53**, 148–64.

Mungham, G. and Pearson, G. (eds) (1976), *Working Class Youth Culture*, London: Routledge and Kegan Paul.

Murdock, G. (1974), 'Mass communications and the construction of meaning', in N. Armistead (ed.), *Reconstructing Social Psychology*, Harmondsworth: Penguin.

Murdock, G. and McCron, R. (1976), 'Consciousness of class and consciousness of generation', in S. Hall and T. Jefferson (eds), *Resistance through Rituals: Youth Subcultures in Post-War Britain*, London: Hutchinson.

Nairn, T. (1988), *The Enchanted Glass*, London: Hutchinson Radius.

Nuttin, J. R. (1984), *Motivation, Planning, and Action: A Relational Theory of Behavior Dynamics*, Hillsdale, N.J.: Lawrence Erlbaum.

Oakes, P. J., Haslam, S. A. and Turner, J. C. (1994), *Stereotyping and Social Reality*, Oxford: Blackwell.

Oakes, P. J., Turner, J. C. and Haslam, S. A. (1991), 'Perceiving people as group members: the role of fit in the salience of social categorisations', *British Journal of Social Psychology*, **30**, 125–44.

Park, R. E. (1927), 'Human nature and collective behavior', *American Journal of Sociology*, **32**, 733–41.

Parker, I. (1989), *The Crisis in Modern Social Psychology – and How to End It*, London: Routledge.

Parker, I. (1990a), 'Discourse: definitions and contradictions', *Philosophical Psychology*, **3**, 189–204.

Parker, I. (1990b), 'Real things: discourse, context and practice', *Philosophical Psychology*, **3**, 227–33.

Parker, I. (1992), *Discourse Dynamics: Critical Analysis for Social and Individual Psychology*, London: Routledge.

Parker, I. and Burman, E. (1993), 'Against discursive imperialism, empiricism and constructionism: thirty-two problems with discourse analysis', in E. Burman and I. Parker (eds), *Discourse Analytic Research: Repertoires and Readings of Texts in Action*, London: Routledge.

Parker, I. and Shotter, J. (1990), *Deconstructing Social Psychology*, London: Routledge.

Parsons, T. (1942), 'Age and sex roles in the United States', reprinted in T. Parsons (1964), *Essays in Sociological Theory*, Chicago: Free Press.

Parsons, T. (1950), 'Psycho analysis and the age structure', reprinted in T. Parsons (1964), *Essays in Sociological Theory*, Chicago: Free Press.

Pinch, T. J. and Clark, C. (1986), 'The hard sell: patter merchanting – and the strategic (re)production and local management of economic reasoning in the sales routines of market pitchers', *Sociology*, **20**, 169–91.

Polkinghorne, D. E. (1992), 'Postmodern epistemology of practice', in S. Kvale (ed.), *Psychology and Postmodernism*, London: Sage.

Pollner, M. (1987), *Mundane Reason: Reality in Everyday and Sociological Discourse*, Cambridge: Cambridge University Press.

Pomerantz, A. M. (1986), 'Extreme case formulations: a way of legitimizing claims', in G. Button, P. Drew and J. Heritage (eds), *Human Studies*, **9**, Special Issue on Interaction and Language Use), 219–29.

Potter, J. (1993), 'Review of K-K. Bhavnani (1991), *'Talking Politics: a psychological framing for views from youth in Britain'*, *Discourse and Society*, **4**, 409–10.

Potter, J. and Mulkay, M. (1985), 'Scientists' interview talk: interviews as a technique for revealing participants' interpretative practices', in M. Brenner, J. Brown and D. Canter (eds), *The Research Interview: Uses and Approaches*. London: Academic Press, 247–69.

Potter, J., Stringer, P. and Wetherell, M. (1984), *Social Texts and Context: Literature and Social Psychology*, London: Routledge and Kegan Paul.

Potter, J. and Wetherell, M. (1987), *Discourse and Social Psychology: Beyond Attitudes and Behaviour*, London: Sage.

Potter, J., Wetherell, M., Gill, R. and Edwards, D. (1990), 'Discourse: noun, verb or social practice?', *Philosophical Psychology*, **3**, 205–17.

Rabbie, J. M. and Horwitz, M. (1988), 'Categories versus groups as explanatory concepts in intergroup relations', *European Journal of Social Psychology*, **18**, 117–23.

Redhead, S. (1990), *The End-of-the-Century Party: Youth and Pop Towards 2000*, Manchester: Manchester University Press.

Reicher, S. (1987), 'Crowd behaviour as social action', in J. C. Turner, M. A. Hogg, P. J. Oakes, S. D. Reicher and M. S. Wetherell, *Rediscovering the Social Group: A Self-Categorization Theory*, Oxford: Basil Blackwell.

Robinson, W. P. (1972), *Language and Social Behaviour*, Harmondsworth: Penguin.

Rose, N. (1989a), 'Individualizing psychology', in J. Shotter and K. J. Gergen (eds), *Texts of Identity*, London: Sage.

Rose, N. (1989b), *Governing the Soul: The Shaping of the Private Self*, London: Routledge.

Rose, N. (1990), 'Psychology as a "social" science', in I. Parker and J. Shotter (eds), *Deconstructing Social Psychology*, London: Routledge.

Ryle, G. (1949), *The Concept of Mind*, London: Hutchinson.

Sabini, J. (1992), *Social Psychology*, New York: W. W. Norton and Company.

Sacks, H. (1972), unpublished lecture, University of California at Irvine (Spring, lecture 3: April 11. Transcribed by G. Jefferson).

Sacks, H. (1979), 'Hotrodder: a revolutionary category', in G. Psathas (ed.), *Everyday Language: Studies in Ethnomethodology*, New York: Irvington.

Sacks, H. (1984), 'On doing "being ordinary" ', in J. M. Atkinson and J. Heritage (eds), *Structures of Social Action: Studies in Conversation Analysis*, Cambridge: Cambridge University Press.

Sacks, H. (1992), *Lectures on Conversation*, edited by G. Jefferson, Oxford and Cambridge, Mass.: Basil Blackwell.

Sacks, H., Schegloff, E. A. and Jefferson, G. (1974), 'A simplest systematics for the organisation of turn-taking for conversation', *Language*, **50**, 696–735.

Said, E. (1978), *Orientalism*, Harmondsworth: Penguin.

Sampson, E. E. (1986), 'What has been inadvertently rediscovered? A commentary', *Journal for the Theory of Social Behaviour*, **16**, 33–40.

Sampson, E. E. (1989), 'The deconstruction of the self', in J. Shotter and K. J. Gergen (eds), *Texts of Identity*, London: Sage.

Sampson, E. E. (1990), 'Social psychology and social control', in I. Parker and J. Shotter (eds), *Deconstructing Social Psychology*, London: Routledge.

Sartre, J-P. (1958), *Being and Nothingness*, translated by H. E. Barnes, Oxford: Basil Blackwell.

Savage, J. (1987), quoted in 'Vault-face', *The Guardian*, 21st April, p. 10.

Schank, R. and Abelson, R. P. (1977), *Scripts, Plans, Goals, and Understanding*, Hillsdale, N.J.: Lawrence Erlbaum.

Schegloff, E. A. (1972), 'Notes on a conversational practice: formulating place', in D. Sudnow (ed.), *Studies in Social Interaction*, New York: Free Press.

Schegloff, E. A. (1988), 'Goffman and the analysis of conversation', in P. Drew and A. Wootton (eds), *Erving Goffmann: Exploring the Interaction Order*, Oxford: Polity Press.

Schegloff, E. A. (1991), 'Reflections on talk and social structure', in D. Boden and D. H. Zimmerman (eds), *Talk and Social Structure: Studies in Ethnomethodology and Conversation Analysis*, Oxford: Polity Press.

Schegloff, E. A. (1992), 'To Searle on conversation: a note in return', in J. R. Searle *et al.*, (eds), *(On) Searle On Conversation*, compiled and introduced by Herman Parret and Jeff Verschueren, Amsterdam and Philadelphia: John Benjamins.

Schegloff, E. A., Jefferson, G. and Sacks, H. (1977), 'The preference for self-correction in the organization of repair in conversation', *Language*, **53**, 361–82.

Schegloff, E. A. and Sacks, H. (1973), 'Opening up closings', *Semiotica*, **7**, 289–327.

Schlenker, B. R. (1980), *Impression Management: The Self-Concept, Social Identity, and Interpersonal Relations*, Monterey, Calif.: Brooks/Cole.

Searle, J. R. (1969), *Speech Acts*, Cambridge: Cambridge University Press.

Sheridan, A. (1980), *Michel Foucault: The Will to Truth*, London: Routledge.

Sherif, C. W. (1984), 'Coordination of the sociological and psychological in adolescent interaction', in W. Doise and A. Palmonari (eds), *Social Interaction in Individual Development*, Cambridge: Cambridge University Press.

Sherif, M. and Sherif, C. W. (1969), 'Adolescent attitudes and behavior in their reference groups within differing sociocultural settings', in J. P. Hill (ed.), *Minnesota Symposium on Child Psychology*, vol. 3, Minneapolis: University of Minnesota Press.

Shotter, J. (1989), 'Social accountability and the social construction of "you" ', in J. Shotter and K. J. Gergen (eds), *Texts of Identity*, London: Sage.

Shotter, J. (1991), 'Rhetoric and the social construction of cognitivism', *Theory and Psychology*, **1** (Special Issue on Cognitivism and its Discontents), 495–513.

Shotter, J. (1992), ' "Getting in touch": the meta-methodology of a postmodern science of mental life', in S. Kvale (ed.), *Psychology and Postmodernism*, London: Sage.

Shotter, J. (1993), *Cultural Politics of Everyday Life: Social Constructionism, Rhetoric and Knowing of the Third Kind*, Buckingham: Open University Press.

Shotter, J. and Gergen, K. J. (eds) (1989), *Texts of Identity*, London: Sage.

Silver, M. and Sabini, J. (1985), 'Sincerity: feelings and constructions in making a self', in K. J. Gergen and K. E. Davis (eds), *The Social Construction of the Person*, New York: Springer-Verlag.

Sinclair, J. McH. and Coulthard, M. (1975), *Towards an Analysis of Discourse*, London: Oxford University Press.

Smith, D. E. (1978), ' "K is mentally ill": the anatomy of a factual account', *Sociology*, **12**, 23–53.

Snyder, M. (1979), 'Self-monitoring processes', *Advances in Experimental Social Psychology*, **12**, 86–128.

Spitzer, S., Couch, C. C. and Stratton, J. R. (1970), *The Assessment of the Self*, Davenport, Iowa: Bawden Brothers.

Steinberg, L. (1993), *Adolescence*, 3rd edition, New York: McGraw Hill.

Stryker, S. (1980), *Symbolic Interactionism: A Social Structural Version*, Menlo Park, Calif.: Benjamin/Cummings.

Stryker, S. (1987), 'Identity theory: developments and extensions', in K. Yardley and T. Honess (eds), *Self and Identity: Psychosocial Perspectives*, Chichester: John Wiley and Sons.

Sugarman, B. (1967), 'Involvement in youth culture: academic achievement and conformity in school', *British Journal of Sociology*, **18**, 157–64.

Tajfel, H. (1969), 'Social and cultural factors in perception', in G. Lindzey and E. Aronson (eds), *Handbook of Social Psychology*, Reading, Mass.: Addison-Wesley.

Tajfel, H. (1972), 'Social categorisation', English manuscript of 'La catégorisation sociale', in S. Moscovici (ed.), *Introduction à la psychologie sociale*, vol. 1, Paris: Larousse.

Tajfel, H. (ed.) (1978), *Differentiation between Social Groups: Studies in Social Psychology*, London: Academic Press.

Tajfel, H. (1981), *Human Groups and Social Categories: Studies in Social Psychology*, Cambridge: Cambridge University Press.

Tajfel, H. (1982), *Social Identity and Intergroup Relations*, Cambridge: Cambridge University Press.

Tajfel, H. and Turner, J. C. (1979), 'An integrative theory of intergroup conflict', in W. C. Austin and S. Worchel (eds), *The Social Psychology of Intergroup Relations*, Monterey, Calif.: Brooks/Cole.

Tannen, D. (1990), 'Demythologizing sociolinguistics: why language does not reflect society', in J. E. Joseph and T. J. Talbot (eds), *Ideologies of Language*, London: Routledge.

Tedeschi, J. T. (1981), *Impression Management Theory and Social Psychological Research*, New York: Academic Press.

Terasaki, A. (1976), *Pre-Announcement Sequences in Conversation*, Social Science Working Paper 99, School of Social Science, University of California, Irvine.

Trilling, L. (1972), *Sincerity and Authenticity*, Cambridge, Mass.: Harvard University Press.

Turner, J. C. (1982), 'Towards a cognitive redefinition of the social group', in H. Tajfel (ed.), *Social Identity and Intergroup Relations*, Cambridge: Cambridge University Press.

Turner, J. C. (1984), 'Social identification and psychological group formation', in H. Tajfel (ed.), *The Social Dimension: European Developments in Social Psychology*, vol. 2, Cambridge: Cambridge University Press.

Turner, J. C. (1985), 'Social categorisation and the self-concept: a social cognitive theory of group behaviour', in E. J. Lawler (ed.), *Advances in Group Processes*, vol. 2, Greenwich: JAI Press.

Turner, J. C. (1987a), 'Introducing the problem: the individual and the group', in J. C. Turner, M. A. Hogg, P. J. Oakes, S. D. Reicher and M. S. Wetherell, *Rediscovering the Social Group: A Self-Categorization Theory*, Oxford: Basil Blackwell.

Turner, J. C. (1987b), 'A self-categorisation theory', in J. C. Turner, M. A. Hogg, P. J. Oakes, S. D. Reicher and M. S. Wetherell, *Rediscovering the Social Group: A Self-Categorization Theory*, Oxford: Basil Blackwell.

Turner, J. C., Hogg, M. A., Oakes, P. J., Reicher, S. D. and Wetherell, M. S. (1987), *Rediscovering the Social Group: A Self-Categorization Theory*, Oxford: Basil Blackwell.

Turner, J. C. and Oakes, P. J. (1986), 'The significance of the social identity concept for social psychology with reference to individualism, interactionism and social influence', *British Journal of Social Psychology*, **25** (Special Issue, The Individual–Society Interface, edited by G. R. Semin), 237–52.

Turner, R. (1974), 'Words, utterances and activities', in R. Turner (ed.), *Ethnomethodology*, Harmondsworth: Penguin.

Turner, R. H. (1987), 'Articulating self and social structure', in K. Yardley and T. Honess (eds), *Self and Identity: Psychosocial Perspectives*, Chichester: John Wiley and Sons.

Turner, R. H. and Gordon, L. (1981), 'The boundaries of the self: the relationship of authenticity to inauthenticity in the self conception', in M. Lynch, A. Norem-Heibesen and K. J. Gergen (eds), *The Self-Concept: Advances in Theory and Research*, Cambridge, Mass.: Ballinger Press.

Vygotsky, L. S. (1978), *Mind in Society: The Development of Higher Psychological Processes*, Cambridge, Mass.: Harvard University Press.

Vygotsky, L. S. (1981), 'The genesis of higher mental functions', in J. V. Wertsch (ed.), *The Concept of Activity in Soviet Psychology*, Armonk: M. E. Sharpe.

Watson, R. (1983), 'The presentation of victim and motive in discourse: the case of police interrogation and interviews', *Victimology*, **8**, 31–52.

Watson, R. and Weinberg, T. (1982), 'Interviews and the interactional construction of accounts of homosexual identity', *Sociological Analysis*, **11**, 56–78.

Weber, M. (1922), *Economy and Society*, vols. I and II, edited by H. G. Roth and C. Wittich, Berkeley, Calif.: University of California Press (1978).

Weber, M. (1985), *The Protestant Ethic and the Spirit of Capitalism*, London: Counterpoint.

Weedon, C. (1987), *Feminist Practice and Poststructuralist Theory*, Oxford: Basil Blackwell.

Wertsch, J. V. (1985), *Vygotsky and the Social Formation of Mind*, Cambridge, Mass.: Harvard University Press.

Wertsch, J. V. (1991), *Voices of the Mind: A Sociocultural Approach to Mediated Action*, Hemel Hempstead: Harvester Wheatsheaf.

Wetherell, M. and Potter, J. (1989), 'Narrative characters and accounting for violence', in J. Shotter and K. J. Gergen (eds), *Texts of Identity*, London: Sage.

Wetherell, M. and Potter, J. (1992), *Mapping the Language of Racism: Discourse and the Legitimation of Exploitation*, Hemel Hempstead: Harvester Wheatsheaf.

Widdicombe, S. (1992), 'Subjectivity, power and the practice of psychology', *Theory and Psychology*, **2**, 487–99.

Widdicombe, S. (1993), 'Autobiography and change: rhetoric and authenticity of "gothic" style', in E. Burman and I. Parker (eds), *Discourse Analytic Research: Repertoires and Readings of Texts in Action*, London: Routledge.

Widdicombe, S. and Woofitt, R. (1990), ' "Being" versus "doing" punk: on achieving authenticity as a member', *Journal of Language and Social Psychology*, **9**, 257–77.

Wiley, M. G. and Alexander Jr., C. N. (1987), 'From situated activity to self-attribution: the impact of social structural schemata', in K. Yardley and T. Honess (eds), *Self and Identity: Psychosocial Perspectives*, Chichester: John Wiley and Sons.

Willis, P. (1977), *Learning to Labour*, Farnborough: Saxon House.

Willis, P. (1978), *Profane Culture*, London: Routledge and Kegan Paul.

Willis, P. (1990), *Common Culture: Symbolic Work at Play in the Everyday Cultures of the Young*, Milton Keynes: Open University Press.

Wittgenstein, L. (1953), *Philosophical Investigations*, edited by G. E. M. Anscombe, Oxford: Basil Blackwell.

Wittgenstein, L. (1981), *Zettel*, 2nd edition, edited by G. E. M. Anscombe and G. H. V. Wright, Oxford: Basil Blackwell.

Woods, P. (1977), *Youth, Generations and Social Class*, Milton Keynes: Open University Press.

Wooffitt, R. (1988), 'On the analysis of accounts of paranormal phenomena', *Journal of the Society for Psychical Research*, **55**, 139–49.

Wooffitt, R. (1992), *Telling Tales of the Unexpected: The Organization of Factual Discourse*, Hemel Hempstead: Harvester Wheatsheaf.

Wooffitt, R. and Fraser, N. (1993), 'We're off to ring the Wizard, the wonderful Wizard of Oz', in G. Button (ed.), *Technology in Working Order Work: Studies of Work, Interaction and Technology*, London: Routledge.

Wowk, M. T. (1984), 'Blame allocation, sex and gender in a murder interrogation', *Women's Studies International Forum*, **7**, 75–82.

Wundt, W. (1900–20), *Völkerpsychologie* (10 volumes), Leipzig: Engelmann.

Wylie, R. C. (1979), *The Self-Concept*, vols. I and II, revised edition, Lincoln: University of Nebraska Press.

Zimmerman, D. H. and West, C. (1975), 'Sex roles, interruptions and silences in conversation', in B. Thorne and N. Henley (eds), *Language and Sex: Difference and Dominance*, Rowley, Mass.: Newbury House.

NAME INDEX

SUBJECT INDEX

accounts, 2, 58, 73, 145, 155, 157, 200–1, 206 n1
  members' own accounts, 2, 22, 28, 137, 186, 202, 225
  academic accounts as members' resources, 137, 180–1, 205, 211, 226–27
Acid House, 13, 14
adolescence, 137–39
  peer groups, 137–38, 147, 157 n1, 158 n2, 215
agency, 31, 32, 109, 146–7, 219, 222
  and determinism, 223–4
authenticity, 5, 6, 19, 108, 140, 145, 151–5, 157, 211–12, 213, 214, 223, 225
autobiography, 27, 145, 156, 180, 208
autonomy, 5, 213, 217

behaviourism, 32

Centre for Contemporary Cultural Studies, 14–15, 18
contrast structures, 123–25, 127–28, 142
conversation analysis, 4–5, 56, 66, 67, 73, 74 n7, 77, 92 n2, 113
  paired actions, 80–81, 82, 86, 96
  conditional relevance, 80
  sequential organisation, 86, 88, 89, 93 n5, 108, 109, 111, 174
  clarification sequences, 86–89, 94–95, 96, 100
  insertion sequences, 95, 97, 111–12
  displacement markers, 88
  self-categorisation, 100
  intersubjectivity, 90, 219
  turn-taking, 77, 79, 92 n4
  sequential contexts, 4
  repair, 80, 97
culture, 15–17, 30, 85

'death of the subject', 4, 45, 50–52, 222–24
discourse analysis, 56, 91, 92 n2
  different types of, 4, 56–59
  and texts, 59–64, 211, 222
Discourse and Social Psychology: Beyond Attitudes and Behaviour, 57–58
discourse(s), 42–44, 50, 53, 59–65, 91
  definitions of, 57–59
  subject positions in, 4, 43, 51, 91, 108, 223
  political implications of, 60–61, 65, 68, 223
  and power, 42–44, 64, 65
Discursive Psychology, 58–59
dramaturgical approach, 24, 26, 47
drugs, 9, 14
dualism, 18, 52, 134
  between individual and action, 133–34
  overcoming social/individual, 3, 45–53, 224–25

ethnomethodology, 47–48, 56, 74 n7, 220, 227 n4
ethogenic approach, 48–49
extreme case formulations, 130, 131, 144

factual statements, 198, 200
formulations, 97–99, 118, 123–24, 176, 202, 216

group affiliation, 157, 160–62, 163, 175, 176, 179, 180, 212, 216

hedonism, 15
hegemony, 16–17

identity, 4, 24, 26
  and social action, 5, 35, 53, 131, 132–34, 135, 214, 218

248